Stress Passages

BY THE SAME AUTHOR:

Guide to Stress Reduction (1985)

Stress Passages

SURVIVING LIFE'S TRANSITIONS GRACEFULLY

L. John Mason, Ph.D.

PHOTOGRAPHS BY
John O'Hara

CELESTIAL ARTS
Berkeley, California

This book is dedicated to my two sons, Matt and Michael, and to the memory of my father. It was their struggles with transitions that have helped inspire this book.

CELESTIAL ARTS
P.O. Box 7327
Berkeley, California 94707

The photograph on page 174 appears by courtesy of the California Milk Advisory Board. All other photographs Copyright © 1988 by John O'Hara.

Cover design by Ken Scott
Text design by Nancy Austin
Composition by Wilsted & Taylor

Library of Congress Cataloging-in-Publication Data

Mason, L. John, 1950–
    Stress passages.
        1. Life change events—Psychological aspects.
2. Stress (Psychology) 3. Stress (Psychology)—
Prevention. 4. Self care, Health. I. Title.
[DNLM: 1. Life Change Events—popular works.
2. Stress, Psychological—therapy—popular works.
WM 172 M289s]
BF637.L53M37 1988   155.9   86-26904
ISBN 0-89087-489-1

First Printing, 1988

Manufactured in the United States of America

1   2   3   4   5   6   91   90   89   88

Contents

Acknowledgments

THIS BOOK would never have been started or completed without David Hinds of Celestial Arts. It was his faith in my work that encouraged this project. My editor, Dorothy Wall, deserves much credit for turning the concepts into readable prose. My family, especially my wife, Barbara Ehlers-Mason, allowed me the time and much of the information that supports the parenting chapters. I wish to thank Holly and John O'Hara for their knowledge and skills in providing photographs to enhance and illustrate this book. Thanks to Jennie Orvino for assistance with graphics. Dr. Cap and Lauren Peck were invaluable in compiling information on child development and parenting. Sharon McKenzie, our birth coach educator, and Vicki Skiver are greatly appreciated for their help, both personal and professional, associated with the prenatal information. In regard to the material on prenatal care, I owe much to the work and training of Dr. David Cheek, MD. The chapter on stress management for death and dying was given a great boost by Dr. Ken Ring's research and writings. Thanks also to my friends at the California Parenting Institute (in Santa Rosa, CA), especially to the director, Robin Bowen. My friends and associates at the Redwood Center deserve recognition for their work in outpatient treatment of chronic pain. Included in this group are Dr. David Scheetz, Arlene Anderson, Kathleen Watson, Dr. Milt Harris, and clinic initiator Deirdre O'Neill. Special thanks to Mary Walker and Dr. Stan Eisenberg. My local bookstore, Eeyore's Books, gave me assistance and support throughout this process, especially Lote Thistlethwaite and Cheryl Maynard. Personal support was also freely offered by John and Nance Silva. I also wish to thank the reference librarians at the Sonoma

County public libraries for their special help throughout this project. Thank you to all my colleagues and friends in biofeedback and behavioral medicine in the Biofeedback Society of America and the Biofeedback Society of California. Finally, I would like to thank my clients, who over the past ten years have taught me much about transitions and stress.

Introduction

SINCE UPDATING the 1980 edition of *Guide to Stress Reduction* in 1985 for Celestial Arts, I have been excited by the prospect of creating an even more useful view of stress management. The *Guide to Stress Reduction* was written to be of service to laypersons or professional counselors who knew that stress management was important to good health and who wanted to have a concise description of various stress management strategies. The relaxation exercises presented in the book were designed for general use, except for a few that had specific applications for several stress-related disorders.

The response to the *Guide to Stress Reduction* was very positive, and many people spoke to me of the beneficial effect the exercises had on their lives. Yet the more I listened to the experiences of my clients, colleagues, and friends, and the more I thought about my own experiences, the more I felt the ideas in this first book could be further refined. I was becoming increasingly aware of the ways in which specific life transitions create stress in our lives, and felt that if we understood these transitions better, we could move through them more easily. I felt that the growth periods through which we all evolve, such as adolescence or midlife, did not have to be as painful and disorienting as they often are. And I felt that the stress reduction exercises could be more specifically tailored to the stresses of each life period.

In working with my private clients, I am continually surprised that very few people really understand or appreciate what a Herculean task it is to cope with life's changes and transitions. People assume that because we all go through these changes, dealing with them must come easily and naturally. For example, it is very common to see new parents, particularly young new parents, quite baffled by the enormous effort it takes to care for their babies, let alone to care for their own needs. These parents had expected to be euphorically happy after the birth of their child, and often appear puzzled by their level of fatigue, or their feelings of resentment toward the baby's demands, or the sudden strain on their marriage. Their poor awareness of the common stresses of parenting can lead to feelings of self-blame, fear, pain, anxiety, and depression. By understanding the normal stresses associated with the transition into parenthood, and by learning specific techniques to reduce the effects of these stresses, transitions such as this one can be survived more gracefully and enjoyed more thoroughly.

The purpose of *Stress Passages: Surviving Life's Transitions Gracefully* is to help people as they move through life's changes. It is not a book written about the theory or psychology of life transitions. It is designed to be a practical, useful guide for self-care. The concept of life transitions was inspired partly by Gail Sheehy's book, *Passages,* which also charts and explores the characteristics of typical life stages. However, while Sheehy's book examines only adult life, my book covers the complete range of human development, from birth to death. And I do not use the theoretical framework that Sheehy uses, but rather present practical suggestions for coping with the stresses associated with each life transition. People in transition or counselors working with this population of people—psychologists, marriage counselors, physicians, clergy, biofeedback therapists, physical therapists, school counselors, childbirth instructors, rehabilitation counselors, hospice groups, drug abuse counselors, sex therapists—can use this book to help recognize sources of stress and to develop a plan to survive transitions with greater control and personal power.

To understand how to cope with stress, we must first understand how our body's stress response works. The stress response is a survival mechanism that we are born with. Often called the "fight/flight" response, it involves a series of physiological changes which enable a person to respond to a dangerous situation by either fighting or fleeing. Heart rate increases and hormones are released which trigger the release of stored body sugar to provide a surge of energy. Respiration increases and breathing becomes more shallow. Skeletal muscles tighten, especially the muscles used for fighting or fleeing the danger: legs, lower back, neck/shoulders, arms, and jaw. Blood flow to the extremities and the abdomen is reduced to provide more blood to the muscles and the brain. Perspiration increases to cool the body after the increases in metabolic rate. Finally, all of the senses are in heightened awareness.

In a life-threatening situation, these physiological responses are totally appropriate. However, the fight/flight response is triggered by emotional stress as well as by actual physical threat; the body knows only one way to respond to stress. Everyday events such as getting stuck in traffic, talking to our parents, or asking for a job or a date can cause some of the physiological changes typical of the stress response. For instance, if you are nervous about asking someone you like for a date, your heart may start to beat more quickly, your respiration increases, and your hands become wet with perspiration.

Not only is the fight/flight response triggered by the seemingly small, everyday stresses of our lives, but these responses can become as habitual and continuous as the source of stress itself. If you had just survived a sudden accident, the physiological changes induced by the stress response would return to normal within a short period of time. If, however, you are feeling a low level of stress every day that you go to work, or every evening when you fight the traffic on your way home, your body is perpetually experiencing some degree of stress response. On a daily basis you may be tightening the muscles in your shoulders and neck, or reducing the blood flow to your abdomen, or releasing higher levels of sugar into your blood stream than you need. You may be unaware of the buildup of tension in your body, until one day you have a neck ache, or pain in your stomach, or you feel jittery and have trouble sleeping.

The physical symptoms of continuous stress are as varied as the individuals who feel them. Some people register stress primarily in their muscular system, others in their digestive system, others in their circulatory system. Symptoms can develop slowly or rapidly. The following is a list of some of the most common stress-related disorders or symptoms:

tension headaches

back pain

neck/shoulder pain or soreness

muscle cramps/spasms

chronic pain

jaw pain/TMJ/dental problems

sleeping problems

fatigue

carelessness/prone to accidents

poor concentration

migraine headache

high blood pressure

cold hands and feet/Raynaud's syndrome/poor circulation

irregular heartbeats

stroke

skin problems

asthma

breathing irregularities

arthritis

stomach pain

digestive disorders

abdominal disorders

constipation

diarrhea

overeating

sexual dysfunction

frequent colds

infectious diseases

cancer

metabolic dysfunction (hypoglycemia, hypothyroidism, etc.)

alcohol or drug abuse

anxiety

depression

emotional instabilities

fears and phobias

learning disabilities

forgetfulness

clumsiness

living in past or future

Most people develop certain weaknesses in their body over time or from an accident, and stresses often manifest in this part of the body. As we get older, we lose flexibility and resilience, and this in turn can lead to increased symptom intensity, duration, or frequency. When stress symptoms flare up, it is common to feel "out of control" or like a "victim." To overcome this feeling, it is important to understand what is contributing to or causing the stress response. Then you must alter your lifestyle or behavior to prevent or minimize the discomforts. This is precisely where stress management—relaxation, exercise, proper diet, and a wellness philosophy—can become important. By controlling your body's responses you can control your life in more positive ways.

Each chapter of this book focuses on one major life transition, beginning with the prenatal and birth experience and ending with the ultimate transition of death. I felt the information in Chapter One on the stresses of pregnancy and birth to be particularly important, as expectant parents often do not have enough information about this major life transition. Chapter Two explores the transition into parenthood and the stresses which arise when the new baby is brought home. Chapter Three covers the stresses of childhood and is designed to help parents better understand and cope with their growing child. The exercises in this chapter are especially designed for children. Chapter Four outlines the typical stresses of adolescence and the transition into the adult world. Chapter Five delves into the wide-ranging stresses of the work world. I feel this is a very important chapter, as the tensions produced by work are a major source of stress-related complaints in the clients I see. Because the stresses vary according to the type of work one does, this chapter is divided into three sections: "white-collar" work, "blue-collar" work, and working women's issues. Chapter Six provides a special look at the problems of stress-related sexual dysfunction. The transitions of midlife are addressed in Chapter Seven. The changes of the middle years are often subtle, but the mind and body are undergoing a substantial transition, and we need to take special care of ourselves during these years. Chapter Eight examines the transition into old age, another major life change which is often poorly understood. Finally, Chapter Nine explores the stresses produced by death and grieving.

The chapters are organized to provide you with easy access to the material you need in order to understand the stresses you are experiencing and to design your own stress reduction program. Each chapter begins with an introduction to the major sources of stress typically accompanying that particular growth period. This overview is not absolutely inclusive, as each individual has a unique set of life circumstances. You may experience sources of stress which are not discussed, and some of the discussion may not apply to you. Sometimes a person may actually be going through several transitions at one time. But the introduction should provide you with an understanding of the most common sources of stress for each life transition.

Following the overview, recommendations for positive lifestyle changes or coping strategies are presented. Next are case studies of people with whom I have worked who were struggling through the life transition discussed in that chapter. These case studies have been selected because they are typical, and they should help create a fuller picture of the common problems and solutions of each growth period. Where it seemed appropriate and relevant, I have shared some of my own life stresses.

After the case studies are specific relaxation techniques which have been modified or adapted to the particular circumstances and stresses of each transitional period. You will find that many of the exercises in the various chapters appear to be similar. This is because the basic relaxation techniques, such as progressive, indirect, or autogenic relaxation, follow certain standard phrases. If you look closely, however, you'll discover subtle alterations in the exercises which are designed to adapt them to specific circumstances and to produce specific results. Finally, each chapter is completed by an annotated bibliography to provide resources for further information.

This book is designed so that you can turn directly to any chapter which is relevant to you; you need not read the book cover to cover, though you may gain additional ideas by reading other chapters. Read the chapter that applies to you several times, until you decide which behavioral changes and exercises seem to make the most sense for you. Practice each exercise for at least two weeks before deciding whether or not it is right for you; the relaxations rarely work overnight. Expect to practice the exercises once or twice daily for four to six weeks before you begin to feel their benefits. The more consistent you are with the exercises, the sooner you should feel the results. Eight to twelve weeks of consistent practice usually brings the maximum results. If you do not practice daily, the exercises can still be helpful. However, it may take longer to develop the maximum skill and confidence with the exercises.

As you begin practicing the relaxation techniques, it is most effective to have someone read the exercise to you. If this is not feasible, consider making an audiotape for yourself. Recording the exercise in your own voice can be very powerful. Make sure you find a quiet time when you will not be interrupted to make the recording. Speak slowly and clearly, and pause to allow time to follow each instruction. You might read the exercise aloud several times before you record it in order to get a feel for the flow and rhythm. Special meditation or relaxation music in the background is also a nice addition. This music can be found at many bookstores, health food shops, and at record or tape stores. If you cannot find this special relaxation music, you may have to order it through the mail.

If you cannot arrange for someone to read the exercises to you and you do not want to make a tape recording, consider ordering one of the relaxation tapes from my inventory, listed in the back of this book. If at all possible, however, I recommend that you try to make your own recording first, as you can tailor it to your specific preferences.

As you read through this book please remember that the awareness of stress and its affect on your body is only half the battle toward controlling stress. The other half of the battle is to apply what you learn to your life by making needed behavioral changes—exercising more, improving your diet, taking time to enjoy the small pleasures of life—and practicing the stress management exercises on a daily basis. I hope the information in this book will serve you. Life's transitions don't have to be painful; when we take control of our stress response, these times of challenge can be growth producing and enjoyable. Good health!

BIBLIOGRAPHY

Benson, Herbert, M.D. with Miriam Klipper. *The Relaxation Response*. New York: Avon, 1975. $3.95.

Good basic book on stress's affect upon the body. Written for the layperson. Recommends a form of TM for relaxation.

Mason, L. John, Ph.D. *Guide to Stress Reduction*. Berkeley, CA: Celestial Arts, 1985. $8.95.

Basic cookbook on relaxation. Various techniques presented word for word, for the layperson or therapist.

Pelletier, Kenneth R., Ph.D. *Mind As Healer, Mind As Slayer: A Holistic Approach to Preventing Stress Disorders*. New York: Delta, 1977. $9.95.

Good basic information on stress response and the research conducted in this field. The chapter on psychophysiology of stress is great but a little too technical for many readers. Very important book for therapists.

AUDIOCASSETTE TAPES

Mason, L. John, Ph.D. *High Blood Pressure Relaxation, Relaxation for Pain,* and *Relaxation for Sleep.* 1988. All are $11.95 and can be ordered from the author.

Specially formulated relaxation exercises designed to help reduce if not eliminate the specific concerns. These guided techniques are most beneficial when practiced regularly.

CHAPTER ONE

Pregnancy & Stress

Introduction

THE MOMENT a woman becomes pregnant, a series of enormous physical, emotional, and lifestyle changes is set in motion. Because these changes happen rapidly and seemingly of their own accord, they are often felt to be highly stressful. At a time when so many things seem beyond control, it's important to remember that the one thing we can control is the way we respond to stress, change, and discomfort.

When I teach stress management classes, I always tell people that being aware of the sources of stress in our lives is half the battle of coping with stress. When we are unaware of the situations that produce stress or of how stress is affecting us, our fear and anxiety levels increase. On the other hand, once we are aware of the stressors in our lives we can learn to relax and respond to them in a positive rather than negative way.

Interestingly, whereas the physiological changes a woman experiences during pregnancy—increased hormone levels, increased appetite, etc.—are all designed to help the baby survive, a pregnant woman's response to stress produces physiological changes to help *her* survive, often at the expense of the baby. In moments of extreme stress, a series of changes occurs in the body. Called the fight or flight response, these changes include a surge of blood to the brain and large muscles so that the organism can either flee the stressful situation or fight it. If a woman is pregnant, the unborn baby's needs may be ignored as this blood rush to the brain and muscles causes blood flow to the fetus to be reduced and nutritional needs to be restricted. While the mother's body is in a state of excitement or fear, her resources are mobilized to fight the stressor, and her body cannot provide as well for the comfort or growth of the fetus. In fact, prolonged or unnaturally high levels of stress can slow if not stop the baby's development. In some extreme cases a woman may even have a spontaneous abortion when under acute stress, a physiological response designed to help the mother survive by ridding her body of the additional burden created by the fetus. When we realize how the effects of stress can work in direct opposition to the needs of the developing fetus, we see how important it is for a pregnant woman to be able to control her stress responses.

What are the major causes of stress for the pregnant woman? The most obvious is the enormous physical change which she is experiencing. Overnight the hormonal system of the body shifts into high gear as the body prepares for the developing fetus. These hormonal changes produce other physical and emotional responses. Nausea in the morning or throughout the day is common. Extreme tiredness as the body adjusts to new demands is also fairly universal. This fatigue can affect the mother emotionally as well as physically, causing heightened sensitivity, depression, or lack of motivation. Her appetite will often change drastically as nutritional needs are increased. Such strong physiological changes may make her feel that her body is "taking over," and that she is not in control.

As the time of childbirth nears, other physiological changes occur to prepare the mother's body for birth. The mother-to-be may experience increasing fatigue, backache, swelling of extremities, frequent urination, bowel problems, sleeping problems, or itchy, stretched skin. All of these symptoms can be anxiety producing. Yet if the mother knows how to relax through these symptoms rather than fight them, she can avoid added worries. In fact, many unnerving physical symptoms are actually positive, healthy ways in which the body is preparing for birth, and to recognize them as such can help reduce anxiety. For instance, contractions, which may have accompanied much of the pregnancy, can become stronger and more frequent as the time of birth nears. These contractions help massage the baby, preparing it to breathe on its own. They also help position the baby and stimulate blood flow to ensure continued nutrition. And the stretching and loosening of certain ligaments, joints, tendons, and muscles during these "warm-up" contractions can make the actual birth easier. If the mother can learn to control her stress response to these symptoms and trust in her body's natural functioning, she will be a better partner to her baby during pregnancy and childbirth.

Though less visible than physical changes, the emotional changes and concerns brought on by pregnancy can produce stress for new parents, too. The most often voiced fear I hear from parents-to-be is whether they will be able to meet their own expectations as a parent. Will they be the perfect "Super Mom" or "Super Dad"? Will they always be able to say just the right thing at the right time, never be angry or tired, and have picture-perfect birthday parties? The only one who seems to hold these extraordinarily high expectations, interestingly, is the parent. It is easy to look at someone else and acknowledge that that person wasn't always the perfect parent, but somehow we always expect ourselves to meet unrealistically high standards. I encourage expectant parents to form realistic expectations about their abilities as parents and to be prepared to make mistakes. After all, would you want to be the child of a "perfect" parent?

Another source of emotional anxiety for expectant parents is concern about their baby's health, at birth and in the future. Will their child be normal and healthy? Will he develop physically, mentally, and emotionally as he should? Along with these more general concerns, many parents have conscious or unconscious ideas about the kind of child they want—boy or girl, blond or brunette, creative genius or football star—and hold silent anxieties about whether their wishes will be fulfilled. I encourage parents to set aside their preconceived ideas and open their hearts to the magic and beauty of the act of creation, celebrating the gift of birth as one of the most amazing experiences they will ever have.

The pregnant mother may feel anxious about her attractiveness and sexuality during pregnancy. Her self-image is undergoing radical change, and while the association with motherhood is usually positive, her large body may make her feel awkward and clumsy. Her partner may also have feelings of insecurity as he feels the mom-to-be becoming absorbed with the growing life within her.

Concern about adjustment to a new life routine and new responsibility is another frequently sounded theme I hear from expectant parents. If this is a first child, the loss of freedom and mobility will indeed be an adjustment, but even if a couple already has children, the added responsibility will affect

the family's routine. The equations that have been maintained between work, fun, and relationships will be thrown out of equilibrium. Time can become a precious commodity, and some recreational or social activities may have to be temporarily suspended or altered. Yet the parent's life needn't totally revolve around the new baby. As one expectant father put it, "I can handle getting up earlier to help change and feed the baby, and not going out to eat as often, but the baby's just going to have to learn to enjoy a soccer game every weekend!"

The additional financial burden of a new baby can also force lifestyle changes and is a common source of stress for parents-to-be. Perhaps the father will have to work longer hours than he would like, or the mother may need to return to work sooner than she would choose. In many cases, the family must do some belt tightening, curtailing certain purchases to accommodate the baby's expenses. And sometimes these financial pressures create other strains, as, for instance, a woman tries to arrange more flexible hours at her job and meets resistance from her employer.

Recent focus on the connection between a pregnant woman's health habits and the health of her baby has caused many women to alter certain health behaviors during pregnancy. Although many women want to make these positive changes, adopting new lifestyle patterns can be difficult and stress producing. A pregnant mother may want to change her diet by cutting down on sugar and eating more protein and fresh fruits and vegetables. She may need to curtail her use of alcohol and caffeine. If she smokes, she may feel pressure to stop. Recent research has shown a connection between mothers who smoke during pregnancy and low birth weight or premature babies. When a mother smokes, blood flow to the unborn baby is constricted. Just as in the fight or flight response, this decreased blood flow reduces nutrition and will have a negative effect on the baby's growth and development. A pregnant woman will also want to review her use of drugs and medications. If the drug is not absolutely necessary, for the sake of the baby, it should probably be avoided.

To find out more about the effects of the mother's health habits on her developing baby, I recommend taking a birth class as early in the pregnancy as possible, especially if it offers information on diet, exercise, and stress management techniques. Although it may be difficult to stop smoking or to say no to that extra cup of coffee, investing in your baby's healthy development during pregnancy is one of the most important investments you will ever make as an adult.

Stress Management Recommendations for Pregnancy

The practice of stress reduction techniques can be one of the most important activities the pregnant mother and her partner engage in as they prepare for their baby. At every stage of pregnancy, from conception to birth, knowing how to relax fully will assist the baby's development, the mother's comfort, and the ease of the pregnancy and delivery. Some research has been conducted to determine whether mothers who practice relaxation techniques, listen to classical music, or talk soothingly to the fetus are actually aiding the baby's healthy development and positive adjustment to future life. While research in this area is far from complete, we do know that a stressful environment is definitely unhealthy for the unborn baby. Excessive noise, smoking, drug use, and poor diet are known contributors to health problems in newborns and low birth weight or premature infants.

Sharon McKenzie, the instructor for the birth class my wife and I attended, maintains that relaxation training is one of the most crucial activities she teaches in her prenatal-childbirth classes. She recommends that couples practice relaxation exercises daily and encourages them to associate the calm state they achieve with pleasing music or a special fragrance. This association can be very helpful during labor, especially if you are in the unfamiliar surroundings of a hospital. The relaxation reflex can be more easily triggered if you take your special music and fragrance with you to help remind you of the deep relaxations previously achieved at home. Much of the information in this chapter was discussed in Sharon's class, and my wife and I benefited greatly from her suggestions.

In addition to practicing relaxation exercises, one of the best stress management strategies during pregnancy is to take a prenatal birthing class, and I recommend you do so as early in the pregnancy as possible. Many people think of birthing classes as only preparation for labor, but in fact these classes can offer much support and information to help you through the first trimester of pregnancy, a critical period in the baby's development. Information about diet and exercise for the pregnant mother is commonly offered in prenatal classes. Being aware of proper diet and exercise as well as the importance of avoiding certain drugs and medications is extremely important during these first three months, as the fetus is particularly susceptible in its early development to the effects of maternal dietary deficiencies and drug use.

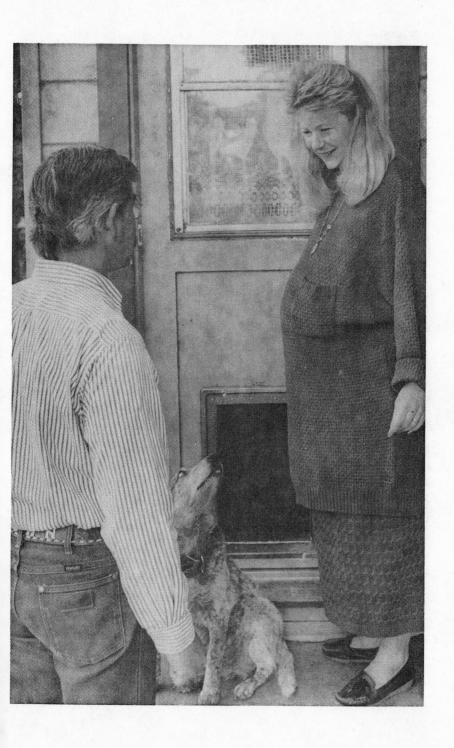

Proper diet and exercise benefit the mother in these early months too, bolstering her energy and often helping to combat nausea. The emotional support which birthing classes provide can be invaluable to the mother throughout her pregnancy, and these classes provide an opportunity for the father to become better acquainted with the facts of pregnancy and birth and to be closely involved with his wife's experience.

Prenatal training classes can also teach techniques to control pain during birth. Certain breathing and massage techniques and the use of certain positions during labor and birth can help reduce discomfort. Desensitization exercises, practiced throughout the pregnancy, can help reduce or eliminate fears about birth. A positive visualization of the birth experience can make parents more confident when the actual moment arrives. It is not an overstatement to say that the inability to relax when under stress is the greatest contributor to pain and discomfort during birth and throughout the entire pregnancy.

Birth classes can also help parents know their options for participating in the birth experience, enabling them to discuss plans knowledgeably with their doctor. Do you want to use breathing techniques instead of anesthetics? If so, how? Do you want your partner present at the birth? Do you want other family members to be present? The more information you gather about what to expect throughout pregnancy and birth, the greater confidence and sense of control you'll have.

Physical exercise is another important technique for relaxation during pregnancy. Exercise helps to dissipate, in a positive way, the tensions that can build as you anticipate your new responsibilities. Walking, bike riding (you can use a stationary bike later in the pregnancy), and especially swimming are excellent exercises for the mother-to-be. A moderate workout will not only promote cardiovascular conditioning, it will also increase blood flow throughout the mother's body, especially to the fetus. Getting in shape, increasing both strength and endurance, can make labor easier, too. And making a commitment to exercise during pregnancy can help to establish regular exercise as a part of your family life.

Massage is another excellent stress reduction strategy for both mother- and father-to-be. Massage helps relax the musculature, can improve communication between partners, and also promotes increased blood flow to the extremities and, for the mother, to the fetus. Some birthing classes teach massage techniques that both partners can use with each other, although late in the pregnancy the mother's ability to massage her partner may be restricted.

Certain massage techniques are specifically useful during labor, such as perineal support massage which can help the mother avoid an episiotomy by relaxing and stretching the skin around the vagina.

Case Study #1

Barbara, my wife, was thirty-nine when we learned we were going to have a baby. Like all expectant parents, we found ourselves experiencing a wide range of emotions: happiness, excitement, fear, sadness, joy, self-doubt, even anger. We spent time discussing how we would like to have this pregnancy and our child develop. Barbara was determined to have a very different experience with this pregnancy than with her first. Her seventeen-year-old son, Matt, had been born in a military hospital at a time when the mother's participation in childbirth was expected to be minimal and standard hospital procedures were not questioned. She had not been well informed about prenatal health care, had been given medication for morning sickness with no information about possible side effects, and had had no support network of family, friends or trained birthing coaches during the pregnancy. She had been alone during the seven hours of her labor, had been given a spinal anesthetic as the baby was born, and was in a recovery room with an IV for eight hours afterward to prevent side effects from the spinal. The baby was whisked away as soon as he was born and she did not see him again until the next morning.

We both wanted to actively participate in this birth experience, to be highly informed about prenatal care, to have family and a birth coach present at the birth, and to keep medical procedures to a minimum. We did not consider a home birth because of Barbara's age, but within the hospital setting we wanted to have the birth be as "natural" as possible.

During the first two months of pregnancy Barbara was nauseous, tired, and weak. She actually lost ten pounds because she could not eat. Yet she was extremely motivated to take good care of herself and the baby. While she was too tired to exercise vigorously, she managed to walk for at least twenty minutes a day. And even if she didn't feel like eating, she drank a high protein drink each day made with brewer's yeast and wheat germ, good sources of B vitamins which help combat nausea and increase energy. We both felt that the stresses of these early months when Barbara was not feeling well were minimized because we felt well informed and able to make good choices about Barbara's health care. Barbara also established a good support network of family and friends early in the pregnancy, so she could call and talk with someone whenever she was feeling low or confused about some symptom.

When Barbara was six months' pregnant we took a birthing class which provided a great deal of information about the parents' rights, responsibilities, and options during pregnancy and childbirth. The training emphasized the importance of diet and exercise and encouraged prospective parents to avoid medication and unnecessary medical procedures except in cases of medical emergencies. Our instructor also included weekly relaxation exercises, and I was pleased when she pulled out my first book, *Guide to Stress Reduction*, to lead the exercises. When she found out I had authored the book, she invited me to lead a relaxation, from which I developed some of the specific exercises listed later in this chapter.

This class was a fantastic aid to us, and we wished we had taken it much earlier in the pregnancy because it offered so much important information and support for the early stages of pregnancy, particularly the first trimester. I also took some special training in stress reduction and hypnosis at this time from David Cheek, MD, whose work is discussed in this chapter. I was intrigued to learn that Dr. Cheek believes labor and delivery should take only three hours, and that if it takes longer it is because stress or anxiety is interfering with the body's natural processes.

During the latter part of the pregnancy Barbara and I eagerly put into practice all that we had learned so far. Barbara continued to exercise, get plenty of rest, and eat well. We did hypnosis together. I made a prenatal stress reduction tape with positive visualizations for her and she listened to it once or twice a day. We later made a desensitization tape to reduce fears about childbirth, and she used it daily during the last six weeks of pregnancy. We did our birthing exercises together. We listened to classical music and special relaxation music. We talked to our unborn baby, hoping to establish a relationship with him. We prepared our house and tried to prepare our lives for the coming of the baby.

Though we continued to have anxieties throughout Barbara's pregnancy about how this new baby was going to affect our lives, we felt strong and in control as the birth date approached. One week before the due date, while we were in a shopping mall, Barbara began feeling contractions, and within three hours and fifteen minutes our nine-pound, four-ounce baby boy was born. Though we didn't have much time, we were able to make it to the hospital, gather our birthing team, including Matt, our son, and help the baby into the world without the use of drugs or an episiotomy. Barbara held the baby as soon as he was born and he slept through his first night at her side.

Case Study #2

Betty was thirty-four years old and single when she became pregnant. After much thought, she made the difficult decision to have her baby without marrying. She was a nurse, so she had a good financial base and felt confident she could provide her baby with a loving, stable home.

Because of her nursing background, she was well informed about the baby's prenatal needs. She understood the importance of proper diet and regular exercise and made sure during her pregnancy that these needs were met. She also avoided taking any drugs or medications throughout her pregnancy. Even though Betty attended to her physical needs conscientiously, she neglected to take her emotional needs as seriously. She knew that the hospital where she was to have her baby offered stress reduction classes, yet she did not take advantage of them. She also did not spend time developing a support network of friends, other pregnant mothers, and professionals. As her pregnancy progressed and the reality of what she was doing began to sink in, she became increasingly anxious and concerned that she would not be able to cope with her and her baby's future. All of the traditional expectations about marriage which she had been raised to believe began to surface, creating doubts in her mind about what she was doing. Because she did not have a good support network or a way to cope with stress, these concerns began to take their toll.

When Betty's labor began, she took herself to the hospital, settled into the alternative birthing room, and then tried to relax. Unfortunately, her feelings of aloneness and vulnerability were only heightened as she struggled with her labor unaided by friends or family. After thirty-six hours of contractions, she had not dilated enough to deliver the baby, and a decision was made to perform a cesarean section. Although other factors certainly could have contributed to Betty's "stuck" labor, I feel that her lack of relaxation training and adequate emotional support was probably a significant reason that her labor did not proceed more easily. It was as if she were unconsciously holding the baby back from its entry into the world because she felt unprepared to deal with the stress of single parenthood.

I did not work with Betty, but heard of her case through a friend. In contrast to Betty's experience is the case of Amanda, another single mom whom I helped with relaxation training during her pregnancy. Amanda is a strong-willed, self-confident woman who runs her own typography business. She came to me when she was three months' pregnant because she wanted to make sure the relaxation and visualization exercises she was doing were adequate. She was highly informed about the importance of self-care during pregnancy, particularly in the first trimester, and didn't want to wait to learn more about relaxation practice until she took a birthing class in her sixth or seventh month.

I was pleased to discover that Amanda was already monitoring her nutritional intake carefully, was getting regular exercise, and had a circle of friends, family members, and professionals to whom she could turn for emotional support. I helped her learn an indirect relaxation exercise similar to the one presented in this chapter, and made a tape for her so she could practice regularly. On the tape I included special visualizations of nutrition flowing easily to the baby, of the baby growing healthily, and of a special love and connection flowing between Amanda and her unborn child. I also encouraged Amanda to continue her yoga, swimming, and gentle bicycling to strengthen her muscles and as general conditioning in preparation for the stress of childbirth. And I recommended that she begin immediately to work with a birth coach in order to develop a firm relationship with her and to be able to benefit from her knowledge and suggestions throughout the pregnancy.

Amanda felt the payoff of her attentive self-care when the time for her baby's birth arrived. She had two hours of preparatory contractions and then 3 1/2 hours of hard labor. Her birth coach and friends were with her in the birthing room, offering love and support. They dimmed the lights, helped Amanda with her breathing, gave her massages, and did a quiet, positive meditation to welcome the baby into the world.

Amanda had a healthy, good-natured baby boy, who slept and ate well right from the beginning. However, he was still a lot of work! Amanda knew she would need to continue taking care of herself after he was born if she didn't want to become a frazzled mom. She arranged to have friends stay with her and do the cooking and housework for the first couple of weeks after the birth, and she continued to rely on her friends and family for emotional support as the baby grew. I think of Amanda as a sterling example of how anxiety about parenting can be transformed into positive self-care.

Relaxation Exercises for Pregnancy

HYPNOSIS AND PENDULUM QUESTIONING

We know that the mind and body work together on many levels to create health/wellness or illness. We also know that the subconscious part of the mind controls about ninety percent of the activity of the brain, including our survival (flight/fight) response mechanism. Thus it makes sense to establish a positive communication link with the subconscious as we attempt to build well-being. Hypnosis and pendulum questioning are excellent mechanisms to develop better communication between the conscious and the subconscious parts of your mind. Through these techniques you can gain a heightened awareness of your subconscious processes and increased control over your body. The mind does not consciously choose illness or other negative behaviors, but often it knows no other option. Hypnosis and pendulum questioning allow you to offer positive suggestions to your subconscious and redirect your body's responses to stress in a positive way.

I learned about pendulum questioning from David Cheek, MD. Dr. Cheek has been a practicing OB/GYN for many years. While assisting mothers in childbirth, he came to believe that stress and anxiety were the prime reasons for a slow or "stuck" labor. He recommends relaxation and breathing exercises for any pregnant woman. Dr. Cheek also is trained in hypnosis and has done research on the use of certain hypnotic techniques to help overcome blocks to easy labors and deliveries. I had attended a couple of his workshops because I have an interest in hypnosis-assisted relaxation. When I heard Dr. Cheek say that the normal childbirth should occur within three hours, I was amazed and slightly skeptical. I told my wife, Barbara, who was several months' pregnant at the time, what I had heard, and we decided to try his procedure for pendulum questioning ourselves. Barbara was thirty-nine years old and I wanted her pregnancy and labor to be as easy as possible.

Because the subconscious mind controls fine motor coordination, the pendulum, held gently between your fingers, can be used to communicate directly with the subconscious. You simply ask the pendulum questions and observe which way it moves to determine the response of the subconscious. If the response is not the one you want, you can ask it politely but firmly to come up with a more positive view. The technique we used is outlined below. If you want to explore this procedure further, you can call a local hypnotherapist to help you. (The training should take only a brief time, perhaps one or two sessions.)

First, get a pendulum that you can hold with your fingers easily. Two feet of string and a house key work fine, though some people prefer fancy crystals or jewelry. Fishing weights work well also. Sit comfortably in a quiet room and hold the pendulum between your thumb and first finger of either hand. Allow about a foot of string between your fingers and the weight. To begin, you need to establish the direction that the pendulum will move to indicate no, yes, or no answer as you ask your questions. The pendulum has four choices of movement: sideways, up and down, in a circle clockwise, or in a circle counterclockwise. Watch the weight, but do not try to move it. Do not try not to move it either. Think of the word yes for a few moments and see which way the pendulum begins to move. Now think of the word no and watch the direction the pendulum moves. Finally, you can establish the movement the pendulum would make if the subconscious mind did not want to answer a difficult or overly direct question.

After you have determined how the pendulum will move to indicate yes, no, or no answer, you can proceed to ask questions of your subconscious mind. Begin by asking if the subconscious mind is willing to answer questions regarding your baby and the pregnancy. If the pendulum moves in the yes direction, then proceed with questions about how long the labor will last (in hours). Do this by asking if the labor will be less than ten hours. If the pendulum indicates yes, ask if the labor will be less than five hours, and so on. You want the subconscious mind to agree with you on some appropriate length of time, hopefully close to three hours. If you have difficulty getting the pendulum to agree and to answer yes, ask if there is a problem. If so, you may need to explore, through yes/no questions, what the source of the problem might be. Be a careful detective in your questioning. Barbara's subconscious wanted a six-hour labor, but we talked it down to a three- to three-and-one-half-hour labor, and that is what occurred. You may also want to ask about the date and time of birth and the weight, length, or sex of the baby. We found out through pendulum questioning that we were going to have a healthy-sized, full-term baby boy. Barbara did, in fact, have a nine-pound, four-ounce baby boy who was healthy and strong. I will not promise that you will get one hundred percent accurate information, but the exercise may prove helpful. You may find that somewhere inside you have resistance or an unresolved feeling that creates an emotional blockage for you with regard to the birth or your future parenting. If you cannot resolve this blockage yourself, you may wish to see a counselor or hypnotherapist who can help you so the pregnancy and labor go more smoothly and easily.

BREATHING TECHNIQUES FOR PREGNANCY AND BIRTH

Slow, relaxed breathing is one of the best ways to handle the stress of pregnancy and birth. Breathing exercises can also benefit the baby, helping him to grow healthily, make the transition into the world more gracefully, and be more relaxed and calm during the first weeks of life.

If you want to test the powerful effect on your baby of your relaxed breathing, try this simple test while you are pregnant. After some moderate exercise, lie down, begin to relax the major muscles of your body, then take three deep slow breaths. Continue breathing slowly and naturally, feeling the cool air as you inhale and the warm air as you exhale. Usually, if you are into at least your eighteenth or twentieth week, you will feel the baby begin to move as you become relaxed. Your relaxation gives him the freedom to move easily. The added oxygen from your deep breathing also stimulates the baby, but be careful not to breathe so deeply that you hyperventilate.

I recommend the slow breathing techniques listed below to manage stress during pregnancy and to allow for the healthy development of your unborn child. I also feel these techniques may be all a mother needs to control pain during labor. However, many birth classes teach specific breathing techniques for use during labor, and if you find these valuable, by all means use them. As with all stress reduction exercises, I recommend that you practice the various techniques until you find the ones that work best for you.

#1. Try this. Lie down flat or stand up straight. Put one hand over your stomach and one hand over your chest, and see which way each hand moves as you inhale. Now which way do your hands move as you exhale? Does your bottom hand move first and outward as you begin the inhale? Does the upper hand then move up and out? On the exhale, do you notice that both hands move in, perhaps forcing the last bit of air out? If so, then you are breathing very well and you can go on to the next breathing exercises. If not, you should practice a bit before you continue, as this breathing technique forms the basis of every stress management exercise.

#2. Now try breathing very slowly while you are in a comfortable position. As you inhale slowly but comfortably, count 1–4. Perhaps you can picture the numbers in your mind, or say them slowly to yourself. Now pause for a moment and count 1–4 again as you hold your breath (slowly, picturing the numbers in your mind if possible). And now as you exhale, slowly and comfortably count 1–8. Let your body relax more deeply as you exhale fully and completely, feeling the warm air as you exhale. You might want to repeat this

for three breaths. Then check to see if you are feeling more relaxed. You may need to check the muscles of your shoulders, neck, and jaw. If you can let these muscle groups relax further, take another slow breath.

#3. Another breathing/counting exercise that works well is to take four slow breaths, counting to eight by counting one on the inhale, two on the exhale, three on the inhale, etc. Try to picture the numbers in your mind or say the numbers to yourself. After counting to eight, check your position, relax your jaw, forehead, neck, and shoulders and repeat the exercise one more time. Within about two minutes you can begin to feel more relaxed and open, releasing tension with each exhale. Remember, go slowly. Do not be in such a hurry to relax!

#4. Take three deep slow breaths. As you lie down or sit back comfortably, allow yourself to breathe slowly. Feel the cool air as you inhale, pause a moment, and then slowly exhale, feeling the warm breath carry away tensions or discomforts. You might try to feel the cool air at the tip of your nostrils. Exhale through your mouth, breathing away the warm air as if it will drift up into the sky like a helium-filled balloon. Let go slowly and easily, becoming more relaxed with every breath. Some people use this exercise not only to relax but to help them drift off to sleep.

#5. Special breathing behavior. This breathing technique works well for active people as it associates deep breathing with a regularly occurring signal in the environment. For instance, if you find yourself eating many small snacks while you are pregnant in order to maintain a consistent blood sugar level, you can use "snack time" as a cue to take a moment to relax. Or remember to stop and relax every time you feel the baby move, or every time the phone rings. Decide upon a "signal" and then each time it occurs, take one slow deep breath, scan your body—let your shoulders drop, jaw relax, arms and legs loosen—and let go of unnecessary tensions. By stopping periodically to release tensions, you prevent them from building to harmful levels.

These various breathing techniques work best when practiced on a regular basis. Find one or two that work well for you, and then use them consistently. I particularly recommend that you begin practicing these exercises, and the others suggested in this chapter, early in pregnancy. Become familiar with them so that when you need them later in pregnancy or during labor your body will respond automatically. If you are unable to begin these exercises in the first trimester, practice with greater frequency, perhaps two or three times a day rather than once a day.

AUTOGENIC TRAINING

The instructions for autogenic training follow a fairly standard format and can be used for any stressful situation. However, once you have reached a state of relaxation, you can combine the autogenic exercise with visualizations which are tailored to your specific situation. In the following exercise I introduce visualizations, once the relaxation has been induced, which focus on the healthy development of your unborn baby. If other issues are causing you stress, such as financial concerns, or concerns about your own health, you can adapt the visualizations to fit your individual needs.

Depending on what your schedule can tolerate and how your pregnancy is going, you may find yourself taking a morning or afternoon rest. This exercise can help revitalize you during these brief periods of recuperation.

Read this exercise slowly (about half normal speaking speed). Pause at each (*). Do not be concerned by mispronunciations or verbal slips. Continue in a calm, even voice.

Find a quiet location where you will not be disturbed. Allow about twenty minutes for this exercise. Sit or lie back comfortably, allowing your arms and legs to remain uncrossed if possible. Let your head be supported and let your shoulders drop into a comfortable position. Check the muscles of your head and face. Let your forehead become calm and smooth. Allow the muscles around your eyes to loosen. Check the muscles of your mouth and jaw to make sure they are relaxed. Finally, allow your eyes to remain closed, remembering that you can open them whenever you need to use them.

Before we begin the relaxation, remember not to try to relax too quickly. In fact, do not try to relax at all. Without any effort you can allow yourself to relax by pleasantly letting go of tensions and discomforts, and then letting yourself drift deeper into a peaceful calmness. To begin the relaxation, take three deep breaths, pausing after you inhale, and then exhaling fully and completely. You might imagine that you release tensions and discomforts as you exhale by just breathing them away. After you have finished these first three breaths, continue breathing slowly and naturally, relaxing more deeply with each slow exhale.

Repeat these phrases to yourself, exactly as they are taken from this exercise, and try to feel your body responding to the commands. If you need to repeat the phrases more than three times to begin to feel results, then continue the repetitions a few additional times.

Repeat this mood phrase to yourself three times: "I am at peace with myself and fully relaxed." Continue breathing slowly and gently.

Begin to feel the muscles of your arms relax as you say, "My right arm is heavy * . . . My right arm is heavy * . . . My right arm is heavy * . . ." Repeat this phrase slowly until you begin to feel the heaviness spreading through your arm. Now turn your awareness to your left arm as you breathe slowly and say to yourself, "My left arm is heavy * . . . My left arm is heavy * . . . My left arm is heavy * . . ." Try to feel the heaviness starting in your arms or feel free to continue slowly repeating this phrase a few more times. Now proceed to your legs. Let them begin to relax as you breathe slowly. Feel the heaviness and relaxation starting in your legs as you slowly repeat, "My right leg is heavy * . . . My right leg is heavy * . . . My right leg is heavy * . . ." You can repeat this several more times if you need to, until you begin to feel the relaxation and the heaviness. Now focus on the left leg and feel it beginning to relax as you say, "My left leg is heavy * . . . My left leg is heavy * . . . My left leg is heavy * . . ." Repeat if needed. With practice you will feel the heaviness more quickly and easily. Now turn your attention to your neck and shoulders. Let them sink into a more comfortable position and let the muscles relax as you breathe gently and say, "My neck and shoulders are heavy * . . . My neck and shoulders are heavy * . . . My neck and shoulders are heavy * . . ." Repeat if needed. Take a deep slow breath and feel the heaviness and relaxation as you begin to sink back into whatever you are sitting or lying upon.

Perhaps you can feel the blood beginning to flow more easily down into your hands or your feet as the blood vessels begin to dilate, as the smooth muscles in the walls of the arteries begin to relax. Focus on the feelings of warmth, or a pulse, or perhaps a tingling feeling in your right hand as you say, "My right arm is warm * . . . My right arm is warm * . . . My right arm is warm * . . ." Repeat this slowly several more times until you begin to feel the warmth or pulse. Heaviness is generally easier for most people to feel than warmth, but with continued practice you can begin to control the blood flow. Now turn your attention to your left arm and say to yourself, "My left arm is warm * . . . My left arm is warm * . . . My left arm is warm * . . ." Repeat if needed. Perhaps you can start to feel the warmth in your arms, and you may feel the blood flowing freely through your entire body. As you breathe slowly and gently, turn your awareness to your legs and say to your-self, "My right leg is warm * . . . My right leg is warm * . . . My right leg is warm * . . ." Repeat several more times to help develop this skill. Move your attention to your left leg and say, "My left leg is warm * . . . My left leg is warm * . . . My left leg is warm * . . ." Repeat if needed. Feel the heaviness and warmth in your arms and your legs as you breathe slowly and gently. Now turn your awareness to your neck and shoulders, and say, "My neck and shoulders are warm * . . . My neck and shoulders are warm * . . . My neck and shoulders are warm * . . ." Repeat if needed. Breathe slowly as you drift for a few moments, feeling the heaviness and warmth spreading pleasantly throughout your body.

Slow and calm your heart by slowly repeating to yourself, "My heartbeat is calm and regular * . . . My heartbeat is calm and regular * . . . My heartbeat is calm and regular * . . ." Repeat if needed. If you experience any discomfort with this phrase, then change to the phrase "I feel calm * . . . I feel calm * . . . I feel calm * . . ." As you breathe slowly, begin to feel the peace and relaxation spreading to every part of your body.

To slow your breathing say to yourself as you breathe into your diaphragm, "My breathing is calm and regular * . . . My breathing is calm and regular * . . . My breathing is calm and regular * . . ." Repeat if needed.

Become aware of the relaxation starting in your stomach region. As you breathe slowly say, "My abdomen is warm and calm * . . . My abdomen is warm and calm * . . . My abdomen is warm and calm * . . . Repeat if needed. If you are in the last trimester of pregnancy, change this phrase to "I am calm and relaxed * . . . I am calm and relaxed * . . . I am calm and relaxed * . . ." Feel the sensations of warmth and relaxation beginning to spread through your abdomen. As you breathe slowly and gently you can remain calm and comfortable as you encourage even more warmth from increased blood flow.

Move on to your forehead and let the muscles of your head and face relax as you say, "My forehead is cool and calm * . . . My forehead is cool and calm * . . . My forehead is cool and calm * . . ." As you breathe slowly, feel the muscles around your eyes, mouth, and jaw loosen and then relax.

Let yourself drift pleasantly in this calmness. As you breathe gently, perhaps you can feel the heaviness in your arms and legs as the muscles relax. * Perhaps you can begin to feel the warmth or pulse of blood flowing more easily down into your hands and perhaps even your feet, like sunshine or a bath gently warming you. Some people feel the warming as if it were a tingling sensation spreading blood more easily into the extremities. * As you enjoy the relaxation you can feel that your heartbeat is calm and regular. *

With practice, you can feel the relaxation more easily and quickly. The warmth of blood flowing into your hands and feet gradually grows easier to control. The relaxation will then carry over with you throughout your day. You will be able to develop the control to see yourself remaining calm and comfortable, enjoying your pregnancy, letting it be pleasurable and productive. The relaxation will aid you in pregnancy and in childbirth. Both will move more smoothly and easily. The baby will respond by developing fully as he feels your love. He will be healthy and full of joy after birth. The relaxation may also help you to bond with your child by reducing stresses and anxiety that may create some distance.

At the end of this relaxation exercise, awaken yourself slowly. Feel the bed or chair beneath you and say, "I am refreshed and completely alert * ... I am refreshed and completely alert * ... I am refreshed and completely alert * ..." Then take a deep breath and stretch, allowing yourself to wake fully, and let the relaxation carry over with you into a fully waking state. You may wish to take another deep breath and stretch, letting the relaxation return with you.

PROGRESSIVE RELAXATION

As with the autogenic training, the progressive relaxation exercise follows a fairly standard format. Once the relaxation is induced, however, you can use positive suggestions and visualizations which address your specific situation. You might picture your state of relaxation helping to relax your baby. Imagine her feeling comfortable and at ease within your womb. Or you might imagine your relaxed state helping the blood flow easily to your baby, bringing vital nutrients to nurture her. Or imagine your feelings of peace and comfort flowing to your child, enveloping her in love. If you have a particular concern or worry, use the visualization to picture a positive outcome to the situation.

Read this exercise slowly (about half normal speaking speed). Pause at each (*). Do not be concerned by mispronunciations or verbal slips. Continue in a calm, even voice.

Find a quiet location where you will not be disturbed. Allow about twenty minutes for this exercise. Sit or lie back comfortably, allowing your arms and legs to remain uncrossed if possible. Let your head be supported and let your shoulders drop into a comfortable position. Check the muscles of your head and face. Let your forehead become calm and smooth. Allow the muscles around your eyes to loosen. Check the muscles of the mouth and jaw to make sure they are relaxed. Finally, allow your eyes to remain closed, remembering that you can open them whenever you need to use them.

The skill of relaxation can be of great value in creating an ideal environment for the unborn baby. As you relax, your blood flows more easily to your baby, bringing him added nutrients. Your feelings of peace and comfort

will help your baby to feel comfortable too, enabling him to grow strong and healthy. The relaxation procedures can also be useful as you face the birthing, then parenting experiences.

Before we begin the relaxation, remember not to try to relax too quickly. In fact, do not try to relax at all. Without any effort you can allow yourself to relax by pleasantly letting go of tensions and discomforts, and then letting yourself drift deeper into a peaceful calmness. To begin the relaxation, take three deep breaths, pausing after you inhale, and then exhaling fully and completely. You might imagine that you release tensions and discomforts as you exhale by just breathing them away. * After you have finished these first three breaths, continue breathing slowly and naturally, relaxing more deeply with each slow exhale.

As you continue to breathe slowly and gently, begin to focus your attention on the muscles in your feet. You may even want to move your toes briefly to see how these muscles feel. Let them rest in the most comfortable position and then use your imagination to see or feel these muscles relaxing even further. Slowly exhale, breathing away any energy or tension in your toes. As you breathe slowly, imagine these muscles becoming more soft and flexible. * Turn your awareness to the muscles of the arch of your foot. The muscles from the ball of your foot below the big toe down to the heel can relax even further. Take a slow breath and then imagine that as you exhale you release the tensions from these muscles. * Now feel the sides and the top of your foot. Can you feel your shoes or socks touching your foot? As you breathe slowly and naturally, can you let the muscles of your foot relax more? You might even be able to feel a pulse or tingling sensation gradually spreading warmth and relaxation to every muscle of your foot. *

Turn your awareness to your lower leg. Can you feel your ankles, * the calves, * your shin bones? * Feel the muscles of your lower legs, and notice that you can relax these muscles even further. Breathe slowly as you feel the muscles softening. You may even feel the knee starting to relax into a more comfortable position. As your awareness increases, your skill at relaxing will also. You will feel your control increasing as you practice letting these muscle groups relax even more. * Now become aware of your upper legs. Feel the large muscles of the sides and top of your legs relax slowly as you exhale the unwanted energies and tensions. * You can now relax the big muscles of the back of your upper legs. As these muscles relax, you might even feel the relaxation spreading up through your pelvic area into the lower back. The big muscles of the leg may loosen so that you can feel the sensation of heaviness down the length of your leg. * Breathe slowly and gently. You might even feel the pulse of blood flowing more freely and easily down your leg into your foot and toes. *

The relaxation can now begin to spread up into your lower back. As the muscles of your back begin to soften, you might feel the relaxation spreading to the other muscles of the back. Feel the muscles of your upper back, including your shoulders, let go even further. Your shoulders may be able to drop down into a more comfortable position. * Feel your head sinking back into the chair or pillow, totally supported, as the muscles of your neck let go even more. * Continue breathing slowly and gently as you feel the relaxation spreading down through your arms. * The muscles of your upper arms may feel loose and comfortable. * Your lower arms, even your wrists, can relax further. As you breathe slowly, feel the sensation of heaviness as your arms sink back into the bed or chair. * The relaxation can slowly drift down into your hands and fingers. * You may feel a pulse of blood flowing freely and easily down into your hands. Feel your hands warm comfortably, letting you drift deeper into comfort and relaxation. *

The muscles of your head and face may be able to relax even more. Your forehead may feel more calm and smooth. * The muscles around the eyes can let go. * Even the muscles of the mouth and the jaw might be able to relax even further. * Slowly breathing away stress, you can control these tensions through relaxation. * The sensations of peace and harmony grow stronger as you allow yourself to drift deeper in this peaceful calmness. *

The relaxation can drift down into your chest. As you breathe slowly, you might feel the relaxation gently spreading to the other muscles of the torso. You can feel your heartbeat, calm and regular. * The relaxation spreads down into your stomach region. * You may be able to feel the sensation of warmth glowing gently in the stomach region. * Imagine that the baby is both comforted and nurtured in an ideal environment. The baby may respond to relaxation by increasing her activity. Continue breathing slowly and gently as you drift peacefully in this relaxation. * Perhaps you can feel the heaviness of your arms and your legs as you learn to control tensions better and better. *

With practice, you will be able to relax more easily and quickly. You will relax more deeply, and the effects will last longer throughout the day. Your awareness of tensions will grow stronger so that you can control your energies and your responses to stressors more effectively.

Relaxation can benefit you and your baby. Your pregnancy may be more calm. The birthing transition can be surprisingly easy, as you bring the baby into the world with grace and love.

If you are using this exercise at bedtime you may wish to drift off into a pleasant sleep, resting fully and awakening refreshed and alert. If you wish to drift off to sleep, continue breathing slowly and focus on the feelings of relaxation in your arms and legs. *

If you wish to awaken now, you can begin to do so. Let yourself gradually return to this room, feeling the bed or the chair beneath you. As you slowly awaken, bring the feelings of calmness, relaxation, health, and happiness back with you into a more fully waking state. Take a deep breath and stretch, letting the calmness return with you. Take another deep breath and stretch, allowing yourself to awaken feeling refreshed and alert, letting the relaxation and calmness continue with you.

INDIRECT RELAXATION

Indirect relaxation is so named because it suggests and provides options for relaxation rather than giving specific commands; thus the relaxation suggestions are "indirect." The instructions provide you with a choice of responses, and you are encouraged to feel how your body reacts in its own unique way. This exercise works powerfully on the subconscious mind, perhaps because the more flexible formula reduces potential resistance to the positive suggestions. Again, I suggest that you become familiar with this technique early in pregnancy so you can benefit from its results throughout your pregnancy and during labor.

Read this exercise slowly (about half normal speaking speed). Pause at each (*). Do not be concerned by mispronunciations or verbal slips. Continue in a calm, even voice.

Find a quiet location where you will not be disturbed. Allow about twenty minutes for this exercise. Sit or lie back comfortably, allowing your arms and legs to remain uncrossed if possible. Let your head be supported and let your shoulders drop into a comfortable position. Check the muscles of your head and face. Let your forehead become calm and smooth. Allow the muscles around your eyes to loosen. Check the muscles of the mouth and jaw to make sure they are relaxed. Finally, allow your eyes to remain closed, remembering that you can open them whenever you need to use them.

Before we begin the relaxation, remember not to try to relax too quickly. In fact, do not try to relax at all. Without any effort you can allow yourself to relax by pleasantly letting go of tensions and discomforts, and then letting yourself drift deeper into a peaceful calmness. To begin the relaxation, take three deep breaths, pausing after you inhale, and then exhaling fully and completely. You might imagine that you release tensions and discomforts as you exhale by just breathing them away. * After you have finished these first three breaths, continue breathing slowly and naturally, relaxing more deeply with each slow exhale.

As you continue to breathe slowly and naturally, you may feel the relaxation beginning in your body. The most important thing to remember when dealing with prenatal stress is that you can take control of your body through awareness and relaxation. So to begin this process, turn your awareness to the sensation of relaxation that is beginning in your arms and hands. You may feel that one arm is more relaxed than the other. * Perhaps one arm may feel a bit heavier than the other arm. The muscles may feel more loose or more flexible than in the other arm. * Or perhaps you feel that one arm is a bit warmer than the other arm. You may feel that the warmth of blood and energy may flow more easily down one arm, as if it were flowing through wide-open blood vessels, slowly but freely moving down into your hand and fingers. You may even feel it slowly pulsing down into your hand. * Or perhaps you find that both arms feel equally relaxed and this would be perfect as well. The only thing that matters is that you breathe slowly and gently as you let yourself drift deeper into that soothing dreamlike calmness. *

As you drift pleasantly, turn your awareness to the sensations of relaxation that may be beginning in your legs and feet. You might feel that one leg is slightly more relaxed than the other. Perhaps you notice that one leg feels a little heavier, as if the muscles of that leg were more loose or flexible than the other leg. * Or as you breathe slowly and gently, you may feel that one leg is slightly warmer, as if the blood and warmth could spread more easily down that leg, drifting down through wide-open blood vessels, * perhaps even pulsing slowly but freely down into your foot and toes. * Or perhaps your legs feel equally relaxed, and that would be perfect also. The only thing that really matters is that you continue to breathe slowly as you allow yourself to drift more deeply into that dreamlike calmness and comfort. *

You may even feel the gradual control of stress and tensions beginning as you sink back into whatever you are sitting or lying upon and the tension just melts away. *

You may even feel the muscles of your back beginning to loosen or soften, and as you breathe slowly, naturally, you might feel the relaxation spreading to the other muscles of your back. * Even your upper back and shoulders may begin to soften or loosen a bit further. Your shoulders may be able to drop into a more comfortable position. * You may feel the control growing stronger as your head sinks back into the pillow or chair, the muscles of your neck begin to let go, and you drift deeper into relaxation. *

As you pleasantly drift deeper into this comfort and calmness, you may be able to feel the muscles of your head and face beginning to relax even further. * Continue to breathe slowly, allowing a soothing, healing wave of relaxation to gently spread down from the top of your head, soothing and cleansing every muscle and cell of your body. You can feel it slowly drifting down to relax the muscles of your forehead, * letting your forehead become calm and smooth. * Let this wave drift down to relax the muscles around your eyes, releasing the tension in these muscles. * The wave then drifts down helping to relax the muscles of your mouth, including your jaw. Let these muscles go loose and limp. * And as you breathe slowly, the wave slowly drifts down to relax the muscles of your neck. Even your shoulders can loosen a bit more. * The relaxation can begin to spread down your arms. * As the wave of relaxation gently drifts down your arms you may even be able to feel it pulsing into your hands. *

The wave of relaxation can drift down through your back and your chest, spreading soothing comfort into your lower back. * The wave of relaxation can spread down through your pelvic area helping to loosen and relax the muscles of your legs even more. * The relaxation slowly drifts down through your legs. Perhaps you can feel it pulsing into your feet, spreading the comfort down, washing the discomfort out of your body. * Even your heartbeat feels more calm and regular as the relaxation gently spreads throughout your body. *

As you allow yourself to drift deeper in this calmness, the soothing relaxation can help you rest and recharge yourself. Your calmness will help your baby to be calm and comfortable, too. As your muscles relax, the baby has greater freedom, and you may feel him begin to move. Your relaxation also allows the blood supply to flow more easily to your baby, nourishing him and allowing him to grow healthily. You can imagine him receiving your love and joy, growing strong as he prepares for his life in the world. As you remain calm and comfortable, you can see the birth going smoothly and easily. See yourself delivering a healthy, beautiful baby, welcoming him into the world with love and acceptance. See yourself healing fully and regaining your energy in those first days, and bonding with even more love with your baby.

If you are using this exercise at bedtime, you may wish to drift into a pleasant sleep in which you rest fully and from which you awaken feeling refreshed and alert. If you wish to drift off to sleep, continue breathing slowly and focus on the feelings of relaxation in your arms and legs. *

If you wish to awaken now, you can begin to do so. Let yourself gradually return to this room, feeling the bed or the chair beneath you. As you slowly awaken, you will bring the feelings of calmness, relaxation, health, and happiness back with you. Take a deep breath and stretch, letting the calmness return with you. Take another deep breath and stretch, allowing yourself to awaken feeling refreshed and alert, letting the relaxation and calmness continue with you.

BIBLIOGRAPHY

Anderson, Mary. *Pregnancy After 30 Workbook*. New York: Faber & Faber, 1984. $7.95.

Special considerations for pregnant women over thirty years of age.

Baldwin, Rahima. *Special Delivery: The Complete Guide to Informed Birth*. Berkeley, CA: Celestial Arts. 1979. $10.95.

Basic guide for care during pregnancy with special emphasis on self-responsibility. Especially for women considering home births. Lots of good information.

Eisenberg, Arlene, Heidi Eisenberg-Murkoff, and Sandee Eisenberg-Hathaway, RN, BSN. *What to Expect When You Are Expecting*. New York: Workman Publishing, 1984. $7.95

Detailed information about pregnancy that can help relieve uncertainty during an uncertain time. Good resource!

Goldbeck, Nikki. *As You Eat, So Your Baby Grows: A Guide to Nutrition in Pregnancy*. New York: Ceres Press, 1978. $1.45.

Very brief but very useful guide to nutrition during pregnancy.

Korte, Diana, and Roberta Scaer. *Good Birth: A Safe Birth*. New York: Bantam, 1984. $7.95.

Important information about all the medical technologies available to you during pregnancy and labor. The pros and cons of each procedure are discussed. Useful to help you make informed decisions about your body and your baby.

McCutcheon-Rosegg, Susan, with Peter Rosegg. *Natural Childbirth: The Bradley Way*. New York: E. P. Dutton, 1984. $14.95.

Good basic information about self-care and self-responsibility during pregnancy for people considering hospital but natural childbirths.

Nilsson, Lennart. *A Child Is Born*. New York: Delacorte Press/Seymour Lawrence, 1966, 1977. $11.95.

Basic physiology of pregnancy and birth. Encourages better self-care by showing the baby's development during all stages of pregnancy. Excellent for dad and any siblings who are curious about what mom is going through.

Samuels, Mike, and Nancy Samuels. *Well Pregnancy Book*. New York: Summit Books, 1986. $14.95.

Good book for stress management and visualization exercises to use during pregnancy. Another book concerned with awareness and self-responsibility for you and your unborn baby.

AUDIOCASSETTE TAPES

Mason, L. John. *Prenatal Stress Management*. 1987. $11.95.

Two guided relaxations designed especially for stress control during pregnancy. Positive visualizations. Music or ocean sounds as background to indirect relaxation or autogenic exercise.

CHAPTER TWO

Parenting & Stress

Introduction

HAVING WORKED with many parents and expectant parents, I have become convinced that parents are providing one of the most vital services for our society, raising the future generation, yet they are not given enough social support nor enough preparation for their demanding roles.

Parenting is an experience which invariably results in increased stress, but most often parents do not fully understand the magnitude of what they are embarking on until they are home from the hospital. It is not until they have been pacing the floor night after night with a colicky baby, or listening helplessly to their child's cries as he suffers from teething that parents understand the impact of this new child on their lives.

Typically, new parents will feel uncertain about their abilities. Will I be a good parent? Can I provide my child with what she needs? Particularly for first time parents, the sense of exploring an uncharted wilderness can be overwhelming. Arriving home from the hospital, they are suddenly on their own. This can be one of the most frightening and stressful times for parents.

Perhaps mom is waiting for her milk to come in, and she worries whether her baby is getting enough nutrition. Perhaps dad is feeling neglected because of his wife's preoccupation with the baby. Perhaps the parents had an exaggerated idea of how close and bonded they would feel with their new child, and the reality does not match their expectations. Or perhaps there are too many "helpers" in the house, and the new family cannot get to know each other in as relaxed or comfortable a way as they would like.

These concerns are compounded by the plethora of practical questions raised as the family structure shifts with the baby's arrival. Who will do the cooking, the cleaning, the shopping, the bill paying? Who will bathe and change the baby? Who will get up in the middle of the night? How will you redistribute the tasks and responsibilities? How will you shape your lives around the baby and how much does the baby need to adapt to your schedules and needs?

After the initial adjustments, further questions continue to arise. Why doesn't your baby sleep through the night? Does your baby sleep too much? Is your baby developing physically and mentally as quickly as other babies you may know? When should mom return to her job? How will you find good, affordable child care? How will mother's self-image be affected if she stays home from work?

With each new stage of development, parents must deal with a new set of stressors. Sometimes it seems that just as you adjust to a particular stage and begin to feel more confident about your parenting skills, a new issue develops. Finally your baby sleeps through the night, but then teething begins, and there you are with a fussy baby and nights of lost sleep again.

Once the child becomes mobile, learning to crawl and then walk, the number of details you must cope with seems to expand. Keeping your house child-proofed and running after an overly active child can exhaust any parent. Allowing your child to learn from his mistakes can be especially trying. It is tempting to protect your child from every mishap, but often letting him discover for himself that, for instance, the cat doesn't like to have his tail pulled, is the most important lesson you can give him.

As the child becomes more self-reliant, learning to feed and dress herself, another difficult parenting stage develops. While you may be happy to be relieved of some tasks, you must also give up a certain degree of control and perhaps even a dependence on your child's helplessness. Learning to support your child as she pulls away from you is an art—one often learned through stressful experiences.

When your child begins school or daycare, his exposure to other people and new situations will increase dramatically. For parents, this can be a time of increased worry. It is important that parents become involved in their child's education, both by helping the child at home and by being familiar with and participating in his school activities. Though involvement may alleviate some parental fears, it can also put new pressures on parents by exerting further demands on their time and energy.

The stresses of parenting will continue as your child grows through each new stage of childhood, adolescence, and even adulthood. However, by becoming more aware of stress-producing events and utilizing stress reduction techniques, parents can ease the strain of these transitions.

Stress Management Recommendations for Parenting

Caring for and loving others is best accomplished when you take the time to care for yourself as well. Self-care should be a high priority for new parents. This means taking time out from work and responsibilities to attend to your own needs for relaxation and pleasure. By attending to your physical and emotional well-being, you will actually increase the energy you have for others. You will also set a positive example for your children, who will learn to model your healthy behavior.

Another very important stress management strategy is to develop good communication skills. For expectant parents, communication is important so that each person is aware of his/her partner's needs, goals, and expectations. Once the baby arrives, it is critical that parents be able to clearly discuss every aspect of their home life, from the sharing of daily tasks and responsibilities, to the parenting needs of the child. Particularly as the child grows older, if the parents do not communicate clearly, the child may receive conflicting messages from her parents, a confusing and stressful situation for everyone concerned. On the other hand, if clear communication exists between parents, children learn these skills from them, and can make a positive contribution to family decision making.

Parents should be aware that nonverbal communication is as important as verbal communication. Touching, hugging, and other simple expressions of love—bringing home a beautifully colored leaf or cooking your child's favorite dinner—should be a daily part of family communication. What you do is often even more important than what you say, as children learn primarily through imitation. It is also important to remember that listening is as important as talking. Unless we really hear our family's needs and concerns, we cannot solve problems or respond adequately.

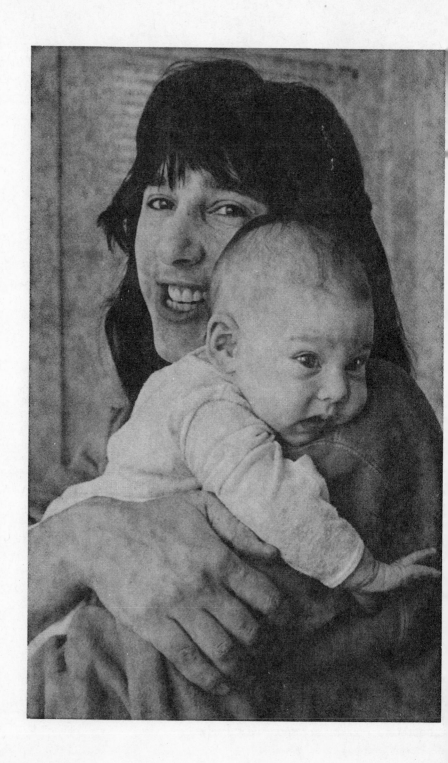

A regular physical exercise program can also greatly help parents with stress management. Regular exercise which stimulates the heart and lungs, such as walking, swimming, biking or jogging, helps you release stored tension which might otherwise result in an emotional blowup. A physical workout can actually free up energy that has been stored as muscular tension, allowing you to use this energy for more positive purposes, such as a project with your daughter or an evening out with your spouse. A physical exercise program also helps you to spend time away from work or other stress-producing situations, providing a break from unhealthy patterns of stress buildup.

Massage can be a very positive stress management strategy for the whole family. Partners can exchange massages as an expression of love and caring, and parents can communicate nonverbally with their children through massage. Very young children especially thrive on the loving physical contact massage provides. Taking the time to relax and soothe each other in this way can help tremendously in reducing family stress and conflict, and can have rewards much larger than many more costly family activities.

Bathing is another relaxation tool that parents and children can utilize. Infants love bath time because they feel warm and comfortable in the water and because this is loving time shared with their parents. Bathing can distract and soothe a cranky child or help an overly tired youngster to relax and prepare for sleep. In many countries, such as Japan and Sweden, family bathing is a ritual which provides time for togetherness and relaxation. If you have access to a hot tub or jacuzzi bath, this comforting experience can become part of your family routine as well.

Other stress reduction techniques which are particularly helpful for parents are detailed in the following section. Many of these exercises can be shared with children. For instance, if mom uses a relaxing breathing technique while she is nursing, she can help calm her baby as well. A youngster can mimic his parent's deep breathing, and while both learn to relax, a strong nonverbal bond is also created between parent and child.

Case Study #1

With their first child, Bob and Sherrie faced many of the typical stresses with which new parents must cope, including an unplanned pregnancy, financial difficulties, fatigue, jealousy, and a colicky baby.

Bob is now twenty-five, has had four years of college, and is a construction worker. Sherrie is twenty-four, has completed two years of college, and works part-time as a secretary. They have two sons, Paul, three and a half, and Michael, nine months.

Sherrie became pregnant when she was twenty-one and still in school. Though she and Bob wanted a family, they had planned to finish school and be more financially stable before having their first child. Instead, Sherrie had to leave her studies, they faced student debts, and Bob was just beginning his work in construction. The disrupted plans and added financial pressure were severe stressors, making both parents tense and adding to the nervousness they already felt as they anticipated their new roles.

Paul's birth went smoothly, but Sherrie's postpartum adjustment was not as easy. Her sleep was broken and restless, her energy was low, and feelings of anxiety and depression seemed to come and go. She often had difficulty concentrating, and at times would respond very slowly to the baby's crying. At the same time, she felt pressured as a new mother to read books on child development and parenting and to be a "perfect" mother. As a result, she would vacillate between being overly concerned about her parenting skills and being lethargic and a bit distant. Bob experienced her as being very absorbed with Paul and having little time for him. He often pressured Sherrie for attention, which made her feel even more burdened.

While Bob was feeling left out, he also felt very encumbered financially. He expressed his general nervousness and frustration through a heightened concern about paying the doctor and hospital bills. Because Sherrie had become pregnant before he started his job, his health insurance would not cover the bills from her pregnancy and birth. Additionally, he and Sherrie had wanted to move into a larger apartment before their first child was born, and he became frustrated that they had been unable to do so. Fortunately, a loan from Bob's parents alleviated some financial stress.

The strain Bob and Sherrie were feeling was compounded by Paul's behavior. Very possibly, Paul sensed his parents' tension and had a hard time relaxing as a result. He did not sleep well, was slightly colicky, and was easily upset. He would cry if the phone rang or when hearing a slightly raised voice. He seemed very sensitive to and irritated by the change in temperature when having his clothes changed. When he teethed he was even more fussy. Both Sherrie and Bob lost sleep and began to doubt their parenting skills.

At this time a counselor they saw recommended that a program of stress reduction might help their communication. They came to me and I helped them learn to use physical exercise and passive relaxation techniques.

They began to use these stress reduction techniques on a regular basis, and the results were encouraging. Not only did they feel better able to handle the stressors in their lives, but Paul seemed to become significantly calmer as his parents learned to relax.

Before Paul turned two, the family was finally able to move to a larger apartment. Home life had settled down, and Bob and Sherrie began planning for a second child. Sherrie was soon pregnant, and this time she was much less anxious. She had less nausea and fatigue in the early months than she had during her first pregnancy. She was able to find time to exercise and practice her mental relaxation routines. She found she had more confidence about the impending birth and fewer doubts about her parenting skills.

Bob also felt much more relaxed. This time health insurance would cover the medical bills, so the financial worries were not as severe. And his improved communication with Sherrie helped to allay his fears about losing her attention.

Though their experience with their first child and the use of relaxation techniques had helped in many respects, the second child still created new stresses. Sibling rivalry became an issue very quickly. After an initial week of enjoying his new brother, Michael, Paul began to regress. He lost interest in toilet training, began to talk baby talk, and even wanted to breast-feed again when he saw the baby nursing. He seemed to need much more attention and physical contact.

Another major adjustment was caused by Sherrie's return to work when Michael was a year old. Sherrie wanted to get out of the house for a few hours each day to have adult contact and conversation, so she was happy to return to her part-time job. Though the job helped meet some of Sherrie's social and intellectual needs, thereby improving her emotional outlook and satisfaction, the entire household had to learn a new routine. Both husband and children had to perform tasks which previously Sherrie had managed, such as making beds, tying shoes, or driving children to daycare.

Child care itself became a new source of stress. Both Bob and Sherrie were concerned about how being in daycare would affect their children. They knew there would be an increased exposure to illness, and that they would have less control over their children's environment. They worried about how the child care providers would influence their children, how the children would respond to being away from home, and how safe the daycare center would be. Fortunately, they were able to find very capable child care providers, and with time they were able to relax as they saw their children respond positively to this new experience.

Case Study #2

Sue was thirty-seven and Mark forty-four when their first baby was born. As older parents, the stresses they felt were somewhat different than those faced by younger couples.

Both Mark and Sue had secure, well-paying jobs, so finances were not an issue when they decided to have a baby. Mark works as a sales representative for several equipment manufacturers, and Sue holds a middle-management position in a large oil company. Sue planned to work until her eighth month and would not have to return to her job until the baby was four months old.

The stresses they felt most susceptible to were caused by overly high expectations of themselves as parents and of their child. Fortunately, they began a stress management program early in Sue's pregnancy because some of their friends had recommended relaxation and visualization to be extremely valuable during childbirth. They found the exercises to be very useful during pregnancy as well, helping to allay their anxiety about the approaching birth and their new responsibilities. Both Sue and Mark found that they were often short-tempered during this time, and they felt the exercises helped them control their outbursts and channel their anxiety in a positive way. Sue also felt her regular use of progressive relaxation techniques increased her energy level. She was able to continue working until her eighth month and did not experience the debilitating fatigue that some pregnant women do.

Sue had a relatively easy four-hour labor, and the first ten days after the baby was born Mark was able to stay home to assist her and help with the baby, Julie. He would get up when Julie woke for her nighttime feeding, change her, then give her to Sue for breast-feeding. This initial time together helped Sue to feel supported, Mark to feel included, and all three of them to bond.

When Julie was eight months old, however, after having been a model baby, she began to become very fussy at mealtimes and refused to eat all her food. She also began resisting bedtime, waking up in the middle of the night more often and sleeping more fitfully. At first these symptoms were attributed to teething, but soon Mark and Sue began to wonder if something else was going on.

We had a consultation and thoroughly discussed Julie's routine and activities. I began to suspect that the parents had been overstimulating Julie because of their overly high expectations for her development. They had been exposing her to classical music and educational TV, using flash cards and other teaching devices to assist her cognitive development, and doing movement exercises with her to encourage her motor development. They tried cutting back on these activities and their expectations of her, and after a short time she seemed to relax significantly and to eat and sleep better. Her parents learned that their daughter needed to develop at her own pace, and that their desire for her to be a child prodigy was neither realistic nor healthy for Julie. When they were able to let go of their unrealistic expectations of her, the family functioned much more smoothly.

The family has continued to practice the stress reduction techniques which they learned during Sue's pregnancy, and both parents feel the benefits of the exercises have carried over into their work lives. Mark notices that he is able to relax at important business meetings more than he used to, and he also feels that his communication skills have improved. He is better able to listen to his clients' concerns and respond positively to them because he is less tense. Sue believes she now uses her time and energy more efficiently at work and manages her staff more smoothly.

Relaxation Exercises for Parents

AUTOGENIC TRAINING

The repeated use of autogenic phrases will give you direct control over your stress response. As you gain this control, you will be able to respond to the stresses of parenting in a positive way. As you practice this exercise, allow yourself to feel the warmth and heaviness beginning in your arms and legs. Over time, you will be able to feel the relaxation in your entire body more quickly and more deeply.

Read this exercise slowly (at about half normal speaking speed). Pause at each * . Do not be concerned by mispronunciations or verbal slips; continue in a calm, even voice.

Find a quiet location where you will not be disturbed. Allow about twenty minutes for this exercise. Sit or lie back comfortably, allowing your arms and legs to remain uncrossed if possible. Let your head be supported and let your shoulders drop into a comfortable position. Check the muscles of your head and face. Let your forehead become calm and smooth. Allow the muscles around your eyes to loosen. Relax the muscles of the mouth, especially the jaw. Finally, allow your eyes to remain closed, remembering that you can open them whenever you need to.

Before we begin the relaxation, remember not to try to relax too quickly. In fact, do not try to relax at all. Without any effort you can pleasantly let go of tensions and discomforts, and then let yourself drift deeper into a peaceful calmness. To begin the relaxation, take three deep breaths, pausing after you inhale, and then exhaling fully and completely. As you exhale, imagine that you are breathing away your tensions and discomforts. * After you have finished the first three breaths, continue breathing slowly and naturally, relaxing more deeply with each slow exhale.

Repeat this mood phrase to yourself three times: "I am at peace with myself and fully relaxed." Continue breathing slowly and gently.

Begin to feel the muscles of your arms relax and feel the sensation of heaviness as you say, "My right arm is heavy * . . . My right arm is heavy * . . . My right arm is heavy * . . ." Repeat several more times if needed until you begin to feel the heaviness and relaxation. Now turn your awareness to your left arm as you breathe slowly, then say to yourself, "My left arm is heavy * . . . My left arm is heavy * . . . My left arm is heavy * . . . Feel the heaviness starting in your arms or feel free to continue slowly repeating this phrase a few more times. Now proceed to your legs. Let them begin to relax as you breathe slowly. Feel the heaviness and relaxation starting in your legs as you slowly repeat, "My right leg is heavy * . . . My right leg is heavy * . . . My right leg is heavy * . . ." You can repeat this several more times if you need to, until you begin to feel the relaxation and heaviness. Now focus on the left leg and feel it beginning to relax as you say, "My left leg is heavy * . . . My left leg is heavy * . . . My left leg is heavy * . . ." Repeat if needed. As you breathe slowly you will feel the heaviness in your arms and legs. With practice you will feel this sensation more quickly. Now turn your attention to your neck and shoulders. Let them sink into a more comfortable position and let the muscles relax as you breathe gently and say, "My neck and shoulders are heavy * . . . My neck and shoulders are heavy * . . . My neck and shoulders are heavy * . . ." Repeat if needed. Take a deep slow breath and feel the heaviness and relaxation as you begin to sink back into whatever you are sitting or lying upon.

Perhaps you can feel the blood beginning to flow more easily down into your hands or feet as the blood vessels begin to dilate, as the smooth muscles in the walls of the arteries begin to relax. Focus on the feelings of warmth, or a pulse, or perhaps a tingling sensation in your right hand as you say, "My right arm is warm * . . . My right arm is warm * . . . My right arm is warm * . . ." Repeat this slowly several more times until you begin to feel the warmth or pulse. For most people, heaviness is easier to feel than warmth, but with continued practice you can begin to control your blood

flow. Now turn your attention to your left arm and say to yourself, "My left arm is warm * . . . My left arm is warm * . . . My left arm is warm * . . ." Repeat if needed. Perhaps you can start to feel the warmth in your arms, and you may feel the pulse of blood flowing freely through your entire body. As you breathe slowly and gently, turn your awareness to your legs and say to yourself, "My right leg is warm * . . . My right leg is warm * . . . My right leg is warm * . . ." Repeat several more times to help develop this skill. Move your attention to your left leg and say, "My left leg is warm * . . . My left leg is warm * . . . My left leg is warm * . . ." Repeat if needed. Feel the heaviness and warmth in your arms and your legs as you breathe slowly and gently. Now turn your awareness to your neck and shoulders, and say, "My neck and shoulders are warm * . . . My neck and shoulders are warm * . . . My neck and shoulders are warm * . . ." Repeat if needed. Breathe slowly as you drift for a few moments, feeling relaxed as heaviness and warmth spread pleasantly about your body.

Slow and calm your heart by slowly repeating to yourself, "My heartbeat is calm and regular * . . . My heartbeat is calm and regular * . . . My heartbeat is calm and regular * . . ." Repeat if needed. If you experience any discomfort with this phrase, change to the words "I feel calm * . . . I feel calm * . . . I feel calm * . . ." As you breathe slowly, begin to feel the peace and relaxation spreading to every part of your body.

To slow your breathing say to yourself as you breathe into your diaphragm, "My breathing is calm and regular * . . . My breathing is calm and regular * . . . My breathing is calm and regular * . . ." Repeat if needed.

Become aware of the relaxation starting in your stomach region. As you breathe slowly say, "My abdomen is warm and calm * . . . My abdomen is warm and calm * . . . My abdomen is warm and calm * . . . Repeat if needed. If you have any serious abdominal problems, such as bleeding ulcers or diabetes, or if you are in the last trimester of pregnancy, change this phrase to "I am calm and relaxed * . . . I am calm and relaxed * . . . I am calm and relaxed * . . ."

Move on to your forehead and let the muscles of your head and face relax as you say, "My forehead is cool and calm * . . . My forehead is cool and calm * . . . My forehead is cool and calm * . . ." As you breathe slowly, feel the muscles around your eyes, mouth, and jaw loosen and then relax.

Let yourself drift in this state of calmness. As you breathe slowly and gently, perhaps you can feel the heaviness in your arms and legs as the muscles relax. * Perhaps you can begin to feel the warmth or pulse of blood flowing more easily down into your hands and feet, like sunshine or a warm bath. Some people feel the warming as a tingling sensation spreading blood more easily into the extremities. * As you enjoy the relaxation, you can feel that your heartbeat is calm and regular. *

With practice, you will feel the relaxation more easily and more quickly. The warmth flowing into your hands and feet gradually grows easier to control. The relaxation will then stay with you throughout your day. You will become more aware of stress and tensions. As you clear away the unnecessary tensions, your ability to be a more successful and patient parent will increase. This will not only help you feel better, but it will benefit the whole family. By taking the time to care for yourself, you will also establish a healthy, self-respecting model for your children.

At the end of this relaxation exercise you can awaken yourself by returning to your room. Feel the bed or chair beneath you and say, "I am refreshed and completely alert * . . . I am refreshed and completely alert * . . . I am refreshed and completely alert * . . ." Then take a deep breath and stretch, allowing yourself to wake fully and letting the relaxation return with you.

INDIRECT RELAXATION

This exercise works especially well when read to you or recorded for playback. Allow yourself to drift as deeply as you wish as you find the sensations of relaxation beginning throughout your body. As with the other exercises, practice will enable you to relax more quickly and more deeply.

Read this exercise slowly (at about half normal speaking speed). Pause at each * . Do not be concerned by mispronunciations or verbal slips; continue in a calm, even voice.

Find a quiet location where you will not be disturbed. Allow about twenty minutes for this exercise. Sit or lie back comfortably, allowing your arms and legs to remain uncrossed if possible. Let your head be supported and let your shoulders drop into a comfortable position. Check the muscles of your head and face. Let your forehead become calm and smooth. Allow the muscles around your eyes to loosen. Relax the muscles of the mouth, especially the jaw. Finally, allow your eyes to remain closed, remembering that you can open them whenever you need to.

Before we begin the relaxation, remember not to try to relax too quickly. In fact, do not try to relax at all. Without any effort you can pleasantly let go of tensions and discomforts, and then let yourself drift deeper into a peaceful calmness. To begin the relaxation, take three deep breaths, pausing after you inhale, and then exhaling fully and completely. As you exhale, imagine that you are breathing away your tensions and discomforts. *

After you have finished the first three breaths, continue breathing slowly and naturally, relaxing more deeply with each slow exhale.

As you continue to breathe slowly and naturally, feel the relaxation spreading through your body. Remember that you can control your body's responses to parental stress through awareness and relaxation. Turn your awareness to the sensation that is beginning in your arms and hands. Perhaps you notice that one arm may feel a bit heavier than the other arm. The muscles may feel more loose or more flexible. * Or perhaps you feel that one arm is a bit warmer than the other arm. You may imagine that the blood and energy flow more easily down one arm, as if moving through wide-open blood vessels slowly but freely into your hand and fingers. * Or perhaps you find that both arms feel equally relaxed. The only thing that matters is that you breathe slowly and gently as you let yourself drift deeper into that soothing, dreamlike calmness. *

And as you drift pleasantly into relaxation, turn your awareness to the sensations that may be beginning in your legs and feet. Perhaps one leg may feel slightly more relaxed than the other. Perhaps you notice that one leg is a little heavier, as if the muscles of that leg were more loose or flexible than the other leg. * Or as you breathe slowly and gently, you may feel that one leg is slightly warmer, as if the blood and warmth could spread more easily down that leg, drifting down through wide-open blood vessels, * perhaps even pulsing slowly but freely down into your foot and toes. * Or perhaps your legs feel equally relaxed. The only thing that matters is that you continue to breathe slowly as you allow yourself to drift deeper into that dreamlike calmness and comfort. *

Feel how you can effortlessly control stress and tension as you sink into whatever you are sitting or lying upon and the tension just melts away. *

You may feel the muscles of your back beginning to loosen or soften, and as you breathe slowly, naturally, you might feel the relaxation spreading to the other muscles of your back. * Even your upper back and shoulders may begin to loosen a bit. Your shoulders may be able to drop into a more comfortable position. * You can feel your effortless control growing stronger as your head sinks back into the pillow or chair, the muscles of your neck begin to let go, and you drift deeper into relaxation. *

As you pleasantly sink deeper into this comfort and calmness, you may be able to feel the muscles of your head and face beginning to relax. * Continue to breathe slowly, allowing a soothing, healing wave of relaxation to gently spread down from the top of your head, soothing and cleansing every muscle and cell of your body. Feel it slowly drifting down to relax the muscles of your forehead, smoothing away any tension. * Then let this wave drift down to relax the muscles around your eyes, releasing these muscles. * Feel the wave drift down to relax the muscles of your mouth, including your jaw. Let these muscles go loose and limp. * And as you breathe slowly, let the wave drift down to relax the muscles of your neck and shoulders. * Feel the relaxation spread down your arms. * As the wave of relaxation gently drifts down your arms, feel it pulsing down into your hands. *

Feel the wave of relaxation moving down through your back and your chest, spreading soothing comfort and relaxation down into your lower back. * Even your heartbeat feels more calm and regular as the relaxation gently spreads throughout your body. * Feel the wave of relaxation spread down through your pelvic area, helping to loosen and relax the muscles of your legs. * Feel the relaxation slowly drift down through your legs. Perhaps you can feel it pulsing slowly into your feet, spreading the comfort, washing the discomfort out of your body. *

As you allow yourself to drift deeper into this calmness, you will begin to feel rested and recharged. Imagine that you are outdoors in a perfect place, on a warm and beautiful day. Choose the most comfortable place to lie down. Feel the warmth from the sun and know that you are well protected and safe from any harm or distractions. As you soak up the warmth from the sun, feel the tensions and discomforts melting away. * The warmth fills you with warm healing energy, and the golden-white light recharges every cell in your body. Even though you remain at peace, feel the warmth of blood flowing freely, carrying oxygen and nutrients and healing energy to bathe every cell. Like a sponge, each cell soaks up nutrients and energy to heal and recharge. Feel the sensations of health, joy, and happiness spreading within you, though you remain calm and comfortable. * Picture yourself filling with strength and energy as your body heals itself. * See yourself in a state of health and happiness, doing something active, perhaps smiling and celebrating in the sunshine. * With practice, this relaxation exercise will become easier, and you will be able to relax more deeply and more quickly. You will be more aware of tension and better able to rid yourself of unnecessary anxieties whenever they may develop. The effects of the relaxation will carry over throughout your day.

Remember that by taking this time for yourself you will be able to help the entire family. Because you are more relaxed, you will be able to create a calmer environment at home and provide a positive example for your children. You will also have more time and energy to do the things that you want to do.

If you are using this relaxation exercise at bedtime, you may wish to drift off into a pleasant sleep from which you will awaken feeling refreshed and alert. If you wish to drift off to sleep, continue breathing slowly and focus on the relaxation in your arms and legs. *

If you wish to awaken now, let yourself gradually return to this room, feeling the bed or the chair beneath you. As you slowly awaken, bring the feelings of calmness, relaxation, health, and happiness back with you into a more fully waking state. Take a deep breath and stretch, letting the calmness return with you. Take another deep breath and stretch, allowing yourself to awaken feeling refreshed and alert, letting the relaxation and calmness continue with you.

PROGRESSIVE RELAXATION

I often recommend this form of relaxation for those just beginning a relaxation program, as it is straightforward and easy to learn. Progressive relaxation has been used widely since the early 1900s for sleep improvement, childbirth, and general relaxation, as well as to enhance yoga exercises and athletic performance. With practice, you should be able to use this exercise to relax anytime, anywhere.

Read this exercise slowly, at about half normal speaking speed. Pause at each * . Do not be concerned by mispronunciations or verbal slips; continue in a calm, even voice.

Find a quiet location where you will not be disturbed. Allow about twenty minutes for this exercise. Sit or lie back comfortably, allowing your arms and legs to remain uncrossed if possible. Let your head be supported and let your shoulders drop into a more comfortable position. Check the muscles of your head and face. Let your forehead become calm and smooth. Allow the muscles around your eyes to loosen. Relax the muscles of the mouth, especially the jaw. Finally, allow your eyes to remain closed, remembering that you can open them whenever you need to.

Before we begin the relaxation, remember not to try to relax too quickly. In fact, do not try to relax at all. Without any effort you can pleasantly let go of tensions and discomforts, and then let yourself drift deeper into a peaceful calmness. To begin the relaxation, take three deep breaths, pausing after you inhale, and then exhaling fully and completely. As you exhale, imagine that you are breathing away your tensions and discomforts. *
After you have finished the first three breaths, continue breathing slowly and naturally, relaxing more deeply with each slow exhale.

As you continue to breathe slowly and gently, focus your attention on the muscles in your feet. Move your toes briefly to notice how these muscles feel. Rest these muscles in the most comfortable position and then imagine them relaxing even more as you slowly exhale, breathing away any energy or tension that you may have in your toes. As you breathe slowly, feel these muscles becoming more soft and flexible. * Turn your awareness to the muscles of the arch of your foot. The muscles from the ball of your foot below the big toe down to the heel can relax even more. Take a slow breath and then imagine that as you exhale you release the tensions from these muscles. * Now feel the sides and the top of your foot. Feel the covers or your shoes and socks touching your foot. As you breathe slowly and naturally, let the muscles of your foot relax even more. Feel a pulse or tingling gradually spreading warmth and relaxation to every muscle of your foot. *

Turn your awareness to your lower leg. Can you feel your ankles, * the calves, * your shin bones? * Feel the muscles of your lower legs, and become aware that you can relax these muscles even more. As you breathe slowly, release any tension and feel the muscles softening. Feel the knee relaxing into a more comfortable position. As your awareness increases, so will your skill at relaxing. With practice, you will let these muscle groups relax even more. * Now become aware of your upper legs. Feel the large muscles of the sides and top of your legs relax slowly as you exhale the unwanted tensions. * Now relax the big muscles at the back of your upper legs. As these muscles relax, feel the relaxation spreading up through your pelvic area into the lower back. Feel the sensation of heaviness down the length of your leg. * Breathe slowly and gently, feeling the pulse of blood flow more freely and easily down your leg into your foot and toes. *

As the muscles of your lower back begin to soften, feel the relaxation spreading to the other muscles of the back. The muscles of your upper back, including your shoulders, can relax even further. Your shoulders can drop into a more comfortable position. * Feel your head sinking back into the chair or pillow, totally supported, as the muscles of your neck relax even more. * Continue breathing slowly and gently as you feel the relaxation spreading down through your arms. * The muscles of your upper arms feel loose and comfortable. * Your lower arms and wrists can relax even more. As you breathe slowly, feel the sensation of heaviness as your arms sink back into the bed or chair. * Feel the relaxation slowly drift down into your hands and fingers. * Feel a pulse of blood flowing freely and easily down into your hands. Feel your hands warming pleasantly, letting you drift deeper into the comfort and relaxation. *

Relax the muscles of your head and face even more. Your forehead can feel more calm and smooth. * The muscles around the eyes can relax. * Even the muscles of the mouth and the jaw can relax further. * Slowly breathe away stress and tension, knowing the relaxation will increase with

practice. * The sensations of peace and harmony grow stronger as you drift deeper into this calmness. *

Feel the relaxation drift down into your chest. As you breathe slowly, feel the relaxation gently spreading to the other muscles of the torso. Feel your heartbeat, calm and regular. * Feel the relaxation spread down into your stomach region. * Try to feel warmth glowing gently in your stomach region. * Continue breathing slowly and gently as you drift peacefully. * Perhaps you can feel the heaviness of your arms and legs as you learn to control tensions better and better. *

With practice, you will be able to relax more quickly and deeply, and the effects will last longer throughout the day. Your awareness of tensions will improve so that you can control your responses to stressors more effectively. Because you take care of yourself, you set a positive example for your family of a healthy, happy adult. Things that may have bothered you in the past will not have the same negative effect upon you. Your patterns of communication will also improve.

If you are using this relaxation exercise at bedtime, you may wish to drift off into a pleasant sleep from which you will awaken feeling refreshed and alert. If you wish to drift off to sleep, continue breathing slowly and focus on the relaxation in your arms and legs. *

If you wish to awaken now, let yourself gradually return to this room, feeling the bed or the chair beneath you. As you slowly awaken, bring the feelings of calmness, relaxation, health, and happiness back with you into a more fully waking state. Take a deep breath and stretch, letting the calmness return with you. Take another deep breath and stretch, allowing yourself to awaken feeling refreshed and alert, letting the relaxation and calmness continue with you.

BREATHING TECHNIQUES

The following breathing exercises are an excellent aid to helping you calm down under pressure and regain proper perspective about what is happening. When the baby is screaming and your two-year-old is throwing food, take a moment to use one of these techniques. You'll find that you will be able to respond to your family with patience and understanding rather than exasperation when you take a moment to calm yourself. The various breathing techniques can also be taught to your children, either directly or through example. When these breathing exercises become a family activity, everyone can experience improved communication and understanding in moments of stress.

The first breathing exercise helps you to relearn proper breathing habits. Though we were all born with the natural ability to breath diaphragmatically, most of us lose this ability as we grow and learn more rigid postures. To relearn good breathing habits, we must be aware of how we breath and practice to change our habits daily. Proper breathing does not use the shoulders or the upper back. Our stomachs should move out gently as we inhale and return as we exhale.

#*1.* Try this. Lie down flat or stand up straight. Put one hand over your stomach and one hand over your chest, and see which way each hand moves as you inhale. Now which way do your hands move as you exhale? Does your bottom hand move first and outward as you begin the inhale? Does the upper hand then move up and out? On the exhale, do you notice that both hands move in, perhaps forcing the last bit of air out? If so, then you are breathing very well and you can go on to the next breathing exercises. If not, you should practice a bit before you continue, as this breathing technique forms the basis of every stress management exercise.

#*2.* Now try breathing very slowly while you are in a comfortable position. As you inhale slowly but comfortably, count 1–4. Perhaps you can picture the numbers in you mind, or say them slowly to yourself. Now pause for a moment and count 1–4 again as you hold your breath (slowly, picturing the numbers in your mind if possible). And now as you exhale, slowly and comfortably count 1–8. Let your body relax more deeply as you exhale fully and completely, feeling the warm air as you exhale. You might want to repeat this for three breaths. Then check to see if you are feeling more relaxed. You may need to check the muscles of your shoulders, neck and jaw. If you can let these muscle groups relax further, take another slow breath.

#*3.* Another breathing/counting exercise that works well is to take four slow breaths, counting to eight by counting one on the inhale, two on the exhale, three on the inhale, etc. Try to picture the numbers in your mind or say the numbers to yourself. After counting to eight, check your position, relax your jaw, forehead, neck, and shoulders and repeat the exercise one more time. Within about two minutes you can begin to feel more relaxed and open, releasing tension with each exhale. Remember, go slowly. Do not be in such a hurry to relax!

#*4.* Take three deep slow breaths. As you lie down or sit back comfortably, allow yourself to breathe slowly. Feel the cool air as you inhale, pause a moment, and then slowly exhale, feeling the warm breath carry away tensions or discomforts. You might try to feel the cool air at the tip of your nostrils. Exhale through your mouth, breathing away the warm air as if it will drift up into the sky like a helium-filled balloon. Let go slowly and easily, becoming more relaxed with every breath. Some people use this exercise not only to relax but to help them drift off to sleep.

BIBLIOGRAPHY

Berends, Polly Berrien. *Whole Child Whole Parent*. New York: Harper & Row, 1983. $9.95.

Good book to read while you are pregnant because it helps with the spiritual and emotional aspects of parenthood which arise before you are confronted by your baby. Many practical parenting suggestions are dealt with, especially for new parents. Talks about clothing, cribs, household needs.

Brazelton, T. Berry. *Infants and Mothers: Differences in Development*. New York: Delta/Seymour Lawrence, 1983. $12.95.

Month-to-month guide for the baby's first year which discusses emotions, development, personality types. Some practical suggestions. Brazelton is a warm, caring physician whose writing style is supportive and easy to read.

Brazelton, T. Berry. *Toddlers and Parents: A Declaration of Independence*. New York: Delta, 1974. $10.95.

One year to thirty months. Sections for working or single parents. Stages toddlers go through and developmental levels to expect.

Durrell, Doris E. *The Critical Years: A Guide for Dedicated Parents*. Oakland, CA: New Harbinger Publications, 1984. $9.95.

Discusses the first three years. Language development, socialization and behavior modification techniques. Some specifics about toilet training, whining, and disobedience.

Ferber, Richard. *Solve Your Child's Sleep Problems*. New York: Simon & Schuster, 1985. $7.95.

Practical, gentle, nontraumatic techniques for helping your child develop good sleep habits (newborn to adolescence). It works!

Greenspan, Stanley, and Nancy Thorndike Greenspan. *First Feelings: Milestones in the Emotional Development of Your Baby and Child*. New York: Penguin Books, 1985. $3.95.

Explains a child's emotional development (to age four) to help parents understand what their child is going through. Helps with parental decision making.

Leach, Penelope. *Your Baby and Child: From Birth to Age Five*. New York: Alfred A. Knopf, 1978. $14.95.

Well written, easy to read guide for parents. Lots of practical information. Presents most of what you may need to know as a parent.

Wyckoff, Jerry, and Barbara C. Unell. *Discipline Without Shouting or Spanking: Practical Solutions to the Most Common Preschool Behavior Problems*. New York: Meadowbrook Books, 1984. $4.95.

Commonsense approaches to limit setting and discipline. Specific behaviors are discussed with step-by-step recommendations for dealing with them appropriately.

CHAPTER THREE

Children & Stress

Introduction

IT MAY SURPRISE us to think that children experience stress just as adults do, but our knowledge of child psychology and development increasingly underscores this fact. Though children are more adaptable than adults, they are still susceptible to the stresses and tensions of day-to-day life. In fact, in some ways children are even more sensitive to the emotions which trigger a stress response—fear, anger, jealousy—because they have not yet developed the mental controls that we learn as adults which serve as a buffer against our feelings.

A child's openness means that she is strongly affected by her environment, responding to both physical and emotional stimuli in an intense way. Excessive light, noise, or activity around the child can all act as stressors. Watching too much TV, particularly programs which depict a great deal of violence, can also produce hyperactivity and other stress symptoms. In addition to physical stimulus, children respond very strongly to the people they are near. Children sense and resonate with the moods of their playmates, siblings, or parents even though they do not yet have the intellectual capabilities to understand or verbalize what they are feeling. If parents or caregivers are tense, angry, or fearful, the child will internalize these emotions, experiencing them in her own body.

The constant newness of a child's life also creates stress. Although new activities are essential to health and growth, they can push a child against his limitations, producing intense anxiety. Developing language and other cognitive skills, learning how to coordinate the body, learning to interact with other people—all of these experiences challenge a child's capabilities. Just as adults become nervous when confronted with a new task, such as a job promotion which involves additional responsibilities, so children can experience tension with each new stage of skill development.

External changes in routine as well as developmental changes can contribute to stress. Switching schools or play groups or moving to a new neighborhood, with the attendant change of friends and/or caregivers, may be experienced as disruptive and stressful. While parents, having made such moves many times, have learned coping skills to help them adapt to these kinds of shifts, children may experience them as highly destabilizing and frightening.

The most profound upheaval a child can experience is that of having parents in conflict and a calm home life disturbed. The home is a child's base of stability, and a child is naturally confused when his parents are unhappy or can no longer live together. Trying to make sense of the turmoil, the child may blame himself for his parents' problems, further adding to his own distress.

Diet is perhaps the most overlooked factor in producing stress. The convenience foods of our modern society are laden with sugar and food additives, and are easily available to our children. A large amount of sugar ingested at once is devastating to the normal blood sugar ratio, particularly for children. Because of their smaller body mass, these blood sugar changes are felt more intensely. A sudden rise in blood sugar triggers the stress response, a condition in which the body is flooded with excess energy and which can result in hyperactive behavior. Moreover, the "junk food" habit produces lifelong dietary patterns which can lead to obesity, heart disease, and even cancer. The proper regulation of diet can go a long way toward reducing stress levels in children and creating future health.

Above all, the lack of love and acceptance are two critical and dangerous stressors in a child's life. Many other stress-producing situations can be adapted to if a child feels loved and accepted by his closest family and friends. As parents we need to express these caring emotions directly and consistently, not just through words, but through touch, smiles, and actions.

Children communicate stress in many ways. Some children become hy-

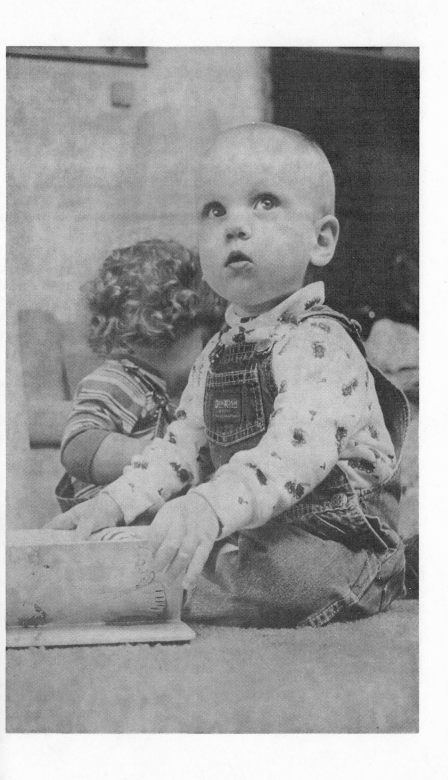

peractive; others may withdraw. Some children exhibit learning disabilities as stress responses. Still others experience "adult" physical symptoms, such as ulcers or headaches, when stress becomes overwhelming. Recognizing the situations which may produce stress for our children and being alert to possible stress symptoms will enable us to respond appropriately when our children need help with stress management.

Stress Management Recommendations for Children

Depending on your child's age, different techniques for controlling stress will be appropriate. What may be effective for your six-year-old may be far from helpful for your infant or your twelve-year-old. While the exercises that are suggested in the next section are organized by age group, don't hesitate to experiment. Try whatever feels right for your child and for you and see what works best. There are no hard and fast rules about stress management techniques for children, but in general the following guidelines are important.

All children need warmth, love, and attention. Sometimes their stress symptoms—hyperactivity or crankiness—are simply a way of asking for love and attention. Try to make a habit of spending special, quality time with each child on a regular basis. Select an activity that you and he particularly enjoy, and make a point of giving him your full attention. Express your caring physically as well as verbally by hugging your child or rubbing his back. Physical affection can create a very powerful bond between you.

Check your expectations of your child. Are they too high or too rigid? Or are you allowing your child the possibility of developing in her own way at her own rate? A child's sense of self-respect is largely reflective of the respect she receives from her parents and other people around her. Of course parents need to provide guidance and set limits, but leaving room for your child to discover her abilities and resources for herself, and letting her know that you respect her choices, will help her to feel calm and comfortable with herself. If your eight-year-old prefers to play with her trucks even though you would like her to read more, your loving approval of her activities will help her to move through each developmental stage in accordance with her own individual needs. This will greatly reduce the stress she may feel from being expected to do things she isn't ready to do or be someone she is not.

Of course, kids can suffer from the confusion of too much freedom or the lack of boundaries as well. Most children will question or test the limits their parents set for them, such as a certain bedtime or a rule about snacks. When you feel the limits you have set are important for you and for your child, being consistent and sticking to these limits will help your child to feel his world is stable and sensible.

Good communication, even with your very young children, is a vital tool for handling and reducing stress. Learning to really listen to your children is as important as clear verbalizing. Listening requires more than just hearing words. Listening involves making eye contact, noticing body language, and being able to respond to your child's feelings as well as his ideas. It is also important to keep an open mind, not interrupt, and not think of a response as he is talking but to wait until he is finished before responding. Speaking at your child's level with language he can readily understand helps him feel you have really listened, too.

Children learn primarily from what they see and feel rather than from what they may be told. As a parent you set an example through your actions that your children will mirror. Be vigilant, for the model you provide will be reflected back to you. If you are a loving parent, able to respect your child's individuality, able to communicate, your children will develop these traits as well. In so doing, their ability to adapt to their environment without undue stress will be heightened.

Finally, I would like to add a cautionary word about TV and stress. I have seen scores of children, particularly adolescents, who come in for help because of poor school grades, low motivation, low energy, low self-esteem, or poor communication skills, and who all watch excessive amounts of TV—often as much as five or six hours a day. I believe, and research has supported this, that these children's symptoms can be attributed, at least in part, to their TV-viewing habits. Television uses twenty- to thirty-second action-packed scenes to hold attention; these children often have short attention spans and difficulty concentrating on longer projects. Television usually presents shallow or stereotypical characters; these children demonstrate poor emotional awareness. Television viewing is a passive activity; these children are often physically unfit because they do not get enough exercise, and they tend to have few hobbies or social activities and low self-motivation. Television does not require verbal interaction with other people; these children demonstrate poor communication skills. While the fact that these kids watch so much TV is often indicative of other emotional and interactional deprivations in the home, I feel TV definitely contributes to the poor intellectual and emotional development and the stress symptoms of the children I see. It is a seductive diversion which, with the exception of educational program-

ming and a few other rare quality programs, is not helping our children to grow.

Not too long ago I met a sixteen-year-old girl at a social event who told me a story that greatly reinforced my feelings about TV. She told me that in the past year she had become an avid reader, truly excited about literature. I was surprised because she struck me as a very fashion conscious, "hip" teenager whom I wouldn't have expected to be so enthused about books. When I asked her what had caused her metamorphosis, she told me the story about a new friend of hers. This girl, also sixteen, had been raised without TV. She was apparently well read, articulate, and able to express an informed opinion on many subjects. This had so impressed my young friend that she decided to turn off the TV and begin reading. Since then her grades had improved and she had discovered interests she never knew she had. Without the numbing influence of TV she felt a whole new world opened up for her.

Case Study #1

Bobby was just six years old when he was referred to me for stress management because he had developed an ulcer. Eating had always been a problem for him, but when he had repeatedly complained of stomach pain, his mother had taken him to a pediatrician. The doctor, upon discovering the ulcer, recommended dietary changes and suggested that relaxation exercises would be helpful as well.

The cause of Bobby's stomach condition was quite evident. His parents were separated at the time I saw him, but they had a long history of splitting up bitterly and then reconciling. The parents sometimes used their son as a pawn in their disagreements, and as they argued over him, Bobby felt responsible for the family's problems. Mealtime, especially dinnertime, was particularly upsetting for him because his parents would quarrel at the table. Sometimes, to distract them from the argument, Bobby would complain of stomach pain. Unfortunately, Bobby's stomachaches themselves often became a point of contention between his parents as they argued about what to do for him.

I helped Bobby practice some breathing exercises and visualization techniques that he could use when he felt tensions building. He learned to do these exercises before naptime or bedtime or when his parents were fighting or getting wound up. I also helped him develop communication skills so he could let his parents know what he was feeling and how their behavior was affecting him. He became able to say to his parents, "I feel uncomfortable because you guys are shouting and no one is listening," or "There's too much noise and I'm feeling pressured. Please, I need to stop and do my breathing exercises. May I be excused to go sit in my room?"

Bobby's ability to call attention to his feelings and to reduce his tension by using the relaxation exercises gave him an increased sense of control over what had previously been an overwhelming situation. He also began to understand that it was not he who had caused the difficulties between his parents. Both the reduction of guilt and his increased empowerment seemed to contribute greatly to the improvement of his symptoms.

For their part, when the parents realized how their behavior was affecting Bobby, they sought counseling, and this had a positive impact on the whole family. The parents also learned to communicate more effectively and to avoid putting Bobby in the middle of their conflicts.

Case Study #2

Ramond was eight years old when I first met with him. He was referred to me because he was hyperactive, rarely staying still for longer than a few seconds, and his behavior had become a problem at school. I was told that even during sleep he appeared restless.

As I talked with Ramond and his parents, I discovered two issues which I felt contributed to his behavior. He was the youngest in the family, and his older brothers and sisters considered him "spoiled" and seemed to tease and taunt him excessively. In order to protect himself, Ramond had learned to lash out emotionally and physically, displaying aggressive and abusive behavior toward other playmates as well as toward his siblings. Ramond also consumed large amounts of junk food, eating candy and cookies and drinking cokes throughout the day. He would become more high-strung and difficult after eating these foods, as the sugar, caffeine, and perhaps some food additives gave him a surge of energy.

I felt several strategies would best help channel and reduce Ramond's hyperactivity. First, I talked with his parents about the need to control the harassment Ramond received from his brothers and sisters. The parents were quick to recognize the need for more attention in this area. Second, I recommended activities which would enable Ramond to release his excess energy in a positive way. Ramond is a very intelligent and naturally curious child whose personality had always been highly active, so I felt trying to suppress his energy would be harmful to his healthy exuberance. Rather, I suggested that if he felt wound up he go outside where he could run, hit a ball, or yell. Active playing and loud verbalizing were healthy outlets and were not destructive when he got out of a confined space.

Tactile experiences are often good for hyperactive children, as they seem to soothe the nervous system. I suggested to Ramond's parents that during the times when he seemed ready to settle down a bit they scratch his back, rub his feet, give him a massage, or let him play with dough. For these calmer times I suggested they also try soothing, warm baths, which can be a wonderful aid to dissipating stored muscle energy, and turning down the lights or the radio to reduce environmental stimuli. Breathing exercises could also be used once the pent-up energy had been vented.

Finally, I encouraged Ramond's parents to curtail his intake of sugar and caffeine. This was the hardest change to make, as Ramond became angry when sweets were withheld. Fortunately, Ramond was perceptive enough to recognize the importance of this measure, and with time he adjusted to the dietary changes.

Within a few weeks of implementing these suggestions, Ramond's teacher reported that his level of disruptive behavior had dropped substantially. While he remained highly active, he was less agitated and aggressive and was able to make the transition to a calmer state more easily.

Relaxation Exercises for Children

Because children's needs change as they grow, this section is divided into two segments: exercises for infants, toddlers, and very young children, and exercises for older, more verbal children. As was suggested in the previous section, however, don't hesitate to try any technique that seems appropriate for your child. This is an area where your sensitivity to your particular child's needs combined with your imagination can allow you to develop innovative methods for helping your child with stress reduction.

FOR INFANTS, TODDLERS, AND VERY YOUNG CHILDREN

Parents need to pay close attention to their young children for signs of stress, as these children usually cannot yet verbalize their tension and anxiety. Watch for signals such as increased or unusual fussiness; tantrums; withdrawal; self-destructive, violent, or antisocial behavior; regression of skills such as sleeping through the night or toilet training; frequent sickness; inability to sleep or oversleeping; or changes in eating habits—all of which can indicate stress or overstimulation.

One of the simplest things a parent can do when a child is exhibiting stress symptoms is to reduce environmental stressors such as excess noise or light. Is the radio or TV blaring? Turn it off, or substitute soothing classical music or a special relaxation tape. Close the windows if a power mower is buzzing or traffic outside your home is heavy. At night, dim the lights or substitute a soft yellow light for that glaring white one. During the day, when you want to have quiet time, draw the blinds to cut down on brightness which can stimulate the child.

Don't forget that the other people in your child's environment can also contribute to his agitation. Ask older children to play their noisy games outside. Check your own level of tension. The more relaxed you are, the easier it will be for your child to relax. Take a few deep breaths and try to slow your breathing. Speak softly and find a comfortable place to sit and compose yourself. By calming yourself, you set an example for your child to follow.

When outside stimuli have been controlled as much as possible, breathing can be used as an effective tool to reduce your child's stress. The following breathing technique uses mimicry to establish a connection with your child and can be especially useful for preverbal children and infants.

Sit near your child or hold him in your lap if he is not too agitated. Begin to imitate his breathing pattern. Each time he inhales you inhale, and each time he exhales, you exhale. Look him in the eye gently as you pace your breathing to his. This should work to trigger his curiosity and catch his attention. Once you have the child's interest, gradually slow your breathing, letting him now imitate you. Continue to slow your breathing until you are taking approximately twelve breaths per minute, then maintain this even rhythm. As you relax your breathing, relax your muscles too, and in this way you can lead your child into a more calm state.

You can mimic movement and sound as well as breathing to make contact with a crying baby or distracted child. The reproduction of your child's own sounds and gestures, when it is not mocking or derisive, is a powerful nonverbal way to let her know you are paying attention to her. For example, one mother came to me when her baby was five months old. The baby was very active and had just learned to swing her head from side to side as if saying no. The mother was worried that this repeated, vigorous movement might injure the child's neck. I showed her how she could mimic the baby's movement as a way to get her attention and then help her calm down. The

mother tried swinging her head from side to side in rhythm with her child, while maintaining eye contact. Any sound the baby made the mother copied as well. The baby was fascinated by the odd behavior of her mother. When the child began looking curiously at her mother, the mom began a circular motion with her hands in front of the baby's face. Once the baby started tracking this movement, the mother began to slow her hands, breathe slowly and deeply, and talk calmly. The baby, happy with mom's attention, learned to follow her mom into a more relaxed posture. Although this relaxation strategy did not work every time, the mother developed a useful relaxation skill and gained a keener sense of her baby's developmental patterns.

Touch is also a powerful tool to help induce relaxation. The tactile contact of gentle massage, cuddling, and hugging can ease a child, even a baby, into a more relaxed state. For infants, massage can include rubbing the arms or legs, gently stroking the back, neck and shoulders, or lightly rubbing the stomach. Young children particularly like back rubs and foot massages. Massage can be a very useful part of the bedtime/naptime ritual. If you have a special nighttime ceremony that includes massage, the child learns to associate this comforting time together with sleep. This positive association helps the child to welcome rather than resist the transition to sleep.

In fact, if the association between massage and rest is well established, this ritual can also be used at other times of the day to calm your child when he is cranky or upset. By establishing patterns of relaxation at an early age, you provide your child with a tool for relaxation that he can use and rely upon in many situations.

Bathing in warm water is another relaxation technique that infants and young children particularly respond to. A bath can be a good distraction to break a bad mood or fussy episode. The bathing ritual can be conducted as a relaxation experience. Use a washcloth and the calming flow of water as a form of massage, gently soothing your childs muscles and skin. Rub down his arms, back, face, and neck with the washcloth, or pour warm water over his stomach or back. As the water gently quiets his nervous energy, a more positive mood will result.

Calm, quiet talk can be a helpful addition to any of the approaches suggested above. For instance, as you bathe your child, you can say to him slowly and in a calm voice: "Isn't the warm water comfortable? . . . Does the water feel nice as it splashes against your skin? . . . Can you feel yourself floating safely? . . . Let the warm water relax you so you can be ready for bedtime (or naptime, dinnertime, etc.) . . . Can you hear the sounds of the warm water? . . . Can you breathe slowly? (You should exaggerate your own slow breathing and slow your voice even further.) . . . The warm water relaxes and comforts you . . . You will be able to sleep deeply all night, waking rested in the morning . . . Let's see if we can remain calm and relaxed as the water drains away and we get ready for bed. . . ."

A melodic human voice is comforting in itself, but if you use language which offers positive images to your child, you will be providing a double benefit. You can tell him he made you feel proud because he played well with his friends or cleaned up his toys without being asked, or made you feel happy when he gave you a hug. While the child is drifting off to sleep, the subconscious mind is most open to suggestion, and these positive messages can have a powerful impact. I feel this is one of the most effective ways in which parents can influence their child's development. Your gentle, relaxing tones and positive verbal suggestion will help calm your child and give him the support he needs to develop a sunny outlook.

As you can see, the techniques suggested above can be combined in an improvised and personalized approach to your child's needs. Here is an example of how you might deal with an infant who is crying and resisting sleep.

First, you might copy the sounds and movements of your baby, the clenched, waving fists and the high-pitched wail. Then, when contact has been made, you can gently pick him up, hugging him and speaking to him in quiet, soothing tones. At this point you can focus on his rapid breathing, pacing your breathing to his, then gradually slowing your breathing and relaxing your muscles to encourage the same relaxation in your baby. As soon as he begins to become less tense, you could use more massage and comforting verbal suggestion. Rub his arms and chest with slow strokes of your palm while you say to him: "Relax so you can rest . . . We love you and we will be in the next room while you sleep . . . Sleep well so you can be rested in the morning . . . You are a good boy . . . You can learn to relax and to allow yourself to drift off to sleep . . . Breath slowly and relax so you can sleep . . . We love you . . . Sleep well . . ." until the baby is finally relaxed enough to sleep.

If your child continues to have sleeping problems, I highly recommend the book by Richard Ferber, *Solve Your Child's Sleep Problems*. My wife and I, as well as many of my clients and friends, have had tremendous success with the techniques it outlines. If all else fails, getting the child outdoors can be a good strategy. Going for a walk or calmly driving around in the car can change a child's mood and provide some relief to the frazzled parent. Fresh air seems to absorb so much negative energy, it's a wonder no one has found a way to bottle it yet.

FOR OLDER, MORE VERBAL CHILDREN

Many of the suggestions for stress management with infants and young children can be used for older children, too. But in addition the parent can use verbal, interactive stress management techniques with the older child. If these exercises are presented as games, children are usually quick to respond. Here is a breathing-focusing game which can help change a child's negative mood.

To begin, ask the child to copy the way you are breathing. Start by taking three deep breaths very quickly. As the child follows your instruction, her mood will change almost immediately. Then take three very slow breaths, pausing between inhale and exhale, and then again between the exhale and the next breath. As the child follows, ask her if she can feel the cool air as she inhales. Then have her notice the warm air as she exhales. Next have her see how slowly she can breathe for two minutes.

This next game combines breathing with awareness of your heartbeat. It is not only fun, but educational. First, teach your child how to put two fingers on his wrist pulse or at the side of the neck, or to put his palm on his chest to count his heartbeat. Help him to figure out how many times his heart beats per minute. When he has done this, make a note of his heart rate and then have him follow your breathing rhythm as you gradually slow your breathing. Time your breathing so that you slow down to twelve breaths per minute, one breath every five seconds. Then slow to one breath every six seconds (ten per minute). You can even try taking one breath every eight seconds. After several minutes of this slow, regular breathing, have the child find and count his heart rate again. Compare this number with the original number. He will discover that when people slow their breathing rate, the heart rate usually slows, too.

Another approach is to have a contest. Kids love contests. Time them to see how long they can hold their breath. Be reasonable; do not encourage them to turn blue. Or time them to see how long they can remain quiet. If the environment is suitable, time them to see who can yell the longest on one breath, or time them for sustained movement. This helps children to unwind by releasing stored tension, and is particularly useful for hyperactive or sugar-laden children.

Other physical activities such as sports, dancing, or active playing can be a good way to release tension. If you are confined to an indoor space, slow movement is a good alternative to more active games. For example, have the child imitate in slow motion the movements of her favorite comic hero. If you are with more than one child, you can have them pose as a group to form

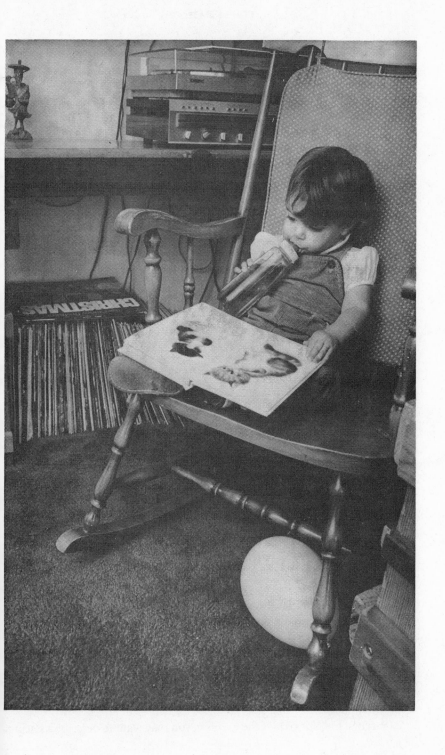

letters or numbers. They have probably seen this done on PBS TV's "Sesame Street." Or have them imitate animals, or pretend to be inanimate objects, such as trees, flowers, or bridges. To maintain the calm mood, have them imitate animals such as turtles or snails, or any animal grazing quietly in a protected pasture. Maybe your future engineer would like to demonstrate what a bridge, tower, or tall building would look like if it could stand for eternity. Redwood trees, swaying palm trees, or branching oak trees are also fun to imitate. Imagine the trees standing silently, feeling the warm breeze, the gentle rays of the sun, or the tickle of birds or squirrels jumping about their branches.

Guided awareness meditation is another relaxation technique which can be fun for the whole family, and it can help build a feeling of family cohesion while everyone learns to relax. Have everyone use his imagination to picture himself outdoors. Have him notice every detail—not only what he would see, but what he would feel, hear, smell.

FAMILY MEDITATION EXERCISE

Begin by having all participants lie down on the floor or on a mat in a quiet room. One person may read the exercise aloud, or the exercise can be taped. Ask everyone to uncross arms or legs, relax shoulders, jaws, forehead, and close the eyes. Then give the following directions:

Take three deep slow breaths, pausing after each inhale and then exhaling slowly and completely. After the first three breaths, continue to breathe slowly and naturally. Allow each breath to help you relax more deeply into a peaceful calmness. Let your arms relax even more. Perhaps you can begin to feel the muscles relax so completely that your arms begin to feel heavy. You may even feel the warmth of energy and blood flowing more freely down into your hands. Maybe you can feel the warmth pulsing slowly into your fingertips.

As you drift more deeply, you may feel your legs relaxing even more. Your legs may begin to feel heavy or warm as you relax further into a peaceful calmness. You may find that your neck and shoulders can settle into a more comfortable position. As you let go with these muscles, perhaps you can let your head sink into the pillow or mat.

Continue to breathe slowly. Make sure your jaw is relaxed, your forehead, and the muscles around your eyes. As your body continues to relax with each breath, use your imagination to see yourself outdoors on a warm and beautiful day.

(Parents: For this part of the exercise, you may want to describe a setting or scene that your family is familiar with, such as a recent or favorite vacation spot, a relative's place in the country, a favorite picnic location, or the family's swimming hole. Use the following suggestions if they are appropriate for your family, or supply your own descriptions.)

Ocean or beach scene: . . . You may see yourself at the beach. Find the perfect place to lie down in the warm sand . . . You may be able to hear the sounds of the waves and the seabirds . . . Feel the warmth from the sun gently shining down on you . . . Perhaps you can even smell the salt air . . . Let your tensions melt away . . . After you have drifted for several minutes in this peaceful calmness, you may wish to walk along the beach and discover the treasures that rest in the sand . . . Maybe you can throw stones into the waves or skip the stones on the surface of the water. . . .

Lake or stream scene: . . . You can see yourself by the lake (or stream) . . . Make yourself comfortable as you settle down into the sand . . . Feel the sunlight gently shining upon you . . . Soak up the warmth as if it could help your tension melt away . . . Listen for the sounds of warm breezes, birds, or of running water . . . Smell the wood, or grass, or the flowers that surround you . . . Sink back into the warm, smooth sand . . . After you drift for several minutes in this peaceful, dreamlike calmness, perhaps you can let go, drift even deeper . . . (pause) Perhaps you explore the beach and find the special treasures that rest by the water . . . Or you may find yourself fishing. . . .

Meadow scene: . . . Picture yourself in a clearing or lush meadow . . . Pick the most comfortable place to lie down in the soft, warm grass . . . Feel the golden sunlight gently shining down upon you . . . Soak up the warmth . . . Perhaps you can hear the sounds of warm breezes or birds or a stream trickling by the meadow . . . Smell the fragrance of the grasses or flowers that surround you . . . Sink into the warm grass as you drift more deeply into a dreamlike calmness . . . (pause) Maybe you can roam about the meadow, watching the birds soaring above you . . . Or maybe you can pick the beautiful wildflowers as you rest and recharge yourself fully and completely. . . .

To end this meditation: . . . Let the memories of these wonderful moments return with you . . . Gently let yourself awaken, bringing the feeling of calmness back with you . . . As you return to this room, feel the floor or mat beneath you . . . You may wish to take a deep breath and stretch, letting yourself awaken fully and completely . . . Let the calmness and relaxation return with you into a fully waking state . . . You may want to take another deep breath and stretch. . . .

After completing this family meditation exercise, talk to one another about your experience. This can be a valuable way to enhance family rapport. Everyone, no matter how young, can share her feelings about the exercise and describe the images which floated through her thoughts. Encourage all members of the family to talk about his or her experience, and help each person to enhance his descriptions and perceptions. For instance, if your child says he pictured himself in the meadow, ask him what he saw or did there, or what he felt that gave him the most pleasure. Encourage him to expand on his descriptions by including colors, sounds, shapes, and textures. Using all of the senses can help expand the limits of consciousness.

It may also be helpful to ask if any part of anyone's meditation seemed uncomfortable or unpleasant. Encourage anyone who had an unsettling image to describe it and then help him control that image by changing it to a more positive one. For instance, it is not uncommon for children to visualize a scary animal and feel frightened. Ask the child to first describe the animal and then ask what he would like to change about the unpleasant image. Help him to visualize himself taming and making friends with the animal. Then ask if that change makes the visualization more enjoyable.

Other family meditation possibilities are to ask everyone to picture a candle flame, or stream, or wave pattern at the ocean. Describe the image in detail at the same time that you encourage slow, deep breathing. Try to remain focused on an image in this way for two to five minutes. This exercise expands concentration abilities, but it takes practice, even for adults.

Some families use chanting or repetition of a simple prayer or singing to form a family meditation. Holding hands while you repeat the chant or song helps your family to remain focused and to bond.

BIOFEEDBACK FOR CHILDREN

Biofeedback is another excellent way to teach relaxation to children. Biofeedback monitoring is a technique which uses simple instruments to measure the body's degree of relaxation. Through this monitoring a person can become aware of the points of tension in his body and learn to control and reduce this tension. Biofeedback equipment can be as simple as an aquarium or photo thermometer to measure hand temperature, a stethoscope to listen to the heart or digestive sounds, or a blood pressure cuff to determine if relaxation has extended to the circulatory system. Another person can even act as a biofeedback machine by holding the subject's arm, leg, or head, providing feedback about how relaxed this part of the body feels, and encouraging further relaxation as needed.

If you want to explore biofeedback with your children at home, I recommend the following exercises:

Temperature biofeedback: For this exercise you'll need an aquarium or photo thermometer (not a fever thermometer) which is easy to read and registers temperatures between 60 and 100 degrees Fahrenheit. Tape the thermometer to the outside of one of your child's index fingers, preferably at the second joint. Do not tape it too tightly. Wait one minute and then read the temperature and record it. Now begin the relaxation technique, such as meditation or visualization, with which your child is most familiar. When the child feels relaxed, have him check the thermometer to see if his temperature has gone up. Eventually, he should try to get his temperature above 90 degrees. When deeply relaxed, his hand temperature should rise above 93 degrees.

When first beginning biofeedback training, it is not unusual to find that one's temperature actually goes down, as one *tries too hard* to relax. With practice your child will learn not to strain, but to simply allow himself to drift into the perfect state of relaxation.

Some people find it helpful to use a visualization exercise which focuses on an image of warmth as the relaxation method used with temperature biofeedback. For instance, you might help your child imagine he is holding his hands up to a warm fire, or putting his hands in warm water. Or he may visualize himself lying in the warm sun on the beach. Encourage him to let the sensations of warmth flow through his hands for a few minutes before checking the thermometer. He will soon learn to feel the rise in hand temperature that indicates a deeper level of relaxation. Temperature training is the easiest kind of feedback to do at home. It is particularly useful for digestive and circulatory problems and autoimmune problems such as allergic responses.

Stethoscope biofeedback: Children are fascinated by their ability to listen to the internal world of their bodies as they use a stethoscope to hear their own heart rate or digestive sounds. They can become familiar with the rumbles or gurgles as the muscles in the walls of the intestines and the stomach fluctuate rhythmically, moving the food along. These sounds should not be too slow or too fast, nor should they be irregular, and with practice children can learn when the sounds are regular and when they need to be speeded or calmed. Encouraging them to first measure their heart rate or the level of digestive activity, and then see how these rhythms change as they practice a relaxation technique is a graphic way to illustrate how relaxation works. Encourage your child to slow her breathing and see how her heart rate slows also, or relax her muscles and hear how her stomach activity relaxes as well, becoming calm and regular. Again, it is often helpful to use a visualization exercise which imitates or suggests the desired bodily change. For example, if your child is trying to slow her heartbeat, have her picture a silver moon slowly setting over a mountain lake. With each slow beat of her heart, she can imagine the moon moving one speck closer to the horizon. If she is trying to calm her stomach, have her imagine ocean waves which roll gently to shore, barely making a ripple along the smooth sand, or the surface of a calm lake which moves gently under a slight breeze. Learning to slow digestive activity can be helpful for problems with diarrhea; speeding digestive activity can help relieve constipation.

Blood pressure biofeedback: A blood pressure cuff can be purchased inexpensively at your local drugstore. The use of this equipment to monitor blood pressure is primarily important for adults. But children will enjoy learning how to use the strange-looking cuff, and this skill will be handy later in their lives. Like adults, children can experience a drop in blood pressure after a relaxation exercise, though it is usually not as pronounced as for adults. If your child does not experience a lowering of blood pressure after relaxation, you may simply want to make a game of taking the measurement itself.

Muscle tension biofeedback: Using another person as a biofeedback machine can be particularly fun for children. Have the child lie down on the floor or bed with his legs straight and his arms at his side. Someone whom the child can trust, either another child or an adult, acts as the biofeedback "machine." The "machine" will carefully and respectfully lift one of the subjects arms or legs. The arm or leg should rest with its complete weight in the "machine's" hands. If the body part is fully relaxed, it will feel heavy and loose as the "machine" gently moves it. If the limb feels stiff, the "machine" can encourage the subject to relax further. The subject must learn to trust his partner and not help move his body in any way. At bedtime, this biofeedback technique can substitute for massage. Gently holding and moving the arms, legs, or head will seem a bit unusual at first, but can quickly lead to new awareness and deeper relaxation. Cradling the head will especially help to teach neck and shoulder relaxation. Muscle tension biofeedback is particularly beneficial for children with headaches, neckaches, sleeping problems, tight jaws, or hyperactive behavior patterns.

Certain biofeedback devices have been designed to operate in conjunction with a video screen. The monitoring system—such as an EMG machine, which measures muscle tension, or a thermometer, which measures skin temperature—can be connected to a video machine so that the changes in the monitoring system produce corresponding changes or movement in an image on the video screen, such as a paddle in a "pong" game. When a subject tenses or relaxes his muscles, for example, the EMG monitor taped to his forehead will register the muscle tension, then feed it to the video equipment, which will show the increase or decrease in tension as a movement of the pong paddle on the video screen. Because children love games, this method of teaching biofeedback can work particularly well, and can hold their attention longer than other relaxation techniques. In fact, it is often easier for children to become proficient at these games than it might be for their parents. In one case I know of, a developmentally disabled boy learned to use biofeedback temperature training to induce relaxation. He was able to warm his hands very quickly, an indication of relaxation. He learned this technique more effectively than his parents, and for the first time had a skill at which he excelled. As a result, he not only learned a valuable relaxation skill, but his self-esteem rose markedly.

Many forms of biofeedback can be easily turned into games for children. Slowing heart rate, warming hand temperature, or changing blood pressure can all be practiced in a "biofeedback Olympics" at home with the entire family, as long as the focus isn't too highly competitve, producing further stress! Your imagination is your only limit in finding ways for your children to use these techniques.

ACTIVE PROGRESSIVE RELAXATION

Another relaxation technique to which older children respond well is Active Progressive Relaxation. The following exercise is particularly useful to help older children relax before bedtime and fall asleep easily.

Create a quiet, warm environment, closing window shades, dimming lights, and eliminating noise or drafts. Have the child lie down in a comfortable position. Have him close his eyes if this does not make him uncomfortable. Repeat the following phrases:

Take three deep breaths, pausing after each inhale and then exhaling fully and completely . . . Breathe slowly and relax more deeply with every breath. During this exercise you will tighten and then relax various parts of your body. To begin, make a fist and hold it tight for a moment . . . then let go . . . Let your hand relax completely . . . Take a breath, and now do the same for the other fist . . . Hold it tight for a moment . . . then let go . . . Let your hand relax completely . . . Now tense your arms, as if you were making big muscles . . . Hold this tension for a moment, and then let go, relaxing your arms completely . . . Take a deep slow breath and let your arms and hands relax even better . . . Now curl your toes, as tightly as you can . . . Hold this tension for just a moment . . . and relax your toes completely . . . Let you feet relax even more as you take a slow deep breath . . . Now point your toes so the backs of your legs tighten . . . hold them even tighter . . . and relax . . . Let your legs relax even more, until they are completely loose and limp . . . Take a slow breath and let the tension go completely . . . Now tighten your shoulders and back as if you were shrugging your shoulders up to your ears . . . Hold this tension for a moment . . . and then relax . . . Take a deep, slow breath, and let your shoulders drop into a comfortable place . . . Now tighten the muscles of your face as if you were squishing your face in toward your nose . . . Tighten your lips and eyes and hold this tension . . . then let go completely . . . Now open your face as wide as you can . . . mouth open, eyebrows high and wide . . . Hold this for a moment and then relax . . . Take a deep slow breath and relax even more . . .

Continue breathing slowly and comfortably . . . Sink back into whatever you are sitting or lying upon . . . Let your arms and legs slowly relax even more, until they feel heavy and comfortable. Drift pleasantly in this state of relaxation . . . as if you were floating on a mattress in a warm pool on a sunny day. (If your child does not like water, have him imagine he is on a magic carpet, floating in the clouds safely and comfortably.)

Parents: Let your child drift in this relaxed and pleasant state for several minutes, then check to see whether his breathing is calm and regular. Let him sleep or awaken him slowly by inviting him to come back to the room, take a deep breath and stretch, waking fully and completely.

CHAPTER FOUR

Adolescence & Stress

Introduction

As EVERYONE who has survived adolescence will attest, this is an awkward, often stressful time. The pressures of growing out of childhood and into adulthood are enormous, as bodies, minds, and emotions ride a roller coaster of change. Beginning to test their wings as young adults, but not yet being completely independent, adolescents feel enormous tugs both forward and backward, and often experience strong, vascillating, and contradictory desires and emotions.

The most visible and obvious changes of adolescence are the physical changes. Puberty is signaled by the onset of menstruation and the development of breasts and hips for girls, and by a deepening voice, facial hair, and increased strength for boys. Both girls and boys experience a growth spurt, skin changes, and increased hormone production, along with the development of other secondary sex characteristics. These various physical changes can sometimes seem to occur at an alarming rate, and the blossoming child must adapt to a radically different self-image in a relatively short period of time. The difficulty in feeling comfortable with a new appearance may lead to clumsiness or awkwardness, and this can weaken self-confidence. Thus, rapid physical change, which itself places stress on the body, also produces emotional stress.

The physical changes which signal adulthood often happen much more quickly than the accompanying emotional changes, so that the adolescent may feel a deep contradiction between his outer appearance and his inner development. For girls, the new attention or attraction from the opposite sex may be more than they are ready for emotionally. For boys, the sudden increase of strength and coordination may not be accompanied by the emotional maturity to control these new abilities.

Emotional stresses result not only from the expectations that accompany physical growth, but from the increasing need to separate from parental authority and control. Freedom is a big issue for the adolescent, but deciding how much freedom, and how soon that freedom will be granted or accepted, is often confusing and difficult for both parent and teenager. The adolescent wants to make decisions, but may not have the experience to make appropriate, "adult" choices. At the same time, unless she has the freedom to act on her own and make mistakes, she will not learn for herself. This push-pull between parental authority and adolescent autonomy often becomes focused on a single issue such as a curfew, or use of the car. The teenager may see the car as a ticket to freedom. Yet she soon realizes it is a major responsibility as well, requiring the ability to know and obey laws, to be safety conscious, to attend to mechanical problems, and perhaps to make a financial commitment. Thus the teenager may feel frustration if she does not have as much freedom as she would like, and fear of new responsibility if that freedom is actually granted. Either way, she will experience the stress that accompanies a life transition.

As adolescents move away from parental authority they are simultaneously constructing an autonomous identity, a sense of self which, though influenced by adults, is independent of them. We've all heard of the teenage "identity crisis." The difficult process of figuring out who we really are starts in earnest during adolescence and is another major source of emotional upheaval and stress.

This is a time of experimentation, of trying on different hats, so to speak, to see which one fits. The sorting out process can be especially confusing today as teenagers find themselves confronted with a sometimes bewildering assortment of options. In any given urban high school, the choice of peer groups ranges from "jocks" to "punks," from "preppies" to "skin heads"—with many other groups in between! The stigma of not belonging can be severe, and a teenager may often feel intense anxiety about being accepted at the same time that he's trying to discover whether this new identity suits him.

Social pressures can also create anxiety for adolescents. The teenager is engaging in many new social behaviors, from attending parties and concerts, to dating, to experimenting with alcohol, drugs, and sex. Even such a simple activity as calling a member of the opposite sex on the phone, which an adult might not think about twice, can be immensely anxiety producing for the teenager who is just learning how to conduct herself socially. At the other extreme, learning about alcohol and drugs and exploring that tantalizing yet confusing thing called "sex" forces teenagers to confront new feelings and make difficult decisions about what they are ready for, decisions which often throw them up against intense peer pressure. The need to belong combined with the need to be true to one's own feelings can create enormous tension.

Mental stresses are strongly felt during adolescence, too. The need to think for oneself, to make decisions which will affect the future, and to learn new, more sophisticated skills places great demands upon the teenager's cognitive abilities. Many adolescents are thinking about college or future vocational training and are feeling pressured to do well in school. Additionally, adolescence is often the time that a person begins his first job. Fears about job performance are common, as is anxiety about getting along with others, developing group cooperation skills, and learning to communicate appropriately. The teenager who finds himself selling paint to a customer who is dissatisfied with the selection must learn to control his own opinions and listen carefully to the other person. Suddenly he realizes that the adult world often requires self-restraint! At the same time, as he gains satisfaction from learning how to take inventory and place orders, he feels the pride of developing a new skill.

Finally, as adolescents grow, they move out of the comfortable circles of home and school and into a larger world. They begin to think about world affairs and the way their lives will be affected by, and can affect, the events around them. Because of the sophistication of today's media, I believe teenagers are exposed more directly than ever before to the disasters and chaos—as well as the possibilities—of the world around them. Each night the terrible litany is pumped into their homes—chemical and nuclear accidents, Middle East wars, terrorism, AIDS. Yet while adolescents are acutely aware of what is going on, they often feel powerless to do anything in response. Anytime we face situations that seem to affect us but do not appear to be under our control, our fear and anxiety level is raised significantly. Add to the fact of world instability and the upheaval at home—the rising divorce rate, the frequency with which families move, and the erosion of the family wage—and we see a picture of increased insecurity for teenagers instead of the stable launching pad, which they need to move smoothly into adulthood.

It is no wonder that teenage suicide is up dramatically and that stress among adolescents is a major health problem.

Yet the same situations that produce stress can also produce growth. When teenagers learn to control their response mechanisms, not through a facade of "coolness," but through real control over their body's responses, they can free up energy to deal positively with the world around them. Relaxation, awareness, and stress management strategies can assist in the growth pattern called adolescence.

Stress Management Recommendations for Adolescents

Because adolescent personalities are not as rigid as those of adults, we often assume that a teenager's flexibility and resilience will allow him to survive these transitional years unscathed. Yet the fact is that during adolescence a person is not only confronting stressful situations just as adults do, he is also developing coping patterns which he will take with him into his adult years. Thus learning to respond in a healthy way to stress is a crucial skill for adolescents.

Physical exercise is perhaps one of the best and most enjoyed forms of stress management for teenagers. Regular aerobic exercise helps to release the energy spurred by the fight or flight response, our body's natural response to stress. When this surge of energy is not released it becomes stored as muscular tension, inhibiting the body's natural, healthy functioning.

I recommend exercises that are not highly competitive, such as jogging, swimming, bike riding, walking or hiking, rowing, jumping rope, dancing, yoga, and aerobics. Avoid exercises that your body does not tolerate; you don't want your stress management program to create stress! Be aware of your limitations and build your exercise program slowly, over time. Be particularly careful if you play competitive sports. They may provide a good workout, but if the competition is too keen, you may not be helping yourself to relax.

Outdoor activities are highly relaxing, as the fresh air seems to absorb stress in a natural way. Getting away from the situation creating stress, whether it be at home or at school, can also provide valuable distance, allowing you to put the stress-producing situation into perspective. Hikes, walks, picnics, fishing, bike rides, sports such as frisbee, baseball, or football, hobbies such as photography, and many other outdoor activities are restful for most teenagers. Simply going outside for a walk may be a strategy that can provide a moment to relax, take a few deep breaths, and have a little time to yourself when things are getting tense.

In addition to physical exercise, good skills of communication are a valuable tool in helping to reduce stress. In fact, knowing how to communicate clearly can often help you avoid altogether the situations that create tension. Because adolescence is a time of such rapid change, being aware of the changes that are taking place and knowing how to talk about them with others is a crucial skill.

Honest communication begins within the self. Before you can communicate clearly with others, you must know what you are feeling and what you want. Relaxation techniques enable you to quiet all the unnecessary internal dialogue which results from your daily encounters and listen to a clearer, truer voice within yourself. The ability to turn off the conscious mind, particularly if it is engaged in negative, destructive ruminations, and become acquainted with a deeper self is crucial to growth and to clear communication. From this state of deep relaxation, a balanced emotional awareness can develop.

In addition to listening to your inner voice, positive communication requires the ability to listen to others. If you watch other people talking, chances are you will find two people speaking at once, not listening, not hearing, and not getting their points across effectively. One reason people do not listen well is because they are busy thinking of answers at the same time they are "listening." Because they are thinking ahead to what they may want to say, they are not clearly absorbing what is being said to them. Listening requires complete attention and a willingness to suspend your own urgent need to express while the other person is talking. Maintaining eye contact will help here, too.

Many people think that good communicators are people with good vocabularies and a "way with words." But, in fact, nonverbal communication makes up a large part of our interactions. So knowing how to communicate well requires an awareness of all the nonverbal ways in which people express themselves. Movements, gestures, voice tone and volume, facial expressions, and many other nonverbal activities make up a large portion of any conversation. Sometimes these forms of expression will contradict a person's words. For instance, a person may say "thank you," but his tone of voice may be icy. The tone of voice, in this case, is communicating the person's feelings more accurately than his words, and must be paid attention to. Learn to notice and respond to these nonverbal forms of communication.

Another important communication strategy is to avoid "blaming" the other person when a problem has occurred. Blaming cuts off communication as the other person usually responds by feeling personally attacked and scrambling to defend herself. If something happens which makes you feel uncomfortable, hurt, or angry, a good response is to describe what you are feeling. For example, if a relative tells you you should not go out with a certain person, or you should dress differently, instead of saying, "Mind your own business!" it would be better to say, "I feel uncomfortable when you tell me how I should behave." The second statement cannot be argued. No one can dispute how you feel. From a statement of your feelings, you can begin a conversation about what could be done to change your feelings of discomfort. If good listening skills are used, this discussion will give both people a chance to become more aware of each other's needs and feelings, and perhaps a compromise can be reached.

Case Study #1

Gary was referred to me for stress management because he was developing an ulcer. He was eighteen when I first saw him, but the symptoms of his stress-related complaint had begun when he was seventeen. As I talked with Gary, I began to recognize a profile which is not unusual for someone at his stage of life. He had recently graduated from high school, was working part time and attending the local junior college, had just moved away from home for the first time, and was developing a relationship with a girlfriend. Gary was experiencing significant change in almost every aspect of his life. Although these changes were positive and growth producing, because they were all occuring at once, they were creating a high level of stress. Gary wanted to be independent, but the challenges he had taken on were feeling more difficult than he had anticipated. Living away from home meant he had to develop many new survival skills. Starting college and maintaining his job at the same time was also difficult. And developing an intimate relationship required new skills of communication and compromise.

We usually experience stress in that part of our body where our physiology is weakest. For Gary, this weak link was his stomach. Since he was a child, he had experienced stomach pain after eating. With the increased stress of his life transition, this tendency toward abdominal sensitivity had become more acute. At the time I saw him he was on a bland diet and had begun taking medication for his ulcer.

After a thorough review of Gary's history, I discussed with him the connection I was seeing between his life changes and his ulcer. It took several weeks for Gary to begin to see for himself the association between feelings of anxiety about school or work and his stomach pain. As Gary's understanding of his condition increased, however, he became very motivated to use stress reduction techniques. I started him on a program of autogenic training and visualization. Because restricted blood flow often contributes to ulcers, autogenic training, which increases blood flow, is particularly useful for this condition. I taught Gary phrases to repeat to himself during his relaxation, which focused on sensations of calmness. After eight weeks of work with me, Gary reported that he could finally feel a sense of control over the degree of warmth in his hands and feet and the feeling of relaxation in his stomach. He also related to me a special visualization which he used after he was deeply relaxed. He imagined himself riding a horse through a sunny, flower-filled meadow. He saw himself happy, strong, and free, glowing with health, a smile on his face. This image gave him such a feeling of happiness and warmth that, though he only experienced the visualization for a few moments, the feeling stayed with him the rest of his day.

In eight weeks Gary was free of any symptoms of his ulcer. His life continues to be challenging and stressful; however, Gary now has the tools to respond positively to his life changes. Gary has learned not only how to control his symptoms, but how to care for himself better.

Case Study #2

Sara came to see me when she was sixteen because she was suffering from headaches almost daily. Her parents had taken her to their family doctor, and after conducting a number of tests and ruling out any serious medical problem, the doctor had discussed with the family the treatment alternatives. Sara could be treated with medication, but there would be potential side effects. Another possibility was to try biofeedback and other stress management techniques to lessen or eliminate the headaches.

As Sara and I discussed her headaches, a clear pattern emerged. The headaches usually began after lunch, became worse before tests at school,

and sometimes were associated with stressful situations such as performances or public speaking. Because the headaches interfered with her studying, they often compounded the pressure of examinations, resulting in a vicious cycle in which the pressure produced a headache, and the headache increased the pressure. The headaches also seemed to have increased as Sara felt more concerned about getting good grades for college. Sara also mentioned other pressures—the fear of losing her popularity if she did too well in school or studied too much, encouragement from her parents to get a part-time job and help save for college, and their repeated expectation that she raise her grades for college.

I started Sara on a program of biofeedback and progressive relaxation. The initial biofeedback measurements I took revealed a great deal of tension in Sara's forehead and jaw. Her need to "bear down" to do well at school seemed to translate into this muscle tension. I used an EMG machine, which measures muscle tension by monitoring changes in the electrical activity of muscles. I placed the machine's sensors on Sara's forehead, and the sensors then transmitted information about the electrical activity of Sara's forehead muscles to a warning tone. When the tone went on, the sensor was registering activity, or tension, in the muscle. When the tone was off, the muscle was at rest.

Sara learned very quickly to control her muscle tension so that the tone would not go on. She was amazed at how clearly she could discriminate between the feelings of tension and relaxation in her muscles. Once she felt this control, she was able to induce a state of relaxation without the use of the EMG machine.

The progressive relaxation exercises also helped Sara to achieve a deep state of relaxation. Because these exercises deal directly with the muscles, they are particularly suited for problems involving muscular tension. As Sara performed the exercise she became aware of each muscle group in her body and its state of tension or relaxation. Within several weeks of regular practice of both biofeedback and progressive relaxation exercises, Sara reported that her headaches were lessening. After six weeks, they were nearly gone. Sara also found that she was sleeping better and feeling more rested and "under control." She even felt that she was studying more efficiently, doing better on tests, and having more time for social activities. By relaxing, she was no longer creating the obstacles which had previously interfered with these activities. Sara still felt pressured at times, but she was better able to control the tension when it occurred. She was also better able to communicate her feelings of anxiety to her parents. She continued her relaxation practice on a regular basis and felt an increased sense of personal power and self-control in many aspects of her life.

Relaxation Exercises for Adolescents

BREATHING TECHNIQUES

If you feel you are not in control of your body or your life, or if you feel out of touch with your body, this information on deep breathing should be helpful. Practice the techniques until you find the ones that work best for you.

The most common physical responses to a stressful situation are increased heart rate, muscle bracing, and changes in breathing patterns. Under stress we tend to first hold our breath and then breath rapidly and shallowly from the upper chest. Of all the physical responses to stress, breathing is the easiest for you to consciously control. Breathing also happens to be one of the best stress management strategies if practiced correctly. In fact, deep slow breathing is at the core of every relaxation technique that I teach. Slow diaphragmatic breathing will help relax muscle groups and can help to slow the heart rate to a normal, relaxed rhythm.

Knowing that deep breathing is good for relaxation is not enough, however. Though we were all born with the natural ability to breath diaphragmatically, most of us lose this ability as we grow and learn more rigid postures. To relearn good breathing habits we must be aware of how we breath and practice to change our habits daily. Proper breathing does not use the shoulders or the upper back. Our stomachs should move out gently as we inhale and return as we exhale.

#1. Try this. Lie down flat or stand up straight. Put one hand over your stomach and one hand over your chest, and see which way each hand moves as you inhale. Now which way do your hands move as you exhale? Does your bottom hand move first and outward as you begin the inhale? Does the upper hand then move up and out? On the exhale, do you notice that both hands move in, perhaps forcing the last bit of air out? If so, then you are breathing very well and you can go on to the next breathing exercises. If not, you should practice a bit before you continue, as this breathing technique forms the basis of every stress management exercise.

#2. Now try breathing very slowly while you are in a comfortable position. As you inhale slowly but comfortably, count 1–4. Perhaps you can picture the numbers in you mind, or say them slowly to yourself. Now pause for a moment and count 1–4 again as you hold your breath (slowly, picturing the numbers in your mind if possible). And now as you exhale, slowly and comfortably count 1–8. Let your body relax more deeply as you exhale fully and completely, feeling the warm air as you exhale. You might want to repeat this for three breaths. Then check to see if you are feeling more relaxed. You may need to check the muscles of your shoulders, neck, and jaw. If you can let these muscle groups relax further, take another slow breath.

#3. Another breathing/counting exercise that works well is to take four slow breaths, counting to eight by counting one on the inhale, two on the exhale, three on the inhale, etc. Try to picture the numbers in your mind or say the numbers to yourself. After counting to eight, check your position, relax your jaw, forehead, neck, and shoulders and repeat the exercise one more time. Within about two minutes you can begin to feel more relaxed and open, releasing tension with each exhale. Remember, go slowly. Do not be in such a hurry to relax!

#4. Take three deep slow breaths. As you lie down or sit back comfortably, allow yourself to breathe slowly. Feel the cool air as you inhale, pause a moment, and then slowly exhale, feeling the warm breath carry away tensions or discomforts. You might try to feel the cool air at the tip of your nostrils. Exhale through your mouth, breathing away the warm air as if it will drift up into the sky like a helium-filled balloon. Let go slowly and easily, becoming more relaxed with every breath. Some people use this exercise not only to relax but to help them drift off to sleep.

These various breathing techniques work best when practiced on a regular basis. Find one or two that work well for you, and then use them consistently. This book is designed to increase your awareness of what you can do to take control of your body and your life, and to help you develop a practical relaxation program that will serve you as you go through the transitions of life.

MEDITATION FOR ADOLESCENTS

Controlling the mind not only helps you relax the body, it also helps you create a bridge to the spiritual self. The spiritual self can assist us when we deal with the multitude of situations over which we have little or no control. The quest for spirituality also encourages self-acceptance and can provide a positive outlet for adolescent energy.

One does not have to be devoted to East Asian philosophies or disciplines to practice meditation. Meditation is the concentrated focusing of one's mind. As with any new skill, learning how to use meditation requires time and patience. With practice, the concentration that at the beginning may be difficult, becomes more natural.

Many forms and styles of meditation exist. Some require that you close your eyes; some suggest you keep your eyes open. Some use a sitting position; others suggest you lie down. It is even possible to meditate while standing. And some forms of meditation combine different styles, while others require a more rigid concentration. The following selection of exercises draws from several different forms to allow you to select those which work best for you.

The most widely used style of meditation among Western cultures is a form of Transcendental Meditation (also called TM). Researchers have studied the use of TM to determine how and in what way it can provide a subject with physiological control over his bodily functions. Herbert Benson, a cardiologist and author of *The Relaxation Response,* has long recommended a form of TM for control of blood pressure and various cardiac disorders. TM uses the repetition of a special word, or "mantra," to help clear the mind. Originally, Eastern Yogis who taught TM to initiates selected a special Sanskrit word for each student to use as his mantra. Dr. Benson suggests that the nondescript word "one" can be repeated over and over to focus the mind during meditation. I often recommend that you use a word that has a stronger, positive connotation such as "love," "peace," or "harmony."

Sit upright in a quiet environment with your eyes closed, repeating your word over and over as you attempt to still your mind. As thoughts or mental insights occur to you, try to let them pass, taking notice, but not becoming focused or absorbed with them. As you repeat your word slowly, release from your mind any other thoughts that invade your consciousness. Let the peaceful feeling of your word fill your mind. After twenty minutes, awaken yourself by taking a deep breath and stretching. The stilling of your mind, with practice, will remain with you as you continue through your day.

Another form of meditation, which allows you to keep your eyes open, is known as Zen meditation. The advantage of this form is that it lets you appreciate the world's natural beauty as you meditate.

Select a visual focus point such as a lit candle, a spot on the wall, a photo or drawing, or a mandala (a drawing or object with a circular design). If you are outside, focus on some object of natural beauty, such as a flower, tree, stream, etc. Sit or stand in a comfortable position as you focus on the selected

object. Keep your mind clear of distracting thoughts or emotions. If thoughts of your daily activities and feelings invade your mind, notice them and gently let them go. Try to keep the image you have selected at the center of your consciousness until its natural beauty fills your mind. As you return to your day after this meditation, the serenity of this meditative state will accompany you.

Do not be discouraged if you seem unable to stop the many thoughts swimming in your consciousness from demanding your attention. The mind will resist being stilled, but with consistent practice you will begin to achieve a peaceful, restful stillness more easily and for longer periods of time.

A third form of meditation I often suggest combines techniques in a way that I have found to be very personally satisfying. Sit upright for twenty minutes in a quiet environment. For the first ten minutes focus your mind on a word, short phrase, or peaceful symbol. Examples might be the words "love," "peace," or "harmony"; the phrases "God is good" or "love is the light"; or a symbol such as a star, cross, or flower. During this ten minutes of focus, do not hold on to any distracting thoughts. Simply let any thoughts that occur to you pass gently through your consciousness and drift away. Return your focus to the symbol or word you have chosen, letting the feeling of peace and harmony which it suggests fill your being. After ten minutes of focus, move into an open meditation. Let your mind become like a blank movie or TV screen. Watch, without attachment, anything that comes up and through your mind. In my experience, some beautiful spiritual insights can come into consciousness in this way. Finally, at the end of your twenty-minute meditation, take a deep breath, stretch, and imagine that you are surrounded by white light. Let the light fill you and bathe you, so that you feel regenerated by this peaceful, loving energy.

During the teenage years, you may find that this practice of Eastern meditation can open special doors for your consciousness that are both pleasant and important for you to move through. The insights gained from practicing meditation can lead to an expansion of consciousness. By tapping the wisdom of your spiritual side, you may be able to experience deeper levels of self-acceptance. Perhaps you will find that problems that used to bother you seem to lose their importance, and you can take them in stride. Through meditation you can learn to honor your mind, body, and your spirit.

VISUALIZATION FOR ADOLESCENTS

Visualization can be used alone or in combination with one of the other deep relaxation techniques. One of the advantages of visualization is that the mental images which you use in the exercises can be changed depending upon your specific needs. For instance, if you want to feel yourself calm and strong as you give an oral presentation in class, you can visualize yourself doing just that. Or if you want to stop smoking, you can visualize yourself putting away your cigarettes for good. Visualization exercises produce greater relaxation, but they can also help you to complete a task or change a habit through the power of positive suggestion. Gaining control over your responses will be a skill that can benefit you for as long as you continue to grow, learn, and seek change. This is perhaps the best definition of true maturity: to be able to learn and grow through new experiences without being knocked off course by stress.

Before you begin your visualization relaxation it may be helpful to review the day's events and write down any important items. In this way you can clear your mind of the details of your day, knowing you can return to these matters when the relaxation is completed. Another good way to clear your mind is to get comfortable and begin breathing slowly and deeply as you imagine yourself outdoors on a clear, sunny day, gazing up into the blue sky. As thoughts or mental distractions pass through your mind, imagine them as colored, helium-filled balloons. Let them drift up into the sky with every slow exhale of your breath. Watch as they drift up and away, perhaps dancing in the warm breezes. As the balloons rise higher and higher, watch them grow smaller. Eventually you see them blow over the horizon, or float so high that they drift from sight. Watch as the sky becomes calm and clear once again. Notice the soothing color of the blue sky as you continue to breathe slowly and naturally. You may even wish to imagine that you can breathe in the cool blue light of the sky as you continue to relax, just letting go.

Turn your attention, gently, to the feelings of warmth. The sun and warm breezes can begin to warm and relax you. Perhaps you can feel the warmth soaking deep within you, allowing tension to melt away. Feel yourself sinking back into whatever you are sitting or lying upon.

(Now select the visualization image that you want to focus upon. The following are some possibilities, but you can imagine anything that will bring you greater relaxation or help you overcome a stressful situation. Use your imagination!)

General relaxation visualization: . . . To continue the relaxation allow yourself to drift deeper into this dreamlike calmness and comfort . . . As you breathe slowly, feel yourself sinking back comfortably into the bed or chair . . . With practice you will be able to relax more deeply and more quickly . . . the relaxation can help you focus your energies for your studies, tests, athletics, or any other task . . . To deepen the relaxation, continue to imagine that you are outdoors on a beautiful day. Feel the relaxation in your arms and legs. You may be able to feel the warmth of blood and energy slowly pulsing down into your hands and feet. As you breathe slowly and peacefully, breathe away any thoughts or discomforts that may come to mind. Let these evaporate in the warm sunshine as the dew might evaporate from the leaves in a meadow on a beautiful spring morning . . . Imagine birds flying freely across the sky, as if they could drift pleasantly on the warm breezes . . . As the relaxation grows stronger, so does your control. Let the relaxation and control carry over with you throughout your day. By taking three slow breaths at any time you will be able to trigger the relaxation and control. Drift for a few more minutes in this pleasant state of deep relaxation, breathing slowly. . . .

When you wish to awaken, imagine that you can return to this room, letting the feelings of calmness and comfort return with you. Let the feelings of relaxation and control remain with you throughout your day. When you wish to awaken completely, take a deep breath and stretch, letting the feelings of health, comfort, and joy return with you to a fully waking state. You may wish to take another deep breath and stretch, feeling wide awake, refreshed and alert . . .

Visualization for making an oral presentation: . . . Continue your relaxation. Let yourself drift as deeply as you can into the dreamlike calmness and comfort . . . To help yourself sink deeply, count backward slowly from five down to one. Picture the number five or say it to yourself and imagine yourself taking a step down a staircase of relaxation. Take a breath and let your arms relax even more . . . Now move down another step as you say the number four to yourself. As you breathe slowly you can feel yourself moving down another step and you can feel your legs relaxing even more . . . Your breathing is calm and regular . . . Your heartbeat is calm and regular . . . And you count the number three as you let yourself drift deeper into the dreamlike calmness. The more you can relax the more control you will have. Pleasantly drift deeper as you count the number two and feel yourself moving gently another step toward complete relaxation. Even the muscles of your neck and shoulders can begin to relax further. Feel the muscles of your head and face let go as your forehead goes calm and smooth. And now take another slow breath as you drift down to one . . . Drift in this state of deep relaxation and comfort. During the day whenever you wish to use this five to one countdown, you will be able to relax and find greater control and calmness.

Now as you continue to drift, imagine that you can maintain this calmness and control, even while doing a difficult task . . . By breathing slowly and controlling your muscle tension any difficult event will go more smoothly and easily . . . As you remain comfortable picture yourself preparing to give an oral presentation. See yourself gathering your information and organizing your notes carefully. See yourself reading and rereading this material so that you have a good grasp of the information. You should also see yourself planning the presentation so the information will be communicated easily and precisely. Now that the hard part is out of the way, take three slow breaths and relax even further. As you drift deeper into calmness, you may want to count down from five to one again . . . Now remain relaxed, breathing slowly and gently, and see yourself moving into position to make your presentation. You have already taken three slow breaths and counted down from five to one to get pleasantly relaxed, so you feel calm as you present your information. The group listens and receives your presentation well. Because you are well prepared the talk is easier than you had expected and you are happy when you complete your presentation. You can even learn from this assignment so that the next presentation will be even better.

Now continue to drift deeper in this state of relaxation and comfort . . . You may need to practice this visualization many times to learn the skill of reaching and then maintaining your relaxation. This skill will develop and can help you throughout your life.

When you wish to awaken, imagine that you can return to this room, letting the feelings of calmness and comfort return with you to a more fully waking state. Let the feelings of relaxation and control remain with you throughout your day. When you wish to awaken completely, take a deep breath and stretch, letting the feelings of health, comfort and joy return with you. You may wish to take another deep breath and stretch, letting yourself feel wide awake, refreshed and alert . . .

Visualization for greater self-acceptance: . . . Continue drifting deeper into this dreamlike calmness. As you feel yourself soaking up the warmth from the sun imagine that you can breathe in the golden sunlight and the warmth. Picture yourself filling with the golden-white light as it glows brightly within you . . . Every cell in your body can be bathed in the golden-white healing light and energy. Every cell is bathed in increased oxygen and nutrients from an easy flow of blood. The cells soak up the perfect amounts of nutrients and energy so they can heal and recharge themselves completely. As the cells grow healthy and strong, you feel the energy of joy, health, and happiness beginning to burn more brightly within you . . . You see yourself in perfect health, smiling and celebrating in the sunshine on this warm and perfect day. Even though you remain relaxed and comfortable, you see yourself active and alive. You maintain this feeling of calmness, control, health, and well-being throughout your day. Let the feelings of joy and happiness burn brightly within your heart along with the golden-white light to allow these pleasant sensations to remain with you. A part of you can grow brighter and stronger. As this part of you grows brighter and stronger, the feeling of joy begins to burn brilliantly within your heart. This is the part of you that sees and understands all of your strengths and your weaknesses. It realizes that your strengths are the tools you use and that the weaknesses are the lessons you have to learn from. As this part of you grows you will find greater self-acceptance and become aware that you are perfect even with your flaws. You must learn to accept these flaws but not be a victim of them. You can change these weaknesses through awareness and control.

As you drift in this state of calmness let these awarenesses sink deep within you to serve you throughout your life. As you develop greater self-love and acceptance you can handle difficult situations in a positive manner. Situations can occur when a choice must be made between what is fashionable or expected of you and what is actually healthy and in your best interest. As you develop more control over your body's response to stress, you become aware that you also have the strength and control to follow the sometimes difficult path of doing what is correct for your friend and ally, your body. Exercising, eating well, and getting the proper rest are necessary for your body to function and grow in the most comfortable way. The transitions to adulthood can be accomplished gracefully and with respect.

You have a choice . . . You can control your response to stress and pressures . . . You can allow yourself to show self-love and greater self-acceptance. You can learn to be fully responsible for your own good health and happiness.

As you let these words burn deeper into your consciousness, let them serve you.

If you wish to slowly and gently awaken, you can begin returning to this room. Let the feelings of relaxation, health, joy, and comfort return with you. If you wish to awaken now, feel the bed or the chair beneath you and slowly awaken. Let the power of choice and control return with you to a fully waking state. You may wish to take a deep breath and stretch, letting yourself become wide awake. If you wish, take another deep breath and stretch, waking completely, feeling refreshed and alert.

AUTOGENIC TRAINING FOR ADOLESCENTS

One of the best ways to gain control over your body's responses to stressful situations is to practice autogenic training. Autogenic training is designed to help you induce the relaxation response by repeating specific phrases to yourself. These phrases help you to feel heaviness and warmth in your body and limbs, a characteristic of relaxation. With four to six weeks of daily practice, you will feel the benefits of these exercises, although continued practice may be needed to attain maximum control. By learning these techniques during adolescence you will gain a skill that can serve you throughout your adult life.

When you first begin practicing these exercises, you may find yourself having difficulty concentrating. With practice, you will be able to focus and maintain your concentration more easily, as you increasingly feel yourself able to control your body's responses.

Read this exercise slowly (about half normal speaking speed). Pause at each (*). Do not be concerned by mispronunciations or verbal slips. Continue in a calm, even voice.

Find a quiet location where you will not be disturbed. Allow about twenty minutes for this exercise. Sit or lie back comfortably, allowing your arms and legs to remain uncrossed if possible. Let your head be supported and let your shoulders drop into a comfortable position. Check the muscles of your head and face. Let your forehead become calm and smooth. Allow the muscles around your eyes to loosen. Check the muscles of the mouth and jaw to make sure they are relaxed. Finally, allow your eyes to remain closed, remembering that you can open them whenever you need to use them.

Before we begin the relaxation, remember not to try to relax too quickly. In fact, do not try to relax at all. Without any effort you can allow yourself to relax by pleasantly letting go of tensions and discomforts, and then letting yourself drift deeper into a peaceful calmness. To begin the relaxation, take three deep breaths, pausing after you inhale, and then exhaling fully and completely. You might imagine that you release tensions and discomforts as you exhale by just breathing them away. * After you have finished these first three breaths, continue breathing slowly and naturally, relaxing more deeply with each slow exhale.

Repeat these phrases to yourself, exactly as they are taken from this exercise, and try to feel your body responding to the commands. If you need to repeat the phrases more than three times to begin to feel results, continue the repetitions a few additional times.

Repeat this mood phrase to yourself three times: "I am at peace with myself and fully relaxed." Continue breathing slowly and gently.

Begin to feel the muscles of your arms relax as you say, "My right arm is heavy * . . . My right arm is heavy * . . . My right arm is heavy * . . ." Repeat this phrase slowly until you begin to feel the heaviness spreading through your arm. Now turn your awareness to your left arm as you breathe slowly and say to yourself, "My left arm is heavy * . . . My left arm is heavy * . . . My left arm is heavy * . . ." Try to feel the heaviness starting in your arms or feel free to continue slowly repeating this phrase a few more times. Now proceed to your legs. Let them begin to relax as you breathe slowly. Feel the heaviness and relaxation starting in your legs as you slowly repeat, "My right leg is heavy * . . . My right leg is heavy * . . . My right leg is heavy * . . ." You can repeat this several more times if you need to, until you begin to feel the relaxation and the heaviness. Now focus on the left leg and feel it beginning to relax as you say, "My left leg is heavy * . . . My left leg is heavy * . . . My left leg is heavy * . . ." Repeat if needed. With practice you will feel the heaviness more quickly and easily. Now turn your attention to your neck and shoulders. Let them sink into a more comfortable position and let the muscles relax as you breathe gently and say, "My neck and shoulders are heavy * . . . My neck and shoulders are heavy * . . . My neck and shoulders are heavy * . . ." Repeat if needed. Take a deep slow breath and feel the heaviness and relaxation as you begin to sink back into whatever you are sitting or lying upon.

Perhaps you can feel the blood beginning to flow more easily down into your hands or your feet as the blood vessels begin to dilate, as the smooth muscles in the walls of the arteries begin to relax. Focus on the feelings of warmth, or a pulse, or perhaps a tingling feeling in your right hand as you say, "My right arm is warm * . . . My right arm is warm * . . . My right arm is warm * . . ." Repeat this slowly several more times until you begin to feel the warmth or pulse. Heaviness is generally easier for most people to feel than warmth, but with continued practice you can begin to control the blood flow. Now turn your attention to your left arm and say to yourself, "My left arm is warm * . . . My left arm is warm * . . . My left arm is warm * . . ." Repeat if needed. Perhaps you can start to feel the warmth in your arms, and you may feel the blood flowing freely through your entire body. As you breathe slowly and gently, turn your awareness to your legs and say to yourself, "My right leg is warm * . . . My right leg is warm * . . . My right leg is warm * . . ." Repeat several more times to help develop this skill. Move your attention to your left leg and say, "My left leg is warm * . . . My left leg is warm * . . . My left leg is warm * . . ." Repeat if needed. Feel the heaviness and warmth in your arms and your legs as you breathe slowly and gently. Now turn your awareness to your neck and shoulders, and say, "My neck and shoulders are warm * . . . My neck and shoulders are warm * . . . My neck and shoulders are warm * . . ." Repeat if needed. Breathe slowly as you drift for a few moments, feeling heaviness and warmth spreading pleasantly about your body.

Slow and calm your heart by slowly repeating to yourself, "My heartbeat is calm and regular * . . . My heartbeat is calm and regular * . . . My heartbeat is calm and regular * . . ." Repeat if needed. If you experience any discomfort with this phrase then change to the phrase, "I feel calm * . . . I feel calm * . . . I feel calm * . . . " As you breathe slowly, begin to feel the peace and relaxation spreading to every part of your body.

To slow your breathing say to yourself as you breathe into your diaphragm, "My breathing is calm and regular * . . . My breathing is calm and regular * . . . My breathing is calm and regular * . . ." Repeat if needed.

Become aware of the relaxation starting in your stomach region. As you breathe slowly say, "My abdomen is warm and calm * . . . My abdomen is warm and calm * . . . My abdomen is warm and calm * . . . " Repeat if needed. If you have any serious abdominal problems, such as bleeding ulcers or diabetes, or if you are in the last trimester of pregnancy, change this phrase to "I am calm and relaxed * . . . I am calm and relaxed * . . . I am calm and relaxed * . . . "

Move on to your forehead and let the muscles of your head and face relax as you say, "My forehead is cool and calm * . . . My forehead is cool and calm * . . . My forehead is cool and calm * . . . " As you breathe slowly, feel the muscles around your eyes, mouth, and jaw loosen and then relax.

Let yourself drift pleasantly in this calmness. As you breathe gently perhaps you can feel the heaviness in your arms and legs as the muscles relax. * Perhaps you begin to feel the warmth or pulse of blood flowing more easily down into your hands and perhaps even your feet, like sunshine or a bath gently warming you. Some people feel the warming as a tingling sensation spreading blood more easily into the extremities. * As you enjoy the relaxation you can feel that your heartbeat is calm and regular. *

With practice you can feel the relaxation more easily and quickly. The warmth of blood flowing into your hands and feet gradually grows easier to control. While you may not be able to control every situation in your life, you can develop control over the way you respond to these situations. As you do, you will gain control of your body and energy so that you can grow without excessive and unproductive stress and anxiety.

At the end of this relaxation exercise, awaken yourself slowly. Feel the bed or chair beneath you and say, "I am refreshed and completely alert * . . . I am refreshed and completely alert * . . . I am refreshed and completely alert * . . ." Then take a deep breath and stretch, allowing yourself to wake fully, and let the relaxation carry over with you into a fully waking state. You may wish to take another deep breath and stretch, letting the relaxation return with you.

PROGRESSIVE RELAXATION FOR ADOLESCENTS

Progressive relaxation is an easy-to-learn and straightforward approach to relaxation. Practiced on a daily basis, it can help you gain awareness and then control of the stress response. Once you've become adept at this exercise, you can abbreviate it to initiate relaxation more quickly. Remember, as with any other technique, progressive relaxation requires regular practice to achieve the maximum benefit. You can adjust the timing or the phrasing of this exercise to best meet your needs.

Read this exercise slowly (about half normal speaking speed). Pause at each (*). Do not be concerned by mispronunciations or verbal slips. Continue in a calm, even voice.

Find a quiet location where you will not be disturbed. Allow about twenty minutes for this exercise. Sit or lie back comfortably, allowing your arms and legs to remain uncrossed if possible. Let your head be supported and let your shoulders drop into a comfortable position. Check the muscles of your head and face. Let your forehead become calm and smooth. Allow the muscles around your eyes to loosen. Check the muscles of the mouth and jaw to make sure they are relaxed. Finally, allow your eyes to remain closed, remembering that you can open them whenever you need to use them.

Before we begin the relaxation, remember not to try to relax too quickly. In fact, do not try to relax at all. Without any effort you can allow yourself to relax by pleasantly letting go of tensions and discomforts, and then letting yourself drift deeper into a peaceful calmness. To begin the relaxation, take three deep breaths, pausing after you inhale, and then exhaling fully and completely. You might imagine that you release tensions and discomforts as you exhale by just breathing them away. * After you have finished these first three breaths, continue breathing slowly and naturally, relaxing more deeply with each slow exhale.

As you continue to breathe slowly and gently, begin to focus your attention on the muscles in your feet. You may want to move your toes briefly to see how these muscles feel. Let them rest in the most comfortable position and then use your imagination to see or feel these muscles relaxing even further. Slowly exhale, breathing away any energy or tension in your toes. As you breathe slowly, imagine these muscles becoming more soft and flexible. * Turn your awareness to the muscles of the arch of your foot. The muscles from the ball of your foot below the big toe down to the heel can relax even further. Take a slow breath and then imagine that as you exhale you release the tensions from these muscles. * Now feel the sides and the top of your foot. Can you feel your shoes or socks touching your foot? As you breathe slowly and naturally, can you let the muscles of your foot relax more? You might even be able to feel a pulse or tingling sensation gradually spreading warmth and relaxation to every muscle of your foot. *

Turn your awareness to your lower leg. Can you feel your ankles, * the calves, * your shin bones? * Feel the muscles of your lower legs, and notice that you can relax these muscles even further. Breathe slowly as you feel the muscles softening. You may even feel the knee starting to relax into a more comfortable position. As your awareness increases, your skill at relaxing will also. You will feel your control increasing as you practice letting these muscle groups relax even more. * Now become aware of your upper legs. Feel the large muscles of the sides and top of your legs relax slowly as you exhale the unwanted energies and tensions. * You can now relax the big muscles of the back of your upper legs. As these muscles relax, you might even feel the relaxation spreading up through your pelvis area into the lower back. The big muscles of the leg may loosen so that you can feel the sensation of heaviness down the length of your leg. * Breathe slowly and gently. You might even feel the pulse of blood flowing more freely and easily down your leg into your foot and toes. *

The relaxation can now begin to spread up into your lower back. As the muscles of your back begin to soften, you might feel the relaxation spreading to the other muscles of the back. Feel the muscles of your upper back, including your shoulders, let go even further. Your shoulders may be able to drop down into a more comfortable position. * Feel your head sinking back into the chair or pillow, totally supported, as the muscles of your neck let go even more. * Continue breathing slowly and gently as you feel the relaxation spreading down through your arms. * The muscles of your upper arms may feel loose and comfortable. * Your lower arms, even your wrists, can relax further. As you breathe slowly, feel the sensation of heaviness as your arms sink back into the bed or chair. * The relaxation can slowly drift down into your hands and fingers. * You may feel a pulse of blood flowing freely and easily down into your hands. Feel your hands warm comfortably, letting you drift deeper into comfort and relaxation. *

The muscles of your head and face may be able to relax even more. Your forehead may feel more calm and smooth. * The muscles around the eyes can let go. * Even the muscles of the mouth and the jaw might be able to relax even further. * Slowly breathing away stress, you can control these tensions through relaxation. * The sensations of peace and harmony grow stronger as you allow yourself to drift deeper in this peaceful calmness. *

The relaxation can drift down into your chest. As you breathe slowly, you might feel the relaxation gently spreading to the other muscles of the torso. You can feel your heartbeat, calm and regular. * The relaxation spreads down into your stomach region. * You may be able to feel the sensation of warmth glowing gently in the stomach region. * Continue breathing slowly and gently as you drift peacefully.

With practice, you will be able to relax more easily and quickly. You will relax more deeply, and the effects will last longer throughout the day. Your awareness of tensions will grow stronger so that you can control your energies and your responses to stressors more effectively.

If you are using this exercise at bedtime you may wish to drift off into a pleasant sleep, resting fully and awakening refreshed and alert. If you wish to drift off to sleep, continue breathing slowly and focus on the feelings of relaxation in your arms and legs. *

If you wish to awaken now, you can begin to do so. Let yourself gradually return to this room, feeling the bed or the chair beneath you. As you slowly awaken, bring the feelings of calmness, relaxation, health, and happiness back with you into a more fully waking state. Take a deep breath and stretch, letting the calmness return with you. Take another deep breath and stretch, allowing yourself to awaken feeling refreshed and alert, letting the relaxation and calmness continue with you.

BIBLIOGRAPHY

Bell, Ruth. *Changing Lives: A Book For Teens on Sex and Relationships.* New York: Random House, 1980. $10.95.

Various articles for teenagers about the changes they are going through. Covers sexuality, emotional, and physical health care.

Madaras, Lynda, with Area Madaras. *The What's Happening to My Body Book for Girls.* New York: New Market Press, 1983. $9.95.

Detailed account of physical changes confronting teenage girls.

Madaras, Lynda, with Dane Saavedra. *The What's Happening to My Body Book for*

Boys. New York: New Market Press, 1984. $9.95.

Detailed account of physical changes confronting teenage boys.

Snider, Dee, with Philip Bashe. *Dee Snider's Teenage Survival Guide*. Garden City, NY: Dolphin Books/Doubleday, 1987. $8.95.

A fun but important guide for dealing with teenage social and emotional issues. Check into this book for information and support.

CHAPTER FIVE

Work & Stress

Introduction

MOST PEOPLE experience some form of job-related stress at some point in their lives. Whether hunting for a job, commuting to a job, learning new job skills and responsibilities, competing for advancement, or just trying to keep a job, a person can feel the anxieties and pressures of the work world. Particularly today, as the shape of our job market is rapidly changing, the uncertainties and fluctuations can take their toll on the worker. Job security is a major issue for people in many sectors of our economy, such as the electronics industry, construction, manufacturing, and agriculture. One of the basic concepts of this chapter is that although the worker does not usually have control over the changes in the marketplace which can drastically affect his day-to-day life, he can control his response to these changes.

In fact, many of the ideas about stress reduction presented in this chapter, and throughout this book, have recently been recognized by top management in many corporations as being significant to the productivity of their workers and the success of their managers. As a part of their management training, many companies now include Peak Performance training sessions. These sessions train managers to function well under stress, and include the use of relaxation and visualization exercises to enhance performance, creativity, and productivity. (See bibliography, *Peak Performance*, by Garfield and Bennett.) The relaxation techniques that have worked well for management can produce positive results for all workers.

Although the worker can do a great deal to minimize negative responses to job-related stress, the employer has a responsibility, too. It is important to recognize that job stress often correlates closely with job satisfaction. The more satisfied a worker is with her job, the better able she will be to handle the stresses which arise as she works. Conversely, people with lower job satisfaction demonstrate an increase in job-related stress symptoms. These stress symptoms can be produced both because a person experiences too little stimulation or challenge on the job and because he experiences too much pressure or challenge. Repetitive, boring job activities can create stress just as much as a phone which never stops ringing and hectic staff meetings. People who work in the computer chip industry, for instance, assembling the same part of the same microcomputer for eight hours a day, often experience high levels of stress. These stresses can lead to physical problems, such as muscle aches or eye strain, or to substance abuse problems, as the worker tries to dull her body's complaints. If employees' tasks are varied throughout the day, and if employees are given more control over their work environment, employers will find they have a healthier and happier work force.

Because the sources and characteristics of job stress vary depending on the type of work one does, this chapter will be divided into three areas of examination: white-collar work, blue-collar work, and working women's issues.

WHITE-COLLAR WORK

Managerial: Management positions provide a high level of responsibility and decision making power. Responsibility and decision making, however, are accompanied by accountability. Managers' decisions inevitably appear in the company's ledger books translated into profits or losses. If the profits of a company do not grow the way its owners or directors expect them to, it is a foregone conclusion that the managers will be replaced by those who will "get the job done." So, pressure from above is an ordinary part of a management position.

Managers also receive a lot of pressure from below—from the employees under their supervision. It is these employees who actually produce the product or services which create the profits. Employee productivity depends on a well-organized workplace and on morale. Managers are responsible in both these areas, and if problems exist among the work force, the manager will feel the pressure. Good communication skills are often a crucial ingredient of effective employee management, too, and if a manager feels uncertain about his interpersonal skills, he may become frustrated or ineffectual.

In addition to pressures from above and below, managers receive plenty of pressure from outside the company—from their competitors. Competition is what business is all about. If managers do not stay ahead of a company's competitors, there go the profits. And there go the jobs. Clearly, this level of responsibility can create much stress.

Managers are also responsible for hiring and firing employees. Hiring the right people requires a special ability to judge talent, and mistakes can be very costly. And firing someone is usually stressful, no matter how great the necessity or how justified the termination. Another highly stressful aspect of managerial jobs may be the responsibility for giving oral presentations. Many people experience extreme stage fright when they must appear before a group, though they are comfortable and competent in other areas of their work.

Though managers exercise a great deal of control in the areas of decision making and employee management, they may feel less control over their own positions. In order to respond to the changing needs of the organization, managers' positions are often reshuffled. As corporations expand or are restructured, managers may be asked to relocate, a change which can subject an entire family to the stress of moving to a new home, new schools, and a new community. Large corporations often require their middle managers to relocate every two to three years. The manager must learn to adapt to new work conditions and to deal with new personnel. Often he must fit into a whole new management system, discovering suddenly that the managerial techniques he has developed over many years are now outmoded and new skills must be learned. Particularly as the manager ages, he or she may become less flexible, less resilient, less able to cope with change. The frustrations he feels can too easily lead to stress-related health problems.

In fact, older managers may be subjected to increasing stress on the job because of a widespread movement in many industries toward hiring and promoting younger managers. Young, innovative managers were behind the spectacular growth of electronics firms in the late seventies and early eighties, and this success has created a trend toward youth in the management field. Whereas older managers with years of experience used to be revered and respected, now they're replaceable. As older managers feel less rec-

ognized and supported, they experience an increase in job burnout and dissatisfaction. This in turn produces an increase in stress-related health complaints as well as an increase in substance abuse.

Small-Business owners: Independent small-business owners experience a unique kind of white-collar stress. They bear full responsibility for an entire operation, and the stress of having everything ride on one set of shoulders can be enormous. Particularly because fifty percent of small businesses fail within the first three years, being at the helm of such an operation can erode even the sturdiest of constitutions. Small-business owners often live a tenuous financial existence, and are responsible for supporting their employees as well as themselves and their families.

In production and service businesses, owners may be required to do everything—bookkeeping, inventory, accounts billing and collecting, ordering, scheduling, marketing, advertising—without expert knowledge of how to do these things. This is not only exhausting, but stressful. The person running a small business either has to learn these skills very quickly or know how to find expert help. Either alternative can provoke a great deal of anxiety.

Professionals: Highly trained professionals working for large organizations may experience another kind of white-collar stress. Engineers, accountants, doctors, nurses, and scientists are often promoted to managerial positions because of their expertise; but they may be completely lacking in managerial skills. Conversely, when they are working under managers who lack their particular expertise, they may feel that they could do a better job of managing than their bosses do, since they understand the work better. Either way, stress is the ultimate result—for everybody. This problem occurs most often in "high-tech" firms, banking and investment houses, and health-care delivery organizations.

BLUE-COLLAR WORK

Blue-collar workers are the trained, semiskilled, and unskilled workers employed by business and industry to provide the labor that gets things made. Blue-collar tasks often involve repetitive, boring, assembly-line work. The lack of stimulation workers experience on the job can be even more stressful than the decision making required of managers.

Stress on the assembly line is well documented. For example, in the midseventies the National Institute for Occupational Safety and Health (NIOSH) documented a phenomenon called "assembly-line hysteria" where a large group of assembly-line workers who were studied developed anxiety symptoms such as hyperventilation. These symptoms were attributed to both the fast pace and repetitive nature of assembly-line work, which created a frenzied response in the worker.

To find out more about work-related stress, NIOSH sponsored a study which examined various jobs and ranked them in terms of the amount of stress experienced by those performing the jobs. They found the highest levels of stress in the following occupations, starting with the most stressful and working down the list: laborer; secretary; inspector; clinical lab technician; office manager; waiter/waitress; miner or machine operator; computer programmer; electrician; house painter; guard/watchman; machinist; mechanic; public relations; registered nurse; sales manager; telephone operator; and warehouse worker.

Environmental conditions are often a source of stress in blue-collar work. Noise is a very important issue on many jobs. Toxic materials such as asbestos, pesticides, and radioactive products affect the health and safety of the employees who must work with them. A workspace which is either too crowded or too isolated is a frequently heard worker complaint. In some of these situations not much can be done to alleviate the environmental stress, but whatever can be done should be. Awareness and caring on management's part can help to minimize some of the problems.

Competition and performance rating are also major stressors in blue-collar jobs. In the building trades, for example, speed and skill are rated on the job-site. If a worker cannot work as fast as everyone else, he or she will not be rehired for the next job. And even speed is often not enough. Older carpenters who know how to work quickly and efficiently are replaced at some point in their working lives by younger, stronger workers. This kind of intense competitive pressure to perform well on the job can be a constant source of stress.

Often the job stressors mentioned above can lead to a further problem for workers: substance abuse. Substance abuse has been linked to low job satisfaction, and many blue-collar workers report low job satisfaction because of their lack of control over job conditions. Almost all decisions about blue-collar jobs are made by management. Workers who are already bored are made even more dissatisfied with their work when they have to submit to what they feel are unfair decisions. Trade unions are supposed to deal with workers' grievances in such matters. In recent times, however, trade unions have often been unresponsive to individual members' needs. Then too, unions have lost a lot of ground in the eighties. Membership has declined and in order to keep wages rising, unions have had to compromise on other issues, such as job conditions or health and retirement benefits.

Fortunately, the detrimental effects of these compromises on worker morale and productivity has become evident to quite a few companies, and in response, many companies are developing programs to promote job satisfaction and decrease stress. The "high-tech" industries have been leaders in this field, particularly with the introduction of recreational facilities and company-sponsored fitness and athletic programs. Japanese-owned and -run firms have also made a significant contribution in this area, encouraging workers to make suggestions for job-site improvements or conducting employee exercise programs. Hopefully, more companies will recognize the need to pay attention to job conditions that produce stress for workers, and to make needed changes.

WORKING WOMEN'S ISSUES

More women are in the work force now than at any other time in history, including the World War II years. Not only are women entering traditional "women's" jobs in larger numbers, but women are competing with men in fields that were closed to them until two decades ago, such as carpentry or fire fighting. Unfortunately, many people believe that for women to advance in these nontraditional fields, they must do much better than their male competitors. This attitude is bound to create pressure and stress for women.

As of the writing of this book in 1987, women were still earning sixty-four cents to every dollar earned by a man. The problem of pay inequity has been perpetuated by the myth that women do not really have to work. Traditionally, women have been seen as the "secondary" breadwinner, working to earn some extra spending money for the family. When women's income is seen as nonessential, lower wages can be justified. Yet the reality today is that fifty percent of the women who are in the work force are there out of economic necessity. Many middle-class families would no longer be middle class without two wage earners. In many other families, women are the sole breadwinner. Clearly, unequal rates of pay are major stressors in working women's lives.

Some men continue to resent the fact that women are in the work world, and this resentment can create negative emotional environments for women on the job. Other men use sexual harassment to convey their feelings of disapproval or unease. Sexual harassment may take the subtle form of verbal abuse, such as comments about a woman's figure or jokes about her "proper" role, or it may consist of more crude physical assault. Harassment of any kind interferes with a woman's job performance and morale and can create severe emotional stress.

Another major source of stress for working women is the fact that they must hold down two jobs, a day job at work and a night and weekend job at home. Current research indicates that although more families are sharing household chores, women continue to carry the major burden of running the home when they work outside the home. Despite the massive influx of women into the job market, a recent study shows that men have only increased their participation in household chores by six percent over the last twenty years (Joseph H. Pleck, "Husband's Paid Work and Family Roles: Current Research Issues," in Helena Z. Lopata and Joseph H. Pleck, eds., *Research in the Interweave of Social Roles,* vol. 3 [Greenwich, CT: JAI Press, 1982], pp. 251–333). To perform both home and office jobs well is extremely difficult and, of course, stressful, especially if there are children in the home.

Even the decision whether to have children or not is a stressor for many working women. If the decision is yes, the next question is, When is the best time? A woman's job requirements must rank with her other considerations in determining her answer. Even when the decision is made, maternity leave and job security vary widely from company to company, and the lack of adequate support in these areas can make the experience of combining work and child rearing extremely difficult.

Then there looms the rather large problem of appropriate and affordable daycare. Most women no longer aspire to becoming "Superwomen." They know that holding down a full-time job while simultaneously running a house and raising children *effortlessly* is a media myth. But women still seem to bear the greater responsibility, and stress, in relation to all aspects of child care: finding good care, transporting the children to and from the daycare, and monitoring their well-being in the child-care situation.

Children are our most important natural resource. If they are not provided with safe, loving, educational environments while their parents are working, the entire nation will be damaged in the future. And, until the government and business interests see fit to address these issues, it looks as if women will continue to shoulder this stressful burden.

One final, little noted source of stress for women results from their almost total lack of role models in some careers. As time goes by, this situation will change, but at present many women—particularly corporate women and women in many blue-collar jobs—are literally pioneers in the work force, and they carry the stress that comes with forging new roles.

Working women need to take special care of themselves because of all the extra stress they encounter as part of their normal work lives. Stress management techniques can help women use their energies positively, so that stress does not add to the burdens of work or interfere with career plans. As women continue to bring their special strengths to their jobs—awareness, compassion, skill at communicating—they can only enrich the world of work.

Stress Management Recommendations for Workers

Stress at work cannot be avoided, as no job is without its pressures and difficulties. But you can learn to manage your response to stress, gaining more control over your body's reactions to anxiety-producing situations. When you manage the stress response on a physical level, your emotions too will become more relaxed and balanced. When an entire wellness program is undertaken, you'll feel the further benefits of increased energy and better health.

WELLNESS PROGRAMS

Many large corporations have instituted various kinds of wellness programs for their employees. These programs take many forms and can be tailored to the needs of a specific company. Programs usually include some of the following: classes and workshops; biofeedback training; relaxation/meditation training; physical exercise programs and facilities; athletic events; behavioral modification training; substance abuse counseling; and individual psychotherapy.

The need for wellness programs is evident when we look at the cost of some of our unhealthy habits. Smoking, for example, has been reported to cost business $27.5 billion a year! ($8.2 billion in direct medical costs and $19.3 billion in indirect costs such as absenteeism.) Alcohol abuse has been estimated to cost business a staggering $44.2 billion a year. In 1980, executive stress cost something between $10 and $20 billion.* These costs are, of course, added to the price of products, so consumers pick up the tab. But more important than the money is what these figures say about the quality of life of thousands of workers.

Some companies simply provide the facilities and the personnel for

*These figures are from *Healthy People in Unhealthy Places: Stress and Fitness at Work*, by Kenneth Pelletier, New York: Dell, 1984.

their wellness programs. Others offer incentives to their employees for participating. For example, some companies offer cash bonuses for the number of laps run on a track or swum in a pool. The companies themselves may receive incentives from their insurance carriers, such as reduced rates on their health insurance premiums, for sponsoring wellness programs.

The cost effectiveness of wellness programs has yet to be completely tabulated. Nevertheless, individual companies have reported, fairly consistently, that their health care and sick leave costs go down and their productivity goes up when a wellness program is instituted.

SELF-CARE

If your company or job does not provide a wellness program, you can still begin to practice self-care. All of the components of a good wellness program are available in most communities. The YMCA, the Heart Association, and the Lung Association are good places to investigate if you need assistance in getting started.

An adequate self-care program must include a balanced diet (low in sweets, fats, and junk foods); an exercise program that includes at least fifteen minutes of continuous exercise to increase the heart rate, three to four times a week; and regular (daily if possible) relaxation exercises.

I recommend the following exercises because they are noncompetitive and you can work out at your own pace: running/jogging; bike riding; swimming; walking; jumping rope; rowing; skating; aerobics; and hiking. If you are not used to exercising, see your physician for a checkup before starting. Begin your program slowly and work up to fifteen minutes a day.

For self-care relaxation work I recommend doing one of the deep relaxation techniques for twenty minutes a day. Select an exercise from this chapter and do it daily for at least a week before deciding it is right for you or moving on to another exercise. In four to six weeks you should notice a difference in how you feel, but it takes eight to twelve weeks to receive the maximum benefit from these exercises. If you are inconsistent in your practice, or are under a great deal of stress, it may take longer to feel results.

When you are doing the exercises properly, you can expect to feel your muscles relax, your breath and heart rate slow, and your hands and feet warm up due to the increase in blood circulation. When you have learned to feel these physical changes, you will also be able to feel calmer and more tranquil mentally and emotionally. Of course, this will take some time and practice.

Beginners have found that making tapes of these exercises and playing them back can be very helpful. The breathing exercises are particularly easy to practice at work because they are so inconspicuous, and they are immediately helpful in reducing work-related stress.

ASSERTIVENESS

Being assertive means that you can communicate your needs or point of view clearly and with confidence. Confidence comes from knowing what you want, knowing that you deserve what you want, and knowing how to get it.

Many people lack this kind of confidence. Often this is the result of low self-esteem or a poor self-image. To increase your self-esteem and to brighten your self-image you must first demonstrate to yourself that you like yourself; that you are worth liking.

Taking the time to relax, exercise, and eat properly are demonstrations that you are worth taking care of, and these actions will increase your self-esteem. In addition, try the following exercise which is designed to bolster feelings of self-worth.

Make a list of all your positive qualities. Write down all the things that you like about yourself, whether it be your compassion for other people, your athletic ability, or something as simple as the color of your hair. Read it aloud in front of a mirror or tape-record your list and play it back, listening to it carefully. Is your tone of voice positive and powerful? Have you chosen your words to emphasize the positive, or do you qualify your statements and make them tentative? Reword your statements, if you need to, to make them shine with conviction, and speak in your most confident tone of voice. You can also read your list to a friend and then have your friend read it to you. Your list should help you feel you are worth taking the time and energy to exercise, eat well, relax, and feel good about yourself.

Another important aspect of self-care which many people overlook, and which is related to self-esteem, is developing the ability to say no. For women in particular, because they have been socialized to be accommodating and compliant, the assertion and forcefulness needed to say no may not come easily. But doing things we don't really want to do is a tremendous drain on our emotional and physical well-being. It is important to think of saying no as a positive rather than a negative assertion. Saying no is really a way of saying what you want by asserting what you won't tolerate. You can say no politely and firmly. You do not need to be either obnoxious or aggressive; but you do have to know how to say no.

Practice saying no into the mirror and the tape recorder. Say it loudly, softly, and with different tones for different moods. Repeat it until you feel comfortable saying it. "No. No. No." Remind yourself that you do not need to excuse yourself for saying it. If the person you say no to does not like it, then he or she must learn how to communicate that response to you. You have a right to say no and to be heard and understood.

COMMUNICATION

Efficient and clear communication is essential in the work world, whether it be between manager and subordinate, seller and customer, or between partners or coworkers. Yet too often, we are not as aware as we could be of the skills of good communication.

Good communication requires first of all quieting the internal dialogue which often prevents us from listening clearly to others. Particularly if we have a lot of negative or destructive ruminations swimming in our minds, we need to learn to still these internal voices. When our internal world is quiet and calm, a balanced emotional awareness can develop and we are more able to see and hear others clearly.

Next, we need to be able to listen. Listening is a developed skill which requires practice and attention. One of the keys to good listening is to avoid formulating a response until the person speaking is completely finished. If we are busy thinking of what we're going to say next, we are probably not absorbing what the speaker is saying. The next time you speak with a coworker or superior, make a point of listening without reacting until she is finished speaking. Then pause a moment, take a deep breath, and let the other person know you have heard what she said before you proceed with your own feelings or opinions. Repeating the other person's main messages for clarification is also useful. You'll be surprised sometimes at the difference between what you heard and what the speaker thought she said. Discussing this difference can be very helpful. In business, mistaken communication can come back to haunt you, so taking the time for clarification is very important.

Paying attention to nonverbal communication is just as important as listening carefully to verbal messages. We communicate through our body language—gestures, eye movement, facial expressions, posture—just as much as through our words. Good communicators know how to listen and respond to this nonverbal communication. For instance, if a worker assures his boss that everything is proceeding smoothly in his department, but fidgets and looks nervously toward the door as he speaks, the manager may want to gently inquire further about some of the specifics of the situation. Make eye contact and use a calm tone of voice when responding to these nonverbal clues. Often a person expresses things through his body when he is uncomfortable articulating them openly. If we remain calm and show respect for the other person's feelings, the other person will more easily feel that he can express his thoughts more directly. Everyone benefits when communication is open and clear.

One other important rule of good communication is to avoid blaming the other person if you are upset or unhappy about something. Blaming cuts off communication, as it usually makes the other person become defensive, and then neither person is able to listen clearly or objectively. If something has happened which you are not pleased about, it is best to convey your feelings about what happened rather than attack the person you feel is responsible. For example, if an associate is constantly interrupting you at a business meeting, it would be better to say, "I feel uncomfortable when I am not allowed to complete my thought," rather than accuse him of being unable to listen. A statement of your feelings cannot be argued. After you state your feeling you can discuss what specific action would help to change your negative feeling. This can lead to a short discussion in which both sides can become more aware of each other's needs and feelings and a compromise can be reached. Even if everyone does not agree, tolerance and respect for another's point of view will help every business situation proceed more smoothly.

TIME MANAGEMENT AND GOAL SETTING

Feeling that there is not enough time to accomplish the tasks at hand is a common complaint of workers, no matter what type of job they may have. For most companies, efficient management of time can mean the difference between showing a profit or a loss. For an individual, managing time well is also a key to being productive and successful.

Though some people report that they work best under pressure, too often, the stress that is produced by feeling pressured actually makes people work less efficiently. When a worker feels harried, accidents increase, communication problems are more likely to occur, and productive energy is absorbed by worry and frustration. Though you may feel you can't take the time out of your hectic day to practice a stress reduction technique, the time you take for relaxation will actually boost your productivity, enabling you to accomplish your tasks more efficiently. I can't stress enough the importance of taking the time to stop and relax, particularly when you're under pressure. Regular relaxation exercises help you to keep your energies focused, your mind open and receptive, and your memory retentive.

In addition to practicing the stress reduction exercises offered in this chapter, you can manage your time more effectively by being aware of some basic time managment techniques. Experts in this area outline several approaches to using time efficiently. Try them out and see which ones work best for you.

One method of time management is to set clear goals and prioritize your job assignments. At the beginning of your day, take a moment to make a list of all that needs to be done. After compiling the list, check off the most important assignments and do them first. Focus your energies on the most difficult tasks, saving the least important and the easiest tasks for last. If a task is especially difficult, allot extra time to do it and arrange well in advance whatever support you may need to accomplish it. Break down large projects into smaller, logical steps. As each task is accomplished, check it off your list to celebrate its completion.

Another approach is to compile a list of tasks and prioritize them, but begin with some of the easier items in order to eliminate a couple of tasks very quickly and gain some momentum before attacking the more difficult jobs. You may need to experiment a bit to see whether you accomplish more by starting with the difficult jobs or the easier ones. You'll also want to consider your boss or supervisor's priorities. If a large job is top priority to her, you may want to tackle it first, even if you prefer to shorten your list as fast as possible by starting with the easier tasks.

Time management experts also offer several other tips. Try not to schedule every minute of your day. Leave some unscheduled time so that you can handle emergencies, interruptions, or last-minute details without having to feel frenzied. You'll work more effectively if you know you have time to deal appropriately with each situation that arises. Try also to control interruptions, such as phone calls and conversations with coworkers. If possible, make yourself available only at certain times for these calls and conversations. You can often use a phone answering machine to screen calls, taking only the ones that are essential to your work and returning the rest later.

Time is often wasted as you wait for other people. You can avoid this by scheduling appointments at specific times and letting people know you stick to your schedule. If you need to phone someone who is difficult to reach, schedule a phone appointment so that you won't be kept waiting. During meetings, make sure you have a specific agenda and stick to it.

Be realistic about the goals you set for yourself. Do not expect Herculean accomplishments from yourself; remember that you are human. Above all, try to think of time as your friend rather than your enemy, as a possibility rather than a limitation. See each day as a time in which you can work productively and feel good about yourself and what you accomplish. Having a positive attitude will go a long way toward helping you achieve the goals that are important to you.

Case Study #1

When I first saw Mike several years ago, he was suffering from stress-related high blood pressure, preulcerous abdominal problems, and tension headaches. His doctor had referred him to me to learn stress management techniques.

Mike knew that his symptoms were related to the stress he felt at work. He is the vice-president of a large financial institution about fifty miles from where he lives. He complained about the commute, work pressures, and interpersonal dynamics at the office.

Mike did not feel that he could at that time do anything to change his long commute or to alleviate the work pressures he was feeling. I suggested that we focus on the areas that he did have control over, and explained to him how he could control his body's response to stress. I made a relaxation tape for him which combined an indirect relaxation exercise with a visualization of calmness and productivity at the office. I suggested that he listen to the tape one or two times a day and explained the benefits that would result.

When Mike returned to see me one week later, he reported little change in his degree of tension. When I asked him about his use of the tape, he replied that he had not had time to listen to it. (This is a typical problem I have to confront with very busy people.) I suggested again that if he listened to the tape and gave it a chance to work, he would find that in the long run it would save time for him.

Mike was still very skeptical and did not seem to believe that taking time out from work could help him to be more productive. In our third session he again reported no change in his symptoms or feelings. I continued to encourage him to listen to the tape one or two times a day and described how much easier his life would become if he did so.

The fourth week that I saw Mike, he appeared in my office looking much more cheerful. He told me that even though he had not believed me, he had tried listening to the tape daily. He reported that during the last week he had slept more deeply and awakened more refreshed than was typical for him. He also said that his headaches had not bothered him for the last several days. I encouraged him to continue using the tape and suggested some breathing exercises that he could use while commuting and during his work day.

Over the next several months of continual practice, Mike experienced a remarkable change in his sense of well-being. He continued to sleep deeply and even began to need less sleep. He was able to relax and listen to music during his long commute rather than feel tense and harried. His blood pressure dropped into the normal range, his headaches and stomach pains disappeared, and he felt he was working much more efficiently. The big surprise to both of us was that with the time he saved at work he was able to take on some creative projects which were a great deal of fun for him. He was actually enjoying his work.

In follow-up visits over the next year, Mike reported that daily relaxation exercises had become part of his everyday routine. In his enthusiasm for the relaxation skills he had learned, he sounded like a recording of my past lectures to him. Mike's is a real success story illustrating the benefits of self-care through stress management.

Case Study #2

Jill's story is an example of the kinds of stress women experience in the work world. Jill had worked very hard to achieve her position as office manager of a large commercial trucking firm. She was also the mother of a preschool-age son, John. And, she took care of her home without outside help. Her decision to seek employment was based both on economics and a desire to develop work skills outside the home.

When she first started working at the trucking firm it was a small operation. Jill was responsible for many different tasks—bookkeeping, scheduling, phones, billing, payroll—in short, she did everything but drive the trucks. Initially, she was the only woman in the office, and often felt that she was excluded from the men's camaraderie, even though her work was certainly as essential to the firm as was the men's. When the firm grew and other women were hired to do office work, they all were occasionally made to feel, through the men's comments and jokes, that they were not as important to the firm as the men who drove the trucks.

After four years, Jill was promoted to the position of office manager and promised a raise after a "trial period." This issue became a source of real stress to her. How much of a trial period did they need? She felt that her bosses were overlooking her already-proven abilities and what an asset she had been to the firm.

When she tried to discuss her raise, she was humiliated and teased about not "dating" her boss. She became very angry and discouraged and began to show signs of stress-related depression. When stomach problems developed a short time later, her doctor recommended her to me for relaxation training.

In our discussions, it became clear that Jill was not fully aware of the balancing act she had been performing in order to meet her obligations as office manager, homemaker, mother, and individual. She did not fully understand that the stress of these various roles had begun to wear her down.

I encouraged her to resume her regular exercise program of swimming three times a week, which she had stopped when she became office manager. I also helped her learn an autogenic training exercise with visualizations to calm her abdominal area. And I taught her some deep breathing techniques which she could use at work when she felt the pressure building. She also learned to use the phone as a cue for relaxation. Each time she heard it ring she took a deep breath and relaxed her muscles before answering it. Jill felt this technique helped improve her communications as well as helping her relax.

Within several weeks Jill reported that she was feeling much stronger physically and less emotionally distraught. She was able to control her tension at work with the breathing exercises, and the autogenic training which she did at home seemed to have a positive effect on her stomach problems. Within a month she reported that her stomach pains had disappeared. As she started feeling better, she became more positive in her outlook and even began to search for another job. She realized that taking care of herself needed to be a top priority.

At work, her boss observed her personality changes and began to worry about losing her. He finally realized how important Jill was to the firm and gave her the long-overdue raise and some additional benefits.

But Jill continued her search for another job because she had realized that she had reached her goal at the trucking firm and that she could not advance any further there. She was more ambitious than she had been, and wanted her future to offer her additional challenges. When Jill took control of her body and emotions using stress management techniques, she was able to take more control over her entire life.

Case Study #3

When Carl came to see me, he was recovering from a low-back problem. He worked as a journeyman carpenter and was expected to work hard and fast. Recurring low-back pain had plagued him for the past five years.

He had learned his trade as a much younger man, at a time when his body was more resilient and able to absorb the physical stresses of his work. He was now in his early forties and was slowing down considerably. He knew that the hard work he had put in over the past twenty years was taking its toll on his body. Yet Carl was earning a good salary, and he did not know any other trade which would pay him as well as carpentry. He had acquired a house, a boat, a truck, and a camper-shell, and had large monthly payments to make on all of them. He measured his success by these possessions, and felt his whole lifestyle would be endangered if he did not receive his regular paycheck.

As Carl continued to work, the irritation in his back increased. He was finally forced to leave his job and receive disability. At the time he did not realize that his financial worries were causing him as much stress as his work. In addition, both physical and mental midlife stresses were exhausting his resources.

His physical therapist, who was supervising him in a daily exercise program, had recommended he come see me. Together, we explored the various sources of his stress problems, but Carl had a hard time seeing the connection between his pain and the stressors in his life, such as his frustration about his financial situation or his anger about the workman's compensation system. He felt that I was suggesting the pain was in his head. I tried to explain that I was talking about the translation of stress and frustration into the physical pain he was feeling in his body.

His doctor had him fitted with a TENS unit, a small battery-operated device which looks like a beeper and is worn on the belt. Wires with electrodes on the end stretch from the TENS unit to a person's sore muscles. Through these wires an electrical current can be sent which stimulates the sensory nerves in the affected muscles and interrupts the pain message. The person wearing the device has control over the duration, volume, and wave pattern of the electrical charge and can adjust it according to the level of pain he is feeling. Using his TENS unit, Carl was able to manage his pain enough that he could continue his physical therapy and exercise program and reduce the amount of pain medication he had been taking.

In addition, I introduced Carl to biofeedback. I began by hooking him up to an EMG machine which measures the level of muscular tension by indicating the level of electrical activity in a given muscle group. In our first session I placed the EMG sensors on the frontalis muscle in Carl's forehead. This muscle reflects the tension of the entire face, including the jaw. Then I placed the sensors on his trapezius muscle at the base of the neck, which reflects the tension in the neck, shoulders, and upper back. Both times the needle on the monitor, which showed the level of electrical activity, clearly demonstrated to Carl how tense these muscle groups were. The EMG machine provided him with the tangible evidence of tension in his body, and helped him to be able to make the connection between this tension and his fatigue and muscle pain.

I then gave Carl a tape with an indirect relaxation exercise, and encouraged him to listen to it at least once a day. The next week when he came to see me he reported that he had had difficulty with the relaxation exercise, finding it too passive. I again hooked him up to the EMG machine to measure his level of muscular tension. Then I led him through the indirect relaxation exercise, and afterward we again measured the level of his muscular tension. We were both delighted to see that the tension was significantly lower after the exercise. Encouraged, Carl continued to use the relaxation tape over the next two months. We continued to use the EMG machine to measure his progress when he came to see me each week.

With time, Carl became comfortable with the indirect relaxation and found that he was sleeping better and experiencing less pain in his back. After three months he was able to stop taking his pain medication, relying only on his TENS unit, relaxation program, and exercise to control his pain. He also cut back on his consumption of coffee, alcohol, and tobacco, all of which inhibit the body's ability to heal.

He began a course of vocational rehabilitation to learn a new trade but gave it up to become a construction supervisor with a firm he had worked for previously. He thought this job would be less physically demanding, but he is still subject to the stresses that accompany supervisory work. He maintains his daily exercise and relaxation program, but he still experiences recurring back pain. When it does occur, however, he knows how to manage it without becoming totally disabled.

Relaxation Exercises for Work Stress

TEN-MINUTE COMMUTE EXERCISE

Read this exercise through and become familiar with it so you can use it on your commute. Or if you have a tape deck in your car, you may wish to tape the exercise and play it while you are driving.

The first step to relaxing is becoming aware of the tension you are carrying in your body. Particularly when you are dashing to work, you are most likely not thinking about how relaxed or tense your muscles are. However, taking just a few moments to focus on your body can make a big difference in how you feel.

When you first get into your car, instead of rushing out of the driveway, take a moment to stop and relax. Take a slow, deep breath, pause a moment, then exhale fully and completely. You may want to roll your neck gently and slowly to release any tensions that may be building.

Now check your body's position. Are you comfortable and relaxed, or are your muscles cramped and tight? Become aware of the muscles which are tense. Drop your shoulders. Relax your jaw. Check your wrists, fingers, buttocks, toes, legs, and chest. Are any of these muscles unnecessarily tight? It is common for these muscles to tense up when you are experiencing stress, but you do not need to wear yourself out by holding tension in these muscles for the whole commute. Feel yourself settling back comfortably into your seat. You can become even more comfortable by loosening your tie, your belt, or even your shoe laces. (Remember to check yourself before you leave the car!) Check the climate of your vehicle. Is it too hot or too cool? Is the air fresh or stale? Make any necessary adjustments to allow for greater comfort. As you begin your commute, make sure your body is as relaxed as possible.

One of the best ways to maintain this state of calmness and relaxation as you drive is to take a deep breath at every stop sign or traffic delay that you encounter. Instead of feeling frustrated and tense, use these delays as your time to relax. Inhale deeply, pause a moment, then exhale fully and completely. Roll your neck gently and check your forehead, jaw, shoulders, and the rest of your body for any tension.

As you are driving you can continue to increase your state of relaxation through several exercises. One is to make a mental list of all of the tasks that you want to accomplish during the day. If you are on your way home, you may wish to review the day and then consider your priorities for tomorrow's work. As you compile your list, make a clear distinction between important tasks and less significant ones. Ask yourself if the outcome of a particular task or issue will make any difference in your life one year from now. If the outcome will be forgotten in one year, then it may not need to be a top priority or a source of anxiety. Try to to keep your responsibilities in perspective and not let them become more important than they need be.

Use this mental list to help yourself feel prepared for the day ahead. But be realistic. Pare down your list as much as possible so that you are not expecting too much of yourself. By sorting the essential from the nonessential tasks, you can avoid carrying unnecessary pressure.

Another exercise which can take your mind off your anxieties and help

you relax on your commute is to notice one new thing on every drive. Notice a tree, a cloud formation, a flight of birds, or an open space in the cityscape. When you spot this new item, take the time to appreciate and remember it. Even if you drive the same route every day, if you look at your surroundings as a source of discovery and pleasure, you will be surprised at what you may notice. When you find something that you enjoy, think about what it is about this image that makes you feel pleasure. Is it the freedom of the bird's flight? The aesthetics of the cloud shapes? Does the color of the sky remind you of some past enjoyment? Keep these positive feelings in your mind as you drive. You may even find that you are no longer thinking about how upset you are with one of your coworkers or how nervous you are about a new assignment. The positive image will help maintain a balance we all need in our lives, reminding you of life's other pleasures and priorities.

If negative distractions surface while you are trying to focus on your new discovery and positive images, try not to become tense. You can learn from negative experiences, even if it's only how to avoid them in the future. Take a breath and relax. Let go of the tensions and regain your calmness. You may even want to focus on your breath for a few moments. Breath slowly, feeling the cool air as you inhale and the warm air as you exhale. Check your shoulders, jaw, and forehead, and relax them if you need to. Let the calmness and relaxation continue with you for the rest of your commute.

When you finish your commute and get out of your vehicle, take another deep breath. Again, gently roll your shoulders and neck, allowing them to relax completely, so you can begin your day in a state of relaxation.

TEN-MINUTE OFFICE RELAXATION

This is an abbreviated relaxation exercise that you may find suitable for use at work. You may wish to tape it if you have access to a tape recorder at work, or you can learn the basics so you can go through the exercise wherever you may be. Before you begin, you may want to make a list of all the tasks that you still have to do. After your relaxation, you can return to work and accomplish these tasks more easily and calmly. You may also want to make sure that someone else will answer your phone or handle any responsibilities that may arise while you are taking these ten minutes for relaxation.

Get into a comfortable position in a place where you will not be disturbed. Loosen any tight clothing. Uncross you legs and let your arms rest comfortably by your sides. Check your shoulders, and let them drop into a more comfortable position. Notice the muscles of your head and face. Let your forehead become calm and smooth. Close your eyes, relaxing the muscles around them. Check the muscles around your mouth, including your jaw. Relax these muscles even further.

Do not try to relax too quickly. Allow yourself to drift into a pleasant calmness and comfort. When you are ready to begin, take three deep, slow breaths. Pause after you inhale, then exhale fully and completely. Begin to release unwanted tension or excess energy as you exhale, feeling tension flow from you with your breath. After the first three breaths, continue breathing slowly and gently, releasing tensions as you exhale and allowing yourself to drift deeper into calmness.

As you breathe slowly, turn your awareness to your arms and hands. Perhaps you can feel the relaxation beginning as the muscles in your arms and hands become loose and comfortable. Breathe slowly and feel the sensation of heaviness in your arms. As you allow yourself to drift deeper into relaxation, take three slow, deep breaths. As you exhale, slowly and completely, perhaps you can feel the warmth of blood flowing freely down your arms into your hands. You may feel the warmth slowly pulsing into your fingers. As you allow yourself to drift deeper into a dreamlike calmness and comfort, you can begin to feel your tensions melting away.

As you breathe slowly and peacefully, turn your attention to your legs and feet. Feel the relaxation spreading as the muscles of your legs begin to loosen. Perhaps you can feel the heaviness in your legs. Take three slow, deep breaths and as you exhale, feel the heaviness growing stronger. Perhaps you can feel the warmth as blood flows more freely down into your legs and feet. You may even feel the warmth slowly pulsing into your toes. Gently allow yourself to drift further into this dreamlike calmness.

As you breathe slowly and naturally, you can feel the muscles of your back beginning to soften and loosen. Feel yourself gaining control of your tensions as you sink back into whatever you are sitting or lying upon. Let your shoulders loosen further as they drop into a more comfortable position. Let your head sink back into the chair or pillow. Let the muscles of your neck loosen and relax even further. You can let yourself drift deeper into a soothing, deep relaxation.

Take the next few moments, as you continue to drift along in deep relaxation, to see yourself outdoors on a beautiful warm day. Imagine yourself finding the most comfortable spot to lie down in the sunshine. As you sink back into whatever you imagine yourself lying upon, the tension just melts away. You can feel the warmth from the sun and the pleasant breezes that brush against you. Perhaps you can even hear the sounds of the ocean or running water, the sound of the birds, or the rustling of the warm breezes. Soak up the sunshine. Imagine that the light and warmth can recharge you, helping to fill you with health and energy. Though you remain relaxed and comfortable, the feelings of joy and happiness can grow brighter within you. Finally picture yourself outdoors in the sunshine, smiling and celebrating. See yourself doing something active that you particularly enjoy.

To awaken, let yourself return to the room, bringing the feelings of calmness and relaxation back with you. Feel the chair or mat beneath you as you gently awaken. Feel the relaxation, the health, and the joy return with you to a fully waking state. As you return to work, you can remain calm and use your energies more effectively. When you wish to, you can take a deep breath and stretch, letting yourself awaken completely. Take another deep breath and stretch, letting the health and calmness carry with you throughout your day.

BREATHING EXERCISES

The breathing exercises offered below are ideal for the busy worker because they can be done anywhere at any time, and can take only a few seconds or a few minutes. They are easily integrated into even the most hectic of work schedules, and should be practiced regularly by anyone who wants to feel more relaxed amidst the pressures of the work world.

Because breathing is an automatic function of our body, we seldom think about the way we breathe. But, in fact, most people breathe shallowly, from the chest, rather than deeply, from the diaphragm. Particularly when we are experiencing stress, we tend to breathe rapidly and shallowly from the upper chest. This kind of breathing may satisfy our need for oxygen, but it does not provide the relaxation that deep, diaphragmatic breathing can. Slow diaphragmatic breathing will help relax muscle groups and can help to slow the heart rate to a normal, relaxed rhythm.

#*1*. Try this. Lie down flat or stand up straight. Put one hand over your stomach and one hand over your chest, and see which way each hand moves as you inhale. Now which way do your hands move as you exhale? Does your bottom hand move first and outward as you begin the inhale? Does the upper hand then move up and out? On the exhale, do you notice that both hands move in, perhaps forcing the last bit of air out? If so, then you are breathing very well and you can go on to the next breathing exercises. If not, you should practice a bit before you continue, as this breathing technique forms the basis of every stress management exercise.

#*2*. Now try breathing very slowly while you are in a comfortable position. As you inhale slowly but comfortably, count 1–4. Perhaps you can picture the numbers in you mind, or say them slowly to yourself. Now pause for a moment and count 1–4 again as you hold your breath (slowly, picturing the numbers in your mind if possible). And now as you exhale, slowly and comfortably count 1–8. Let your body relax more deeply as you exhale fully and completely, feeling the warm air as you exhale. You might want to repeat this for three breaths. Then check to see if you are feeling more relaxed. You may need to check the muscles of your shoulders, neck, and jaw. If you can let these muscle groups relax further, take another slow breath.

#3. Another breathing/counting exercise that works well is to take four slow breaths, counting to eight by counting one on the inhale, two on the exhale, three on the inhale, etc. Try to picture the numbers in your mind or say the numbers to yourself. After counting to eight, check your position, relax your jaw, forehead, neck, and shoulders and repeat the exercise one more time. Within about two minutes you can begin to feel more relaxed and open, releasing tension with each exhale. Remember, go slowly. Do not be in such a hurry to relax!

#4. Take three deep slow breaths. As you lie down or sit back comfortably, allow yourself to breathe slowly. Feel the cool air as you inhale, pause a moment, and then slowly exhale, feeling the warm breath carry away tensions or discomforts. You might try to feel the cool air at the tip of your nostrils. Exhale through your mouth, breathing away the warm air as if it will drift up into the sky like a helium-filled balloon. Let go slowly and easily, becoming more relaxed with every breath. Some people use this exercise not only to relax but to help them drift off to sleep.

#5. Special breathing behavior. This breathing technique is particularly recommended for people with hectic jobs, as it associates deep breathing with a regularly occurring signal in the environment. For instance, if your phone rings constantly or you are continually opening a file drawer, you can use these cues to take a moment to relax. Or remember to stop and relax every time you look at the clock. Decide upon a "signal" and then each time it occurs, take one slow deep breath, scan your body—let your shoulders drop, jaw relax, arms and legs loosen—and let go of unnecessary tensions. If you have difficulty remembering your cue, give yourself a visual aid by putting a piece of colored tape on the face of the clock or the top of the phone. Each time you glance at the clock or reach for the phone, the tape will remind you to take a moment to relax. By stopping periodically to release tensions, you prevent them from building to harmful levels.

These various breathing techniques work best when practiced on a regular basis. Find one or two that work well for you, and then use them consistently. Within a short time you should feel yourself devloping greater control of your body and your life.

MEDITATION

Meditation is an Eastern form of relaxation which requires a high degree of discipline. If concentration is essential to your work, you may find meditation highly useful, as it encourages the development of mental focus and concentration. However, meditation requires a good deal of practice and the ability to control your mind. If you want to feel the benefits of relaxation more quickly, you may find the Western styles of relaxation—autogenic training, indirect relaxation, progressive relaxation, or visualization—more attractive. These Western relaxation techniques do not require the kind of focused concentration on one item that meditation does, because their primary purpose is relaxation, not concentration.

I suggest you try the three meditation techniques outlined below for yourself to determine whether they are an effective relaxation tool for you. Many people find meditation to be highly relaxing, and once you are comfortable with the practice, meditation can be easily integrated into your work schedule. Instead of taking a coffee break, take twenty minutes to sit in a quiet place and clear your mind of the day's clutter. You can experience a remarkable degree of rejuvenation from these few moments of concentrated relaxation.

Many forms and styles of meditation exist. Some require that you close your eyes; some suggest you keep your eyes open. Some use a sitting position; others suggest you lie down. It is even possible to meditate while standing. And some forms of meditation combine different styles, while others require a more rigid concentration. The following selection of exercises draws from several different forms to allow you to select those which work best for you.

Transcendental Meditation: The most widely used style of meditation among Western cultures is a form of Transcendental Meditation (also called TM). Researchers have studied the use of TM to determine how and in what way it can provide a subject with physiological control over his bodily functions. Herbert Benson, a cardiologist and author of *The Relaxation Response,* has long recommended a form of TM for control of blood pressure and various cardiac disorders. TM uses the repetition of a special word, or "mantra," to help clear the mind. Originally, Eastern Yogis who taught TM to initiates selected a special Sanskrit word for each student to use as his mantra. Dr. Benson suggests that the nondescript word "one" can be repeated over and over to focus the mind during meditation. I often recommend that you use a word that has a stronger, positive connotation such as "love," "peace," or "harmony."

Sit upright in a quiet environment with your eyes closed, repeating your word over and over as you attempt to still your mind. As thoughts or mental insights occur to you, try to let them pass, taking notice, but not becoming focused or absorbed with them. As you repeat your word slowly, release from your mind any other thoughts that invade your consciousness. Let the peaceful feeling of your word fill your mind. After twenty minutes, awaken yourself by taking a deep breath and stretching. The stilling of your mind, with practice, will remain with you as you continue through your day.

Zen Meditation: Another form of meditation, which allows you to keep your eyes open, is known as Zen meditation. The advantage of this form is that it lets you appreciate your surroundings as you meditate.

If you are at work, find a place to sit, either inside or outside, which has a view that is aesthetically pleasing to you. If your surroundings are not visually enjoyable, you may want to bring an object to work with you which provides you with visual pleasure, such as a flower, a photo or drawing, or a mandala (a drawing or object with a circular design). You will use this object, or some other pleasing object in your environment, as a visual focal point. If you are outside, focus on some object of natural beauty, such as a flower or tree.

Sit or stand in a comfortable position as you focus on the selected object. Keep your mind clear of distracting thoughts or emotions. If thoughts of your daily activities and feelings invade your mind, notice them and gently let them go. Try to keep the image you have selected at the center of your consciousness for twenty minutes, until its natural beauty fills your mind. As you return to your day after this meditation, the serenity of this meditative state will accompany you.

Do not be discouraged if you seem unable to stop the many thoughts swimming in your consciousness from demanding your attention. The mind will resist being stilled, but with consistent practice you will begin to achieve a peaceful, restful stillness more easily and for longer periods of time.

Yogic Meditation: A third form of meditation I often suggest combines techniques in a way that I have found to be very personally satisfying. Sit upright for twenty minutes in a quiet environment. For the first ten minutes focus your mind on a word, short phrase, or peaceful symbol. Examples might be the words "love," "peace," or "harmony"; the phrases "God is good" or "love is the light"; or a symbol such as a star, cross, or flower. During this ten minutes of focus, do not hold on to any distracting thoughts. Simply let any thoughts that occur to you pass gently through your consciousness and drift away. Return your focus to the symbol or word you have chosen, letting the feeling of peace and harmony which it suggests fill your being. After ten minutes of focus, move into an open meditation. Let your mind become like a blank movie or TV screen. Watch, without attachment, anything that comes up and through your mind. In my experience, some beautiful spiritual insights can come into consciousness in this way. Finally, at the end of your twenty-minute meditation, take a deep breath, stretch, and imagine that you are surrounded by white light. Let the light fill you and bathe you, so that you feel regenerated by this peaceful, loving energy.

AUTOGENIC TRAINING FOR WORK STRESS

The autogenic training exercise is easy to learn and can be a potent tool for combating the stresses of work. Developed by Western Europeans, autogenics may be easier for the Western person to relate to than an Eastern relaxation technique, such as meditation. This relaxation will not solve all your problems, but it will help you control your responses to the normal pressures and tensions of the work day.

You can practice the complete exercise at home until you are comfortable and familiar with it and are feeling the results. If your practice is consistent, you should reach this point within six weeks. Then you can try using it at work during a twenty-minute break. Even if you have only ten minutes at work to find a quiet place to relax, you can create an abbreviated version by simply moving through the phrases with less repetition or more selectively. With practice, even in the middle of your hectic workday you will be able to evoke the peacefulness which this exercise brings.

Read this exercise slowly (about half normal speaking speed). Pause at each (*). Do not be concerned by mispronunciations or verbal slips. Continue in a calm, even voice.

Find a quiet location where you will not be disturbed. Allow about twenty minutes for this exercise. Sit or lie back comfortably, allowing your arms and legs to remain uncrossed if possible. Let your head be supported and let your shoulders drop into a comfortable position. Check the muscles of your head and face. Let your forehead become calm and smooth. Allow the muscles around your eyes to loosen. Check the muscles of the mouth and jaw to make sure they are relaxed. Finally, allow your eyes to remain closed, remembering that you can open them whenever you need to use them.

Before we begin the relaxation, remember not to try to relax too quickly. In fact, do not try to relax at all. Without any effort you can allow yourself to relax by pleasantly letting go of tensions and discomforts, and then letting yourself drift deeper into a peaceful calmness. To begin the relaxation, take three deep breaths, pausing after you inhale, and then exhaling fully and completely. You might imagine that you release tensions and discomforts as you exhale by just breathing them away. * After you have finished these first three breaths, continue breathing slowly and naturally, relaxing more deeply with each slow exhale.

Repeat these phrases to yourself, exactly as they are taken from this exercise, and try to feel your body responding to the commands. If you need to repeat the phrases more than three times to begin to feel results, then continue the repetitions a few additional times.

Repeat this mood phrase to yourself three times: "I am at peace with myself and fully relaxed." Continue breathing slowly and gently.

Begin to feel the muscles of your arms relax as you say, "My right arm is heavy * . . . My right arm is heavy * . . . My right arm is heavy * . . ." Repeat this phrase slowly until you begin to feel the heaviness spreading through your arm. Now turn your awareness to your left arm as you breathe slowly and say to yourself, "My left arm is heavy * . . . My left arm is heavy . . . My left arm is heavy * . . ." Try to feel the heaviness starting in your arms or feel free to continue slowly repeating this phrase a few more times. Now proceed to your legs. Let them begin to relax as you breathe slowly. Feel the heaviness and relaxation starting in your legs as you slowly repeat, "My right leg is heavy * . . . My right leg is heavy * . . . My right leg is heavy * . . ." You can repeat this several more times if you need to, until you begin to feel the relaxation and the heaviness. Now focus on the left leg and feel it beginning to relax as you say, "My left leg is heavy * . . . My left leg is heavy * . . . My left leg is heavy * . . ." Repeat if needed. With practice you will feel the heaviness more quickly and easily. Now turn your attention to your neck and shoulders. Let them sink into a more comfortable position and let the muscles relax as you breathe gently and say, "My neck and shoulders are heavy * . . . My neck and shoulders are heavy * . . . My neck and shoulders are heavy * . . ." Repeat if needed. Take a deep slow breath and feel the heaviness and relaxation as you begin to sink back into whatever you are sitting or lying upon.

Perhaps you can feel the blood beginning to flow more easily down into your hands or your feet as the blood vessels begin to dilate, as the smooth muscles in the walls of the arteries begin to relax. Focus on the feelings of warmth, or a pulse, or perhaps a tingling feeling in your right hand as you say, "My right arm is warm * . . . My right arm is warm * . . . My right arm is warm * . . ." Repeat this slowly several more times until you begin to feel the warmth or pulse. Heaviness is generally easier for most people to feel than warmth, but with continued practice you can begin to control the blood flow. Now turn your attention to your left arm and say to yourself, "My left arm is warm * . . . My left arm is warm * . . . My left arm is warm * . . ." Repeat if needed. Perhaps you can start to feel the warmth in your arms, and you may feel the blood flowing freely through your entire body. As you breathe slowly and gently, turn your awareness to your legs and say to yourself, "My right leg is warm * . . . My right leg is warm * . . . My right leg is warm * . . ." Repeat several more times to help develop this skill. Move your attention to your left leg and say, "My left leg is warm * . . . My left leg is warm * . . . My left leg is warm * . . ." Repeat if needed. Feel the heaviness and warmth in your arms and your legs as you breathe slowly and gently. Now turn your awareness to your neck and shoulders, and say, "My neck and shoulders are warm * . . . My neck and shoulders are warm * . . . My neck and shoulders are warm * . . ." Repeat if needed. Breathe slowly as you drift for a few moments, feeling heaviness and warmth spread pleasantly about your body.

Slow and calm your heart by slowly repeating to yourself, "My heartbeat is calm and regular * . . . My heartbeat is calm and regular * . . . My heartbeat is calm and regular * . . ." Repeat if needed. If you experience any discomfort with this phrase then change to the phrase "I feel calm * . . . I feel calm * . . . I feel calm * . . ." As you breathe slowly, begin to feel the peace and relaxation spreading to every part of your body.

To slow your breathing say to yourself as you breathe into your diaphragm, "My breathing is calm and regular * . . . My breathing is calm and regular * . . . My breathing is calm and regular * . . ." Repeat if needed.

Become aware of the relaxation starting in your stomach region. As you breathe slowly say, "My abdomen is warm and calm * . . . My abdomen is warm and calm * . . . My abdomen is warm and calm * . . ." Repeat if needed. If you have any serious abdominal problems, such as bleeding ulcers or diabetes, or if you are in the last trimester of pregnancy, change this phrase to "I am calm and relaxed * . . . I am calm and relaxed * . . . I am calm and relaxed * . . ."

Move on to your forehead and let the muscles of your head and face relax as you say, "My forehead is cool and calm * . . . My forehead is cool and calm * . . . My forehead is cool and calm * . . ." As you breathe slowly, feel the muscles around your eyes, mouth, and jaw loosen and then relax.

Let yourself drift pleasantly in this calmness. As you breathe gently perhaps you can feel the heaviness in your arms and legs as the muscles relax. * Perhaps you can begin to feel the warmth or pulse of blood flowing more easily down into your hands and perhaps even your feet, like sunshine or a bath gently warming you. Some people feel the warming as a tingling sensation spreading blood more easily into the extremities. * As you enjoy the relaxation you can feel that your heartbeat is calm and regular. *

With practice you can feel the relaxation more easily and quickly. The warmth of blood flowing into your hands and feet gradually grows easier to control. The relaxation will then carry over with you throughout your day. It is important to remember to breathe slowly in stressful situations, to help release any building tensions. As you become comfortable with this relaxation technique you will be more aware of tension in your body and you will automatically be able to let go of this unwanted stress. The release of stress will free up your time and energy so you can work more productively and efficiently throughout your workday.

You may wish to spend a moment enjoying the feelings of deep relaxation. See yourself remaining calm and comfortable in your work environment. See yourself happily succeeding with an activity that may have given you problems or anxiety in the past. You will now have better control over your body's responses to even the most stressful of tasks.

At the end of this relaxation exercise, awaken yourself slowly. Feel the bed or chair beneath you and say, "I am refreshed and completely alert * . . . I am refreshed and completely alert * . . . I am refreshed and completely alert . . ." Then take a deep breath and stretch allowing yourself to wake fully, and let the relaxation carry over with you into a fully waking state. You may wish to take another deep breath and stretch, letting the relaxation return with you.

INDIRECT RELAXATION FOR WORK STRESS

The ease with which the indirect exercise can be learned and used makes it particularly suitable as you begin a stress management program. The subtle but powerful messages will help you become aware of and then "let go" of unwanted tensions that rob you of your energy and distract you from efficient work patterns.

Make a tape of the exercise or have someone read it to you and practice it at home daily for four to six weeks before judging its positive effects on your life. Once you are familiar with the exercise and can practice it without listening to the tape, you can try using it during a break at work. When you feel tense or tired during your workday, take twenty minutes to take care of yourself and relax. The positive results will stay with you throughout your day.

Read this exercise slowly (about half normal speaking speed). Pause at each (*). Do not be concerned by mispronunciations or verbal slips. Continue in a calm, even voice.

Find a quiet location where you will not be disturbed. Allow about twenty minutes for this exercise. Sit or lie back comfortably, allowing your arms and legs to remain uncrossed if possible. Let your head be supported and let your shoulders drop into a comfortable position. Check the muscles of your head and face. Let your forehead become calm and smooth. Allow the muscles around your eyes to loosen. Check the muscles of the mouth and jaw to make sure they are relaxed. Finally, allow your eyes to remain closed, remembering that you can open them whenever you need to use them.

Before we begin the relaxation, remember not to try to relax too quickly. In fact, do not try to relax at all. Without any effort you can allow yourself to relax by pleasantly letting go of tensions and discomforts, and then letting yourself drift deeper into a peaceful calmness. To begin the relaxation, take three deep breaths, pausing after you inhale, and then exhaling fully and completely. You might imagine that you release tensions and discomforts as you exhale by just breathing them away. * After you have finished these first three breaths, continue breathing slowly and naturally, relaxing more deeply with each slow exhale.

As you continue to breathe slowly and naturally, you may feel the relaxation beginning in your body. The most important thing to remember when dealing with work-related stress is that you can take control of your body through awareness and relaxation. So to begin this process, turn your awareness to the sensation of relaxation that is beginning in your arms and hands. You may feel that one arm is more relaxed than the other. * Perhaps one arm may feel a bit heavier than the other arm. The muscles may feel more loose or more flexible than in the other arm. * Or perhaps, you feel that one arm is a bit warmer than the other arm. You may feel that the warmth of blood and energy may flow more easily down one arm, as if it were flowing through wide-open blood vessels, slowly but freely moving down into your hand and fingers. You may even feel it slowly pulsing down into your hand. * Or perhaps you find that both arms feel equally relaxed and this would be perfect as well. The only thing that matters is that you breathe slowly and gently as you let yourself drift deeper into that soothing dream-like calmness. *

As you drift pleasantly, turn your awareness to the sensations of relaxation that may be beginning in your legs and feet. You may feel that one leg is slightly more relaxed than the other. Perhaps you notice that one leg feels a little heavier, as if the muscles of that leg were more loose or flexible. * Or as you breathe slowly and gently, you may feel that one leg is slightly warmer, as if the blood and warmth could spread more easily down that leg, drifting down through wide-open blood vessels, * perhaps even pulsing slowly but freely down into your foot and toes. * Or perhaps your legs feel equally relaxed, and that would be perfect also. The only thing that really matters is that you continue to breathe slowly as you allow yourself to drift more deeply into that dreamlike calmness and comfort. *

You may even feel the gradual control of stress and tensions beginning as you sink back into whatever you are sitting or lying upon and the tension just melts away. *

You may even feel the muscles of your back beginning to loosen or soften, and as you breathe slowly, naturally, you might feel the relaxation spreading to the other muscles of your back. * Even your upper back and shoulders may begin to soften or loosen a bit further. Your shoulders may be able to drop into a more comfortable position. * You may feel the control growing stronger as your head sinks back into the pillow or chair, the muscles of your neck begin to let go, and you drift deeper into relaxation. *

As you pleasantly drift deeper into this comfort and calmness, you may be able to feel the muscles of your head and face beginning to relax even further. * Continue to breathe slowly, allowing a soothing healing wave of relaxation to gently spread down from the top of your head, soothing and cleansing every muscle and cell of your body. You can feel it slowly drifting down to relax the muscles of your forehead, * letting your forehead become calm and smooth. * Let this wave drift down to relax the muscles around your eyes, releasing the tension in these muscles. * The wave then drifts down helping to relax the muscles of your mouth including your jaw. Let these muscles go loose and limp. * And as you breathe slowly, the wave slowly drifts down to relax the muscles of your neck. Even your shoulders can loosen a bit more. * The relaxation can begin to spread down your arms. * As the wave of relaxation gently drifts down your arms you may even be able to feel it pulsing into your hands. *

The wave of relaxation can drift down through your back and chest, spreading soothing comfort and relaxation down into your lower back. * Even your heartbeat feels more calm and regular as the relaxation gently spreads throughout your body. * The wave of relaxation can spread down through your pelvic area, helping to loosen and relax the muscles of your legs even more. * The relaxation slowly drifts down through your legs. Perhaps you can feel it pulsing slowly down into your feet, spreading the comfort down, washing the discomfort out of your body. *

As you allow yourself to drift more deeply in this calmness, the soothing relaxation can help you rest and recharge yourself. Perhaps you can imagine that you are outdoors in a perfect place, on a warm and beautiful day. Choose the most comfortable place to lie down. Feel the warmth from the sun bathing your body. As you begin to soak up the warmth you can feel your tensions and discomforts melting away. * The warmth can fill you with healing energy, and the golden-white light can help to recharge you fully and completely. You remain at peace, feeling the warmth of blood flowing freely to every cell of your body, carrying oxygen and nutrients and healing energy to bathe every cell. Each cell like a sponge can soak up the perfect amount of nutrients and energy to help heal and recharge you. You may begin to feel sensations of health, joy, and happiness burning more brightly within you, though you remain calm and comfortable. * Perhaps you can picture yourself filling with strength and energy as your body heals itself. * See yourself in a state of health and happiness, doing something active, perhaps smiling and celebrating in the sunshine. * As you practice this relaxation exercise you will be able to relax more deeply and quickly. You will be more aware of tensions and begin to develop confidence that you can rid yourself of unnecessary anxieties whenever they may develop. The effects of the relaxation will begin to carry over throughout your day.

As you become comfortable with this relaxation, your awareness and control will continue with you throughout the day. You will feel more patient with any interactions that you experience. This patience will help to create a better environment at work and allow you to be a more positive example for your coworkers. You will also find that you have more time and energy to do the things that you want to do. Remember that by taking the time to relax, you will be able to be more productive.

If you are using this exercise at bedtime you may wish to drift into a pleasant sleep, resting fully and awakening refreshed and alert. If you wish to drift off to sleep, continue breathing slowly and focus on the feelings of relaxation in your arms and legs. *

If you wish to awaken now, you can begin to do so. Let yourself gradually return to this room, feeling the bed or the chair beneath you. As you slowly awaken, bring the feelings of calmness, relaxation, health, and happiness back with you into a more fully waking state. Take a deep breath and stretch, letting the calmness return with you. Take another deep breath and stretch, allowing yourself to awaken feeling refreshed and alert, letting the relaxation and calmness continue with you.

BIBLIOGRAPHY

Garfield, Charles A., Ph.D., and Hal Zina Bennett. *Peak Performance: Mental Training Techniques of the World's Greatest Athletes*. Los Angeles: Tarcher, 1984. $13.95.

Theory of peak performance defined and described. Helpful for developing concentration and learning to use the powers of your mind to increase your performance in athletics or work.

Gherman, E. M., M.D. *Stress and the Bottom Line: A Guide to Personal Well-Being and Corporate Health*. New York: AMACOM, 1981. $16.95.

Introduction to the effects of stress on the body and on work performance. Many facts and statistics.

Goldberg, Phillip. *Executive Health: How to Recognize Health Danger Signals and Manage Stress Successfully*. New York: McGraw Hill 1978. $4.95.

Stress defined. Health strategies and programs described.

Harragan, Betty Lehan. *Games Mother Never Taught You: Corporate Gamesmanship for Women*. New York: Warner Books, 1977. $4.95.

A useful guide that has been around for ten years. It may help prepare women for business, particularly management positions.

Pelletier, Kenneth R. *Healthy People in Unhealthy Places: Stress and Fitness at Work*. New York: Dell, 1984. $8.95 (Delta paperback edition).

Very thorough examination of stress in the workplace, including the expenses in time and money of stress related ailments. Many wellness programs are described as possible models for interested corporations.

AUDIOCASSETTE TAPES

Mason, L. John. *Stress Management for Commuters* and *Ten Minute Stress Management for the Office*. 1988. Both are $11.95.

Relaxations for the commute to and from work. Ten-minute exercises for busy people to use at work.

CHAPTER SIX

Sexual Dysfunction & Stress

Introduction

THE EXPRESSION of our sexuality is not only a physical act, but an emotional one. Enjoyable sex involves both mind and body; it depends not only on what we do with our bodies, but on how we feel about what we do. If we are relaxed and comfortable with ourselves and our sexual partner, it is easier to experience sexual fulfillment than if we are tense or worried. In fact, sex therapists say that very few sexual problems are due to faulty "equipment" or difficulties with the mechanics of sex. Rather, the most common contributors to sexual dysfunction—along with poor communication skills and lack of information about sexual functioning—are feelings of inadequacy or insecurity, concern about sexual performance, or worries about other aspects of one's life, such as work or money.

Imagine yourself, for a moment, in a stressful situation. Perhaps your car has gone into a skid on a wet winter road. As you bring the car to a stop and breath a sigh of relief that nothing serious has happened, the last thing on your mind would be languishing in your lover's arms. The reason for this is physiological as well as emotional. In a moment of stress or danger, your body reacts with the fight/flight response, a series of physiological changes which prepare your body either to fight the source of danger or flee. These physiological changes counteract or interfere with sexual functioning.

During the fight/flight response, the heart beats faster and breathing becomes shallow. Blood, carrying nutrients and oxygen, surges to the brain and major muscles, enabling the person to run or fight. At the same time, blood flow to the digestive or reproductive organs is restricted, as the need to digest food or have sex is not essential for survival. Adrenaline (epinephrine) and nor-adrenaline (nor-epinephrine) are released into the bloodstream, causing the release of blood sugar which provides instant energy. But these hormones also diminish sexual excitation.

So while the fight/flight response has great survival value in truly dangerous situations, it works in direct opposition to the relaxation response, which is necessary to enhance or stimulate sexuality. Moreover, the stressful situation which triggers the fight/flight response does not have to be truly life threatening. Emotional stress triggers the fight/flight mechanism just as if real physical danger were present. Thus fear of sexual failure, fear that one's partner will expect too much, or fear of rejection by one's partner can all trigger the stress response and reduce sexual functioning. With this in mind, this chapter will present specific stress management techniques as they apply to the most common sexual dysfunction problems. In men, two forms of dysfunction—impotence and premature ejaculation—appear to be stress-related responses. Frigidity and preorgasmic condition are the female equivalents to impotence and premature ejaculation. Infertility and low sexual satisfaction are two stress-related conditions that affect both sexes.

I highly recommend a book by Alex Comfort, *The Joy of Sex*, an excellent reference guide which answers many questions about sexuality. It covers the issues in a very sensitive, adult manner without too much psychological jargon or intellectualizing.

Stress Management Recommendations for Sexual Dysfunction

IMPOTENCE

Impotence is usually defined as the inability to achieve or maintain an erection. Although an impotent man may become aroused and want to make love, he cannot. This inability will often make him feel that his masculine identity is damaged or destroyed. Impotence can be caused by poor diet, fatigue, or the effects of drugs, alcohol, or nicotine. Health problems, such as hardening of the arteries, hepatitis, diabetes, or depression, can also interfere with male potency. And sometimes impotence can be caused by external circumstances which are easily changed, such as the lack of privacy, temperature extremes, or distractions like TV or radio.

But in seventy to eighty percent of impotence cases, stress and anxiety have been proved to be the major contributing factors. Impotence is often associated with stressful life transitions, such as drastic career or family changes. Even positive life transitions such as a job promotion have been known to trigger potency problems. Fears about sexual performance, fear of rejection, or fear of failure are also common causes of impotence. In most cases, the problem can usually be corrected through relaxation, improved diet, adequate rest, and patient cooperation from the sexual partner.

Clearly, a thorough physical checkup is essential if impotence is an ongoing problem. It is important to remember, however, that most men have a problem with impotence at some time in their lives. Often it is only a temporary condition and is frequently cured by a good night's sleep.

If you are unsure whether your impotence problems are due to physical causes or emotional stress, try the Postage Stamp Exercise that follows before consulting a physician.

STAMP EXERCISE FOR STRESS-RELATED IMPOTENCE

First obtain a roll of perforated stamps from the post office. You can use either postage stamps or trading stamps with equal effectiveness. Then, for three nights in a row, just before going to sleep encircle the base of your penis with a single layer of stamps, snug but not too tight. Make sure that the perforations are not broken.

Most men experience erections while sleeping as a result of normal dreaming patterns. If an erection is achieved during sleep, in the morning the perforations between stamps will be broken. You may assume that you are capable of normal erections and that your impotence problem is emotional rather than physical in origin. Care must be taken, of course, not to thrash about while sleeping to avoid breaking the perforations in any other way. Three nights with this test should help to remove any doubts.

A more scientific version of this potency test can be administered by trained researchers using mechanical monitors. Naturally, this costs a great deal more than the price of a few stamps. Ask your physician about such a scientific test.

If you take the postage stamp test and determine that your problem is an emotional one, your next step should be to try the relaxation techniques recommended below. Be patient. Let go of high expectations. Try to keep your mind in the present; don't fantasize about the future or relive the past. If these relaxation exercises do not help you within six to eight weeks, consult a psychotherapist and/or sex therapist.

Recommended: To achieve and maintain an erection the relaxation response must be stimulated and the fight/flight response negated. Autogenic relaxation training, visualization, and desensitization exercises are the three components for an effective self-treatment program. Massage techniques can also help to establish loving physical contact without the pressure or expectation of making love. Biofeedback training and sex therapists are recommended for those needing professional help. *The Joy of Sex* and Masters and Johnson's book, *Human Sexual Inadequacy*, are recommended reading for more information.

PREMATURE EJACULATION

Men suffering from this complaint cannot voluntarily control their ejaculatory reflex. Once they become sexually aroused, they reach orgasm too quickly to afford their partners or themselves much pleasure. Some men ejaculate after several minutes of foreplay, others immediately upon penetration of the vagina. Different explanations for this behavior exist, ranging from neurosis, to hostility between the partners, to excessive sensitivity of the penis. In any case, stress, excitement, and anxiety usually are considered to be the major factors in its occurrence, and they can be resolved. Moreover, the earlier in life that this problem is tackled, the more easily the premature ejaculation habit is broken.

Many men who suffer from this complaint employ a commonsense technique to deal with it. They shift their attention to nonsexual thoughts during intercourse and thereby delay intense erotic arousal. Once aroused, however, they still cannot control their ejaculations and often feel sexually inadequate and guilty about not satisfying their partners.

Recommended: A formula described by Alex Comfort in *The Joy of Sex* is said to be very effective in dealing with this problem. Basically, it requires the man to masturbate a short time before intercourse. Either the man can masturbate himself or his partner can do it for him. This eliminates the overeager excitement aspect of the problem. It works well for young men who have no difficulty achieving and maintaining another erection a short time after masturbating. It is less effective for older men.

Comfort also recommends holding sexual sessions with a partner in which it is agreed beforehand that intercourse will not take place. Only practice in achieving and maintaining an erection is permitted.

For older men, the "start and stop" technique first developed by James Semans as long ago as 1956 has a very high success rate in dealing with this problem. Semans believed that the distinguishing feature of premature ejaculation is the rapidity of the orgasm reflex. His treatment goal was to prolong the reflex. To accomplish this, the man's sexual partner is directed to stimulate the man's penis until he feels he is just about to have an orgasm. At that point, the man must signal his partner to stop. When he feels that he has recaptured control, they begin again, until the sensations that signal ejaculation are felt and again he signals her to stop. The couple is instructed to practice this "start and stop" method for several hours per session, for several weeks until the man learns to tolerate stimulation for longer and longer periods of time. This method has improved the sex lives of thousands of men without the intervention of any other techniques.

Visualizations, desensitizations, and relaxation techniques are all helpful for premature ejaculation problems. During these exercises, visualize yourself remaining calm and relaxed, enjoying sex with a prolonged erection, until mutual climax occurs. If all else fails, see a sex therapist. Very few men who have actively tried to change their sexual patterns continue to suffer from premature ejaculation.

FRIGIDITY

Frigidity in women is a term that can mean (1) the complete absence of sexual feelings, (2) the inability to reach orgasm, or (3) a combination of both. Emotional, psychological, and physical issues may contribute to this condition. Consequently, care must be taken to tailor any treatment plan to the individual woman's needs.

Hormonal imbalances and pelvic inflammation or pain are well-known causes of this dysfunction. Some common psychological and emotional reasons for its occurrence include: fear of losing control, fear of rejection or abandonment, and/or the belief that "nice" girls don't enjoy sex. Underlying anxiety, such as financial worry, job insecurities, or family problems may be involved as well. Regardless of the cause or causes, if a woman considers sex to be an ordeal, then a great deal of stress is generated, and, of course, stress only intensifies the already unhappy situation.

A relaxed, sensuous atmosphere that allows the natural unfolding of sexual responses to develop is essential in helping nonresponsive women. To create such an atmosphere the woman and her partner must learn to communicate openly and honestly about their sexual desires and fears.

Masters and Johnson developed a technique they called the "sensate focus" for treating frigidity. This consists of having the couple forego intercourse and orgasm completely for several sessions. At first, they are only permitted to caress and fondle each other's body and to discuss what they enjoy and what they don't. In later sessions they add light, teasing genital play, concentrating on clitoral stimulation, with the woman guiding the man's actions verbally and nonverbally. Only when manual genital stimulation produces a definite increase in the woman's sexual responsiveness do they begin experimenting with sexual intercourse.

Often these sessions evoke painful feelings and great resistances which must be discussed and resolved before sexual activity resumes. Obviously, the outcome of this treatment depends on the depth and commitment of the couple's relationship. If the partners are patient and communicate honestly, the great majority of women in such relationships learn to enjoy sex and to reach orgasm.

Recommended: A complete and thorough physical checkup is essential. Relaxation exercises combined with visualizations of sexual enjoyment and satisfaction are helpful, as are desensitization exercises. Mutual massage helps to create a comfortable, relaxed, and sensuous environment. You may also wish to share massages without the expectation of sexual encounter. Many sex therapists believe that self-stimulation and masturbation are the best ways to begin to experience sexual pleasure. What is learned in self-exploration can be communicated to one's partner. The chapter on frigidity in *The Joy of Sex* is excellent for additional information and so is Masters and Johnson's *Human Sexual Inadequacy*.

PREORGASMIC CONDITION

The most common sexual complaint that women relate is difficulty in reaching orgasm. Such women are called preorgasmic. In most cases, this difficulty can be traced to stress, trauma, or lack of information about the location and sensitivity of a woman's clitoris. If the man is sexually sophisticated, and the couple's communications are open, honest, and caring, then trauma and stress may be the source of the problem. If this is the case, therapy may be helpful. It need not be long-term therapy, as the satisfactory resolution to this problem can occur within weeks or months. But if underlying stress is the major cause of the problem, it is essential to deal effectively with the issues that generate the stress. Worry—about money, rejection, fear of pregnancy, AIDS, or whatever—is not conducive to the relaxed frame of mind necessary to "let yourself go."

Recommended: Open, honest communication is essential. Women are slower than men to become sexually aroused and their arousal signs are much less obvious. Often a woman has been culturally conditioned to put her partner's needs ahead of her own. She may have to learn how to express her own needs. Her partner may have to learn how to accept her expression of her needs as nonthreatening, nonaggressive behavior.

As with prematurely-ejaculating men, self-exploration and masturbation can help a woman find ways to please herself, ways she can then communicate to her partner. Vibrators have been used by some couples to good effect. Mutual massage can help create a relaxed, sensuous atmosphere. You can agree before a massage session not to have intercourse in order to reduce feelings of pressure.

Relaxation is vital to a sensuous, pleasing sexual experience. Autogenic training is an excellent place to start, as it helps you to increase the blood flow to your extremities, warming and relaxing you . When you can relax, trust, and enjoy yourself and your partner, you can truly "let go" and appreciate the pleasures of your own sexuality.

I recommend *Messages: The Communication Book* (see bibliography) for further information on communicating well with your sexual partner. Also, *The Joy of Sex*, as previously noted, has excellent information for preorgasmic women.

DYSMENORRHEA

Dysmenorrhea is the medical term for any unpleasant symptoms that women experience shortly before or at the onset of their monthly periods. Two distinct sets of symptoms are recognized: spasmodic and congestive.

Spasmodic period pain is experienced as cramps in the lower abdomen and genital area and is most often diagnosed in young women. A growing body of evidence suggests that spasmodic dysmenorrhea disappears after a woman has had a child. Why this is so is not clearly understood, but it may be related to the stretching and relaxation of the uterine muscles that occur in childbirth.

Congestive period pain occurs just before a woman's period begins and takes the form of bloating and aching in the abdomen and genitals. It may be accompanied by nausea, fatigue, irritability, and other unpleasant symptoms.

It is important to see a gynecologist if dysmenorrhea is severe and persistent, as the symptoms may indicate organic malformation. Remember, though, that stress will exacerbate any or all of these symptoms, and, in some cases, it may be the primary cause. Stress management techniques can lessen and sometimes eliminate the symptoms of dysmenorrhea.

It is best to begin a stress management program before the onset of your period. Expect several menstrual cycles to pass before you experience the full benefit of your stress reduction program.

Recommended: Autogenic training or indirect relaxation exercises can help relax the muscles in the abdomen and pelvic areas. Combine these relaxations with visualizations of blood flowing to the area to help in the healing and flushing process and reduce cramping. Desensitization exercises which focus on overcoming abdominal pain can also be combined with the relaxations. Massage sometimes has a beneficial effect. Many women receive great comfort from the age-old remedy of heat applications. Use a heating pad or a hot-water bottle to reduce muscle spasms. Lifestyle changes can also help ease the symptoms of dysmenorrhea. Increasing physical exercise, especially stretching exercises for the pelvic area; reducing or eliminating caffeine consumption and cigarettes; eating a well-balanced diet and increasing your intake of calcium, vitamins B and C, and trace minerals; and taking the time to rest and relax are all recommended.

INFERTILITY

Infertility—the inability to conceive a child—can be a traumatic event for people who truly desire children. It is widely accepted that stress is a very important factor in human fertility. Stress has been known to cause spontaneous abortions and the absence of stress promotes both conception and healthy pregnancies. The physiological and/or chemical problems creating infertility may be the result of stress factors at work either in the male or female body. Before resorting to expensive fertility tests, a couple unable to conceive should give careful consideration to the possible ways in which stress may be contributing to this problem. It is surprisingly common that an "infertile" couple will conceive after they released the pressure for conception by adopting a child.

The fight/flight response discussed earlier in this chapter can significantly affect fertility. The hormone activity and blood flow patterns elicited by the stress response create an inhospitable atmosphere for successful fertilization. In the woman, the stress response causes blood flow to the uterus and ovaries to be decreased, so that blood can be rushed to the muscles and brain in preparation for fighting or fleeing the source of danger. This makes conception less likely. Additionally, the hormones released by the stress response may make it more difficult for the sperm to successfully reach the egg, or may irritate the unfertilized egg, making it less susceptible to fertilization.

In the man, stress may lower the quantity and quality of sperm production, because of either blood flow patterns or hormone changes. Also, too much physical stress can create higher temperatures in the scrotum, a condition which contributes to male infertility. To develop properly, sperm need to be in an environment which has a temperature lower than normal body temperature. Relaxation and cool, unconstricting garments may be helpful for healthy sperm development.

In both men and women, diet, smoking, alcohol consumption, and certain drugs and medications may be contributing factors to infertility.

Recommended: Relaxation exercises, such as indirect relaxation or autogenic training, combined with visualizations can be helpful for infertility problems. You can visualize the ideal amount of blood and nutrition flowing easily to the sexual organs, creating a receptive environment for conception and for the healthy development of the embryo. For other appropriate visualizations, read the chapter in this book on prenatal development or consult with a knowledgeable health care provider.

LOW SEXUAL SATISFACTION

Low sexual satisfaction may appear to be the least serious of the sexual dysfunctions discussed here, but unsatisfying sexual relations can create such misery and unhappiness they can spoil every aspect of an otherwise healthy, happy relationship. Both men and women are affected by it, and most people experience it at some time in their lives.

Low sexual satisfaction can result from drug and alcohol abuse, depression, anxiety, lack of self-esteem, and even extreme fatigue. Ignorance about human sexual response and poor communication can also result in low sexual satisfaction. Because stress can contribute to all of the above problems, stress management is helpful in their prevention and treatment. Stress can obscure sensations of pleasure, beauty, and happiness in a haze of distractions; relaxation can enhance one's sensual response to another person and to the world.

Recommended: Any of the stress management techniques which you feel comfortable with, such as indirect relaxation or progressive relaxation, combined with visualizations of sexual pleasure and fulfillment are of benefit. I recommend reading *The Joy of Sex* and Masters and Johnson's book, *Human Sexual Inadequacy*, to add to your understanding of sexuality and perhaps add diversity to your sexual experiences and open new doors to further pleasure. It is also important to take care of yourself by eating well, exercising, and getting enough rest.

Case Study #1

Jane came to see me for two reasons. She had been trying to conceive for some time without success, and she had suffered painful dysmenorrhea since she had left home to attend college. At the time she made an appointment with me she was in her late twenties, attractive, in good health, and had always taken good care of herself.

Her career in real estate, although moderately stressful, provided her with many satisfactions. Her personal life, after much struggle, had blossomed and she had recently begun a happy marriage and wanted to begin a family.

She was convinced after consultations with many doctors that not much could be done for her dysmenorrhea, and that her infertility problem could only be helped with expensive laboratory techniques or fertility drugs. She did not want to try fertility drugs, except as a last resort, because she had known a woman who had used them and had experienced many difficulties and complications because of their use. Opting for a more conservative treatment, Jane had been referred to me for biofeedback and stress management training.

As we discussed her history, Jane began to draw the connections be-

tween her major life changes and her stress-related complaints. Leaving home to attend college had been the biggest change in her young adult life, and it was only then that she had begun to experience painful menses. Her marriage, although happy, had followed many unsuccessful relationships during which her level of sexual desire had diminished.

She had always given her sexuality lower priority than her career or taking care of herself in other ways, but she reported that her sexual relations with her husband were "easy, comfortable, and fairly satisfying."

We discussed the effect of stress on sexuality, and the connections made a lot of sense to her. I explained that when we are tense, on an unconscious level our body is triggering the stress response in the autonomic nervous system, which in turn constricts blood flow into the abdomen, sexual organs, and the extremities. As she absorbed this information, her anxiety level decreased. She began a program of autogenic training combined with visualizations designed to increase the blood flow to the abdomen and increase the warmth and calmness of the sexual organs. She also maintained her balanced diet, continued to walk, bike, or swim three to four times a week, and got a good night's sleep every night.

After she became comfortable with the autogenic relaxation, I introduced her to biofeedback temperature training. By taping a fish tank thermometer to the outside of the second joint of her index finger, or to the ball of the foot at the base of the big toe, she could measure the temperature of her hands and feet at the beginning and end of the relaxation. This gave her a chance to tangibly see how the autogenic exercise increased the blood flow to, and thus the temperature of, her extremities. The increased blood flow to the extremities was a signal that she was learning to "let go" of unconscious stress.

Within two months of beginning the autogenic training, Jane found her periods became much less painful. She also began experiencing heightened levels of sexual pleasure. Her increased control of stress helped her to communicate more effectively with Phil, and she felt their relationship grew even stronger. As she learned to "let go" of tension, she also learned to let go in other areas of her life. She put aside her hopes of conceiving and redevoted herself to her career.

Shortly thereafter she became pregnant. It is not unusual to find that when a woman stops trying to get pregnant, she more easily becomes pregnant, because the stress involved in "trying" releases hormones which create a less than ideal environment for fertility. Jane was delighted to be pregnant, and felt that stress control techniques would continue to be of use to her as she and her husband raised their child.

Case Study #2

Bob came to me because of a stress-related impotence problem. His despair over his impotence had been so great that he had been considering a penile implant, but his doctor referred him to me for stress management training.

Bob is a healthy man in his midthirties. He enjoys his work as a sales representative for an electronics firm except when job-related travel keeps him away too long from his wife and two young sons.

In our first discussions, he reported that he had suffered from premature ejaculation during his early sexual encounters as a young man. Since he had settled down with his wife, premature ejaculation had not been a problem until after the birth of their first son. With his wife's patience and understanding they had worked through the difficulty reasonably well.

At the time their second son was born, however, Bob was also experiencing a great deal of work-related stress. His firm was nearly absorbed by a much larger one in a corporate takeover bid, and he felt great anxiety during the negotiations. He also began to suffer from low energy at that time.

Between the stresses of work and the new baby, Bob's sexual drive became very erratic, going from nonexistent to insatiable and back to nonexistent. A short time later, he began to experience impotence and consulted his doctor, who sent him to me.

I immediately introduced him to autogenic training to achieve a deep relaxation and lessen his anxieties. I made a twenty-minute tape for him which I suggested he listen to twice a day. After about six weeks of practice he began to feel the results of the relaxation, and was able to achieve a deeply relaxed state. At this time I added a desensitization exercise which he could use once he was fully relaxed from the autogenic suggestions. The desensitization exercise was designed to help him overcome his impotence by taking the emotional charge off his sexual performance. As we talked and worked together, Bob began to see the connections between the stresses of work and parenting and his impotence, and this also helped him to feel less anxious and concerned that there was something wrong with him.

Bob enlisted the support and understanding of his wife, too. They learned to play light, teasing games with each other without expecting or anticipating sexual intercourse to follow. Once they removed the performance pressure, they found their sexual charge was rekindled, and normal sexual intercourse became possible again.

Bob continued studying stress management techniques for some time until his normal energy levels were restored. He was delighted to find that his improvement in well-being meant he had greater energy at work, too, and felt that his work performance and satisfaction improved along with his sex life.

Relaxation Exercises for Sexual Dysfunction

BREATHING DESENSITIZATION

When the body begins to manifest the stress response, many systems are affected. The system that is easiest to consciously control and relax is the respiratory system. Combining breathing exercises which slow and deepen your breath with desensitization can be particularly helpful for problems of impotence, premature ejaculation, frigidity, low sexual satisfaction, preorgasmic condition, or "performance anxiety."

Before starting this exercise, remember that desensitization requires some practice. You may need to repeat this exercise many times before you develop the control and confidence you would like.

To begin, make a list of the concerns which most often get in the way of your sexual satisfaction. Consider any issue which may create anxiety for you, whether it is job pressure or child-care concerns, or whether it is more directly related to your sexuality, such as fear of rejection or fear of "letting go." Once you have identified the sources of your anxiety to the best of your ability, check to see if you can make any adjustments in your life to eliminate some of these anxieties. Can you reduce your work load? Can you arrange for more child care? If you are able to change any of the anxiety-producing situations, you may find that your sexual tensions are reduced. If some of the distractions are in areas over which you feel little control, however, you can still change your attitude or response to the problem. You may not be able to change a stressful situation which occurred in your childhood, but you *can* learn to change your response to the feelings which that experience raises.

As you think about the problem areas which interfere with your sexual pleasure, you may experience some uncomfortable feelings about past activities or relationships or about future expectations. By confronting these discomforts in a gradual, gentle way, they can be overcome.

Select one of your lesser fears or anxieties to start with. Make a list of all the uncomfortable aspects of this situation. For example, if you have a fear of being sexually unattractive to your partner because you are several pounds overweight, list all of the feelings which this fear elicits. Are you concerned that your partner will compare you to a former lover? Are you comparing yourself to a time when you were younger and slimmer? Are you worried that your lover will not be as excited as you would like him/her to be? Do you imagine that he/she will not call you again? Start from the beginning and work through all of the mental fears that you may have. Do you notice that as you do this you start to feel physically uncomfortable? If you are feeling an unpleasant response, where in your body is it? How does it feel? Is your stomach upset, your heart racing, your jaw tight? Has your breath quickened? Are you sweating? Does your back hurt?

Now imagine that you will encounter this uncomfortable situation four months in the future. Does it still make you feel physically uncomfortable? If not, imagine that the situation will occur in three months, or two, or two weeks. Find the point at which your body's fear response is triggered. This will be the starting place for your desensitization. After you have relaxed with the breathing exercise which follows, you will begin your desensitization by mentally placing yourself at the point where you first feel anxious and then imagining yourself moving through all of the stressful feelings until you successfully and happily complete the activity which had previously seemed uncomfortable.

To begin the breathing exercise, find a place where you feel safe and comfortable and will not be disturbed. (You can substitute the autogenic relaxation in this chapter for the breathing exercise if you find it more relaxing.) Sit or lie back comfortably. Let your arms and legs remain uncrossed. Check your shoulders, neck, and jaw for tension. Take a breath and begin to let go of any unwanted thoughts or tensions. Do not try to relax too quickly; in fact, do not try to relax at all. Just let go of tensions slowly and easily. When you are ready to begin, take three deep slow breaths, pausing after you inhale, then slowly exhaling. Imagine that as you exhale, your warm breath releases unwanted tension. After the first three breaths, continue breathing slowly and naturally. Feel yourself drifting deeper into a dreamlike state of comfort and control . . . Now you are going to count backward from twenty down to one. As you slowly count backward, you can imagine yourself safely stepping down into a peaceful calmness. As you count backward, you can feel your body slowing down and relaxing even further . . . At twenty you take a step down deeper into relaxation . . . At nineteen you can begin to feel yourself letting go of stress . . . At eighteen you drift deeper into this dreamlike state of comfort and you can feel your arms starting to relax better . . . Take a deep slow breath and count the number seventeen . . . As you breathe slowly and gently you can feel yourself letting go of stress and tensions . . . Your legs can relax even further as the muscles become more loose and comfortable . . . As you drift down to sixteen your breathing is calm and regular . . . You can feel yourself taking another step deeper into this dreamlike quiet and calm . . . As you slowly move down to fifteen, perhaps you can feel your shoulders relaxing further, dropping down so that your head is totally supported by the pillow or chair . . . As the muscles of your back start to loosen and soften with relaxation, you can take another deep breath . . . As you slowly exhale count the number fourteen and feel yourself drifting deeper into the dreamlike calmness . . . Counting backward to thirteen, you continue to breath slowly, feeling your body slowly ease into a comforting rhythm . . . Your heartbeat is calm and regular . . . Your mind is becoming more calm and clear . . . As you drift down another level, you count the number twelve, letting go . . . Pleasantly you drift down to the number eleven, breathing very slowly and comfortably . . . You begin to feel the muscles of your head and face starting to relax . . . Counting down to ten you are starting to feel the effects of relaxation and comfort. Your arms and legs may feel heavy and relaxed . . . As you drift down to nine your jaw relaxes even futher . . . Breathing slowly and gently you can feel the muscles around your eyes relaxing . . . Drifting down to eight you can feel the control of deep relaxation beginning as you feel yourself sinking into whatever you are sitting or lying upon . . . As you count the number seven you can drift more deeply into the complete calmness and comfort . . . You breathe very slowly and easily, letting go even further with every slow, gentle breath . . . As you drift down to six, you can feel your forehead becoming calm and smooth . . . You can sink as deeply as you want into the restful comfort . . . counting down another step, you take a deep breath and see the number five . . . As you drift in this pleasant relaxation, remember that you can enjoy this relaxation whenever you wish by taking the time to relax . . . By breathing slowly you can relax anytime . . . You can drift down to four, letting your mind become calm and still . . . Your body relaxes and rests peacefully as you drift down another level to the number three . . . You can remain at this level of calmness or go even deeper as you continue to breathe slowly . . . At two you are very relaxed and comfortable . . . You can control tension by practicing this relaxation regularly . . . By breathing slowly you can become calm and comfortable . . . As you drift deeper into this dreamlike calmness you count the number one . . . Feel the peaceful control of deep relaxation . . . Continue breathing slowly and evenly as you drift . . .

Now that you are relaxed, you can remain relaxed as you see yourself slowly and easily moving through the situations which have previously made you uncomfortable . . . Imagine yourself moving through each step of the stressful situation, from the moment when you first feel discomfort until you

have successfully and happily completed the encounter . . . You remain relaxed, knowing that the encounter will be pleasant and satisfying . . .
Breathe slowly . . . If you start to become tense, stop and relax until you can
picture yourself remaining calm . . . See yourself enjoying yourself and yet
comfortable . . . Remember to go slowly and to practice this many times so
you can maintain your deep relaxation . . . Stay in this relaxed state until you
have completed the desensitization exercise.

If you are using this exercise at bedtime you may wish to drift off to
sleep . . . If you are going to sleep continue breathing slowly . . . Rest well
and when you awaken you will be refreshed and alert.

If you wish to awaken now, then you can begin to do so . . . See yourself
returning to this room, gently awakening to feel refreshed and alert . . . Feel
the chair or the bed beneath you, and slowly awaken, bringing the feelings of
relaxation, calmness, and comfort back with you . . . You may wish to take a
deep breath and stretch, allowing yourself to awaken fully and completely
. . . You may want to take another deep breath and stretch, becoming wide
awake.

Be gentle with yourself as you practice this breathing/desensitization
exercise. Do not expect too much, and do not push yourself through your list
of anxieties, but take them one at a time. Practice one situation over and over
until you can move through it calmly and peacefully before you take on another.

For certain anxiety-producing situations, you may want to add to the
mental desensitization a slow, well-planned, real-life desensitization. This
requires actually working through your fear with your partner. Good communication skills, trust, and patience are essential, and you may want to en-
list the help of a skilled psychotherapist or counselor.

MASSAGE

Massage can help you to relax and can help build trust and communication
between you and your partner. For this reason massage can be very helpful in
overcoming the performance anxiety that often causes or intensifies certain
sexual dysfunctions such as impotence, premature ejaculation, frigidity, or
preorgasmic condition. Massage can be used to enhance lovemaking or it can
be nonsexual. An agreement should be made before the massage as to which
it will be, so the partners know what to expect. Sometimes one or both of the
partners would like to enjoy a relaxing massage without feeling pressure to
have sex, and this should be respected.

Massage can be light and sensual. This type of caress can be used as sexual foreplay. Massage can also be more firm, working to relax various muscles. Because people benefit differently from the various strokes and pressures, communication between the massager and the receiver is vital. Do not expect your partner to know exactly how and where to massage. Learn to communicate your needs and desires. The massager can ask, "Is this pressure ok? How does this feel?" The receiver should feel free to say, "That feels great" or "That is uncomfortable."

The following instructions are for a full body massage for relaxation. The complete massage can take an hour or longer, so it is important to find a time when you will not be interrupted. You can also plan to do only part of the body at one session.

Make sure the temperature of the massage room is warm and comfortable, but not too warm for the person giving the massage. A massage table is not essential, but it does provide more comfort for the massager and easier access to the various muscles of the body. If the massage is given on the floor or bed, the comfort of the massager may determine the length of the massage. Fifteen or twenty minutes on one's knees may be a necessary limit.

If you are using oil for the massage you may want to spread a sheet on the floor, bed, or massage table. You can create your own lubricant by adding some vegetable oil to your favorite skin lotion. A ratio of 1:10, oil to lotion, will provide a frictionless massage as the oil stays on the surface and the lotion sinks into the skin.

When giving a massage keep in mind that the large muscles, such as the quads-front upper legs, hamstrings-rear upper legs, and calves respond well to a kneading action. Small muscles or areas such as the neck and lower back may need only thumb pressure. I recommend that you read the books on massage recommended at the end of this chapter for fuller instructions on the various techniques and styles of massage that can be used. Employing a variety of techniques can keep the massage experience interesting and fresh.

Hands or feet: A good place to start a massage is with the hands or feet. Assume a comfortable position. Take several deep slow breaths to ground your energy and focus on the massage. Lay your hands gently on the receiver's body for a moment to make the initial contact. Then firmly, yet with gentle loving respect, rub the palm of the hand or the sole of the foot. If the sole of the foot is too ticklish for some people, begin stroking the heel or the top of the foot, and save the sole of the foot until the person is more relaxed. Work down every finger or toe, rubbing with your fingers and thumbs as firmly as the recipient is comfortable with. The ankles, wrists, and back of the hand also need to be relaxed. Pulling strokes can work better than deep circular motions on these areas, but check with the recipient to see what works best. Take your time. The slow gentle strokes will be relaxing and comforting. Both partners can breathe slowly while the massage is being given to aid the relaxation and to help release any anxieties caused by the intimate touching. Breathe . . .

Back and shoulders: Like the hands and feet, the back and shoulders are safe, nonsexual places to focus in the first part of a massage. The person receiving the massage can begin by lying face down, arms at her sides or under her head, however she is most comfortable. Oil or lotion will help to reduce friction and to increase the long, comfortable strokes of this therapeutic massage.

The massager can use his fingers to firmly trace around the bones and down the full length of various muscles, helping the receiver to relax and stretch these muscles. You may find it useful to look at a simple anatomy book which shows the positions of the muscles so that you know the direction in which they run. You can also find simple charts or diagrams which show basic front and rear views of the body's musculature. Start with a light stroke, gradually working more deeply, rather than starting with a strong stroke. If your partner wants a deeper massage than you can give, repeating a firm stroke may be a good substitute for strength.

After working the shoulders and around the shoulder blades, you can move to the muscles along the spine and the lower back. Work along both sides of the spine, moving two to three inches out from the midpoint. Either you can use a rubbing stroke with your full hand or you can apply circular pressure around each vertebrae with your fingertips, a technique borrowed from acupressure and shiatsu. Gentle repetition will work wonders.

Slowly work down into the lower back. If this region is tender, apply pressure toward the legs rather than down into the back. Some firmness will help the muscles to relax, but you can use a press and release stroke if the lower back can't tolerate too much pressure.

If you want to massage only the neck and upper shoulders, the receiver can lie on her back. (A massage table comes in very handy here, as it makes these areas more accessible.) You can cradle the receiver's head in one hand and rub the neck, shoulder, or head with the other hand. This should be done slowly, with great respect. Massage can help develop trust and a strong connection between two people when it is respectful and caring. Breathe . . .

Legs and buttocks: After the back is relaxed, while the receiver is still lying on her stomach, you can move on to a massage of the legs and buttocks. Move down the back of the upper legs and down the lower legs with a firm, even stroke. If you started with the back rather than the hands or feet, you can now massage the feet, using the suggestions given above. Trace the bones and muscles around the ankles as well, as tension is often stored in these joints. You can work down the legs and then back up to the buttocks. If you are giving a nonsexual massage, use a firm stroke into the backs of the upper legs and buttocks. Some people with sexual anxieties often hold great amounts of tension in the muscles of the legs and buttocks, so respect and gentle patience may be needed.

Breathe . . .

Arms: After completing the back and legs, the receiver can turn over onto her back. The arms and hands, if not done previously, can be massaged. You can lift and stretch the arms as well as knead the muscles. Be sure to communicate with your partner about what stroke, what movement, and what amount of pressure works best. This is an excellent opportunity to build trust.

Breathe . . .

Chest and stomach: If the receiver is comfortable having the chest and stomach massaged, these parts of the body can be worked on next. Again, firm and respectful massage strokes are best used unless a sensual massage has been planned.

Breathe . . .

Head and face: Finally, you can massage the head and face. With slow, circular strokes the forehead and muscles of the eyebrows can be massaged. The jaw and cheekbones can be relaxed with easy, firm strokes tracing the bones and muscles. The head can be gently cradled between both hands and then slowly lifted and rocked from side to side. You can gently pull the head while holding it to help the neck relax futher. Be careful not to pull too hard. Be gentle!

The receiver should be fully relaxed by now, perhaps even asleep. Let her drift in this state of relaxation until she is ready to get up. Make sure she is warm.

Practice with both giving and receiving massage can help develop trust and openness between partners. These positive effects will spill over into intimate sexual experiences. Our needs for physical contact, intimacy, and support are just as important as the need for release of sexual tension. Massage can enhance the enjoyment and loving connection between partners, whether or not it is combined with a sexual experience.

In fairness, it should also be said that massage is not for everyone. If one partner is not enthusiastic about massage, you may want to discuss your feelings with each other and see if a compromise can be reached. Keep in mind that it does not mean that your partner does not love you if he/she does not want to participate in this experience.

In addition to the massage techniques presented here, other types of massage include Swedish, Esalen, acupressure, shiatsu, and reflexology (foot massage). Other forms of massage are coming into recognition as well. If you wish to gather further information, check your local bookstore or library. Many excellent books are available on this subject. Massage classes are also offered in most areas of the country for individuals or couples who wish to have firsthand instruction.

AUTOGENIC RELAXATION FOR SEXUAL DYSFUNCTION

The autogenic organ specific phrases used in this exercise help counter the stress response by inducing relaxation. With practice, repetition of the relaxation commands in this exercise will enable you to reverse any habitual reaction to stress that has interfered with your sexual satisfaction. As you become more aware of how tension affects your body, you will be able to interrupt the stress response and allow your body to feel comfort and pleasure.

Read this exercise slowly (about half normal speaking speed). Pause at each (*). Do not be concerned by mispronunciations or verbal slips. Continue in a calm, even voice.

Find a quiet location where you will not be disturbed. Allow about twenty minutes for this exercise. Sit or lie back comfortably, allowing your arms and legs to remain uncrossed if possible. Let your head be supported and let your shoulders drop into a comfortable position. Check the muscles of your head and face. Let your forehead become calm and smooth. Allow the muscles around your eyes to loosen. Check the muscles of the mouth and jaw to make sure they are relaxed. Finally, allow your eyes to remain closed, remembering that you can open them whenever you need to use them.

Before we begin the relaxation, remember not to try to relax too quickly. In fact, do not try to relax at all. Without any effort you can allow yourself to relax by pleasantly letting go of tensions and discomforts, and then letting yourself drift deeper into a peaceful calmness. To begin the relaxation, take three deep breaths, pausing after you inhale, and then exhaling fully and completely. You might imagine that you release tensions and dis-

comforts as you exhale by must breathing them away. *   After you have finished these first three breaths, continue breathing slowly and naturally, relaxing more deeply with each slow exhale.

Repeat these phrases to yourself, exactly as they are written from this exercise, and try to feel your body responding to the commands. If you need to repeat the phrases more than three times to begin to feel results, then continue the repetitions a few additional times.

Repeat this mood phrase to yourself three times: "I am at peace with myself and fully relaxed." Continue breathing slowly and gently.

Begin to feel the muscles of your arms relax as you say, "My right arm is heavy * . . . My right arm is heavy * . . . My right arm is heavy * . . ." Repeat this phrase slowly until you begin to feel the heaviness spreading through your arm. Now turn your awareness to your left arm as you breathe slowly and say to yourself, "My left arm is heavy * . . . My left arm is heavy * . . . My left arm is heavy * . . ." Try to feel the heaviness starting in your arms or feel free to continue slowly repeating this phrase a few more times. Now proceed to your legs. Let them begin to relax as you breathe slowly. Feel the heaviness and relaxation starting in your legs as you slowly repeat, "My right leg is heavy * . . . My right leg is heavy * . . . My right leg is heavy * . . ." You can repeat this several more times if you need to, until you begin to feel the relaxation and the heaviness. Now focus on the left leg and feel it beginning to relax as you say, "My left leg is heavy * . . . My left leg is heavy * . . . My left leg is heavy * . . ." Repeat if needed. With practice you will feel the heaviness more quickly and easily. Now turn your attention to your neck and shoulders. Let them sink into a more comfortable position and let the muscles relax as you breathe gently and say, "My neck and shoulders are heavy * . . . My neck and shoulders are heavy * . . . My neck and shoulders are heavy * . . ." Repeat if needed. Take a deep slow breath and feel the heaviness and relaxation as you begin to sink back into whatever you are sitting or lying upon.

Perhaps you can feel the blood beginning to flow more easily down into your hands or your feet as the blood vessels begin to dilate, as the smooth muscles in the walls of the arteries begin to relax. Focus on the feelings of warmth, or a pulse, or perhaps a tingling feeling in your right hand as you say, "My right arm is warm * . . . My right arm is warm * . . . My right arm is warm * . . ." Repeat this slowly several more times until you begin to feel the warmth or pulse. Heaviness is generally easier for most people to feel than warmth, but with continued practice you can begin to control the blood flow. Now turn your attention to your left arm and say to yourself, "My left arm is warm * . . . My left arm is warm * . . . My left arm is warm *

. . ." Repeat if needed. Perhaps you can start to feel the warmth in your arms, and you may feel the blood flowing freely through your entire body. As you breathe slowly and gently, turn your awareness to your legs and say to yourself, "My right leg is warm * . . . My right leg is warm * . . . My right leg is warm * . . ." Repeat several more times to help develop this skill. Move your attention to your left leg and say, "My left leg is warm * . . . My left leg is warm * . . . My left leg is warm * . . ." Repeat if needed. Feel the heaviness and warmth in your arms and your legs as you breathe slowly and gently. Now turn your awareness to your neck and shoulders, and say, "My neck and shoulders are warm * . . . My neck and shoulders are warm * . . . My neck and shoulders are warm * . . ." Repeat if needed. Breathe slowly as you drift for a few moments, feeling the heaviness and warmth spreading pleasantly about your body.

Slow and calm your heart by slowly repeating to yourself, "My heartbeat is calm and regular * . . . My heartbeat is calm and regular * . . . My heartbeat is calm and regular * . . ." Repeat if needed. If you experience any discomfort with this phrase then change to the phrase, "I feel calm * . . . I feel calm * . . . I feel calm * . . ." As you breathe slowly, begin to feel the peace and relaxation spreading to every part of your body.

To slow your breathing say to yourself as you breathe into your diaphragm, "My breathing is calm and regular * . . . My breathing is calm and regular * . . . My breathing is calm and regular * . . ." Repeat if needed.

Become aware of the relaxation starting in your stomach region. As you breathe slowly say, "My abdomen is warm and calm * . . . My abdomen is warm and calm * . . . My abdomen is warm and calm * . . ." Repeat if needed. If you have any serious abdominal problems, are diabetic, or are in the last trimester of pregnancy, change this phrase to "I am calm and relaxed * . . . I am calm and relaxed * . . . I am calm and relaxed * . . ." Feel the sensations of warmth and relaxation beginning to spread through your abdomen into your sexual organs. As you breathe slowly and gently you can remain calm and comfortable as you encourage even more warmth from increased blood flow. Repeat, "My genitals are warm and comfortable * . . . My genitals are warm and comfortable * . . . My genitals are warm and comfortable * . . ." With practice you feel an increase of blood into the reproductive organs. As you remain calm you can begin developing a sense of confidence and relaxation, gaining greater control over your sexuality.

Move on to your forehead and let the muscles of your head and face relax as you say, "My forehead is cool and calm * . . . My forehead is cool and calm * . . . My forehead is cool and calm * . . ." As you breathe slowly, feel the muscles around your eyes, mouth, and jaw loosen and then relax.

Let yourself drift pleasantly in this calmness. As you breathe gently, perhaps you can feel the heaviness in your arms and legs as the muscles relax. * Perhaps you can begin to feel the warmth or pulse of blood flowing more easily down into your hands and perhaps even your feet, like sunshine or a bath gently warming you. Some people feel the warming as if it were a tingling sensation spreading blood more easily into the extremities. * As you enjoy the relaxation you can feel that your heartbeat is calm and regular. *

With practice, you can feel the relaxation more easily and quickly. The warmth of blood flowing into your hands and feet gradually grows easier to control, until you will be able to consistently warm your hands to 93 degrees and your feet to 90 degrees. The relaxation will then carry over with you throughout your day. You will be able to develop the control to see yourself remaining calm and comfortable, enjoying your sexuality, letting it be as pleasurable as you may wish.

At the end of this relaxation exercise, awaken yourself slowly. Feel the bed or chair beneath you and say, "I am refreshed and completely alert * . . . I am refreshed and completely alert * . . . I am refreshed and completely alert * . . . I am refreshed and completely alert * . . ." Then take a deep breath and stretch, allowing yourself to wake fully, and let the relaxation carry over with you into a fully waking state. You may wish to another deep breath and stretch, letting the relaxation return with you.

INDIRECT RELAXATION FOR SEXUAL DYSFUNCTION

The following relaxation exercise is one of the most effective stress management techniques that has been formulated for stress-related sexual dysfunction problems. It is designed to help you control stress and anxiety by gradually inducing the relaxation response. The gentle process of slowing your breath and letting go of distracting thoughts and tensions allows you to achieve a pleasant and relaxed state.

Read this exercise slowly (about half normal speaking speed). Pause at each (*). Do not be concerned by mispronunciations or verbal slips. Continue in a calm, even voice.

Find a quiet location where you will not be disturbed. Allow about twenty minutes for this exercise. Sit or lie back comfortably, allowing your arms and legs to remain uncrossed if possible. Let your head be supported and let your shoulders drop into a comfortable position. Check the muscles of your head and face. Let your forehead become calm and smooth. Allow the muscles around your eyes to loosen. Check the muscles of the mouth and jaw to make sure they are relaxed. Finally, allow your eyes to remain closed, remembering that you can open them whenever you need to use them.

Before we begin the relaxation, remember not to try to relax too quickly. In fact, do not try to relax at all. Without any effort you can allow yourself to relax by pleasantly letting go of tensions and discomforts, and then letting yourself drift deeper into a peaceful calmness. To begin the relaxation, take three deep breaths, pausing after you inhale, and then exhaling fully and completely. You might imagine that you release tensions and discomforts as you exhale by just breathing them away. * After you have finished these first three breaths, continue breathing slowly and naturally, relaxing more deeply with each slow exhale.

As you continue to breathe slowly and naturally, you may feel the relaxation beginning in your body. The most important thing to remember when dealing with a sexual dysfunction is that you can take control of your body through awareness and relaxation. So to begin this process, turn your awareness to the sensation of relaxation that is beginning in your arms and hands. You may feel that one arm is more relaxed than the other. * Perhaps one arm may feel a bit heavier than the other arm. The muscles may feel more loose or more flexible than in the other arm. * Or perhaps you feel that one arm is a bit warmer than the other arm. You may feel that the warmth of blood and energy may flow more easily down one arm, as if it were flowing through wide-open blood vessels, slowly but freely moving down into your hand and fingers. You may even feel it slowly pulsing down into your hand. * Or perhaps you find that both arms feel equally relaxed and this would be perfect as well. The only thing that matters is that you breathe slowly and gently as you let yourself drift deeper into that soothing dreamlike calmness. *

As you drift pleasantly, turn your awareness to the sensations of relaxation that may be beginning in your legs and feet. You might feel that one leg is slightly more relaxed than the other. Perhaps you notice that one leg feels a little heavier, as if the muscles of that leg were more loose or flexible than the other leg. * Or as you breathe slowly and gently, you may feel that one leg is slightly warmer, as if the blood and warmth could spread more easily down that leg, drifting down through wide-open blood vessels, * perhaps even pulsing slowly but freely down into your foot and toes. * Or perhaps your legs feel equally relaxed, and that would be perfect also. The only thing that really matters is that you continue to breathe slowly as you allow yourself to drift more deeply into that dreamlike calmness and comfort. *

You may even feel the gradual control of stress and tensions beginning as you sink back into whatever you are sitting or lying upon and the tension just melts away. *

You may even feel the muscles of your back beginning to loosen or soften, and as you breathe slowly, naturally, you might feel the relaxation spreading to the other muscles of your back. * Even your upper back and shoulders may begin to soften or loosen a bit further. Your shoulders may be able to drop into a more comfortable position. * You may feel the control growing stronger as your head sinks back into the pillow or chair, the muscles of your neck begin to let go, and you drift deeper into relaxation. *

As you pleasantly drift deeper into this comfort and calmness, you may be able to feel the muscles of your head and face beginning to relax even further. * Continue to breathe slowly, allowing a soothing healing wave of relaxation to gently spread down from the top of your head, soothing and cleansing every muscle and cell of your body. You can feel it slowly drifting down to relax the muscles of your forehead, * letting your forehead become calm and smooth. * Let this wave drift down to relax the muscles around your eyes, releasing the tension in these muscles. * The wave then drifts down helping to relax the muscles of your mouth, including your jaw. Let these muscles go loose and limp. * And as you breathe slowly, the wave slowly drifts down to relax the muscles of your neck. Even your shoulders can loosen a bit more. * The relaxation can begin to spread down your arms. * As the wave of relaxation gently drifts down your arms you may even be able to feel it pulsing into your hands. *

The wave of relaxation can drift down through your back and your chest, spreading soothing comfort into your lower back. * Even your heartbeat feels more calm and regular as the relaxation gently spreads throughout your body. * The wave of relaxation can spread down through your pelvic area, helping to loosen and relax the muscles of your legs even more. * The relaxation slowly drifts down through your legs. Perhaps you can feel it pulsing slowly down into your feet, spreading the comfort down and washing the discomfort out of your body. *

INDIRECT RELAXATION

As you experience the perfect state of relaxation and comfort, you can continue to drift along pleasantly. Relaxation gives your body a chance to rest and heal. In this state you will be able to express your sexuality openly and freely. You will feel your sexuality blossom into a satisfying physical sharing. Your body will remain relaxed as you enjoy every act of closeness and pleasure. You will be able to communicate freely to your partner to have your needs and desires perfectly satisfied. This increased communication will bring further closeness and pleasure between you and your partner with every encounter. Your body will be open and receptive to a wonderful state of enjoyment. (If you are desiring increased fertility, this relaxation exercise will greatly enhance the physical conditions that allow conception. Relaxation helps balance your hormonal levels and increase the blood flow into your sexual organs.)

If you are using this at bedtime you may wish to drift into a pleasant sleep, resting fully and awakening refreshed and alert. If you wish to drift off to sleep, continue breathing slowly and focus on the feelings of relaxation in your arms and legs. *

If you wish to awaken now, you can begin to do so. Let yourself gradually return to this room, feeling the bed or the chair beneath you. As you slowly awaken, you will bring the feelings of calmness, relaxation, pleasure, and happiness back with you. Take a deep breath and stretch, letting the calmness return with you. Take another deep breath and stretch, allowing yourself to awaken feeling refreshed and alert, letting the relaxation and calmness continue with you.

BIBLIOGRAPHY

Comfort, Alex, M.D., Ph.D. *The Joy of Sex: A Gourmet Guide to Love Making*. New York: Fireside, 1972.

A positive approach to exploring human sexuality free of moral dogma. Direct information about pleasures of and problems with sexual activity. Useful techniques to reduce problems.

Downing, George. *The Massage Book*. New York: Random House, Bookworks, 1972. $8.95.

Basic massage book that is simple and straightforward.

Greenwood, Sadja, M.D. *Menopause Naturally: Preparing for the Second Half of Life*. San Francisco: Volcano Press, 1984. $10.00.

Very complete book about the physical changes of menopause for women in this stage of midlife adjustment. Many helpful suggestions.

Kaplan, Helen Singer, M.D., Ph.D. *The New Sex Therapy: Active Treatment of Sexual Dysfunctions*. New York: Brunner/Mazel, 1974. $17.50.

Decent review of information about and treatments of sexual dysfunctions.

Lidell, Lucinda, et al. *The Book of Massage: The Complete Step-by-Step Guide to Eastern and Western Techniques*. New York: Fireside Books, 1984. $10.95.

Well-illustrated and photographed basic text on massage. Many styles and various message strokes are demonstrated.

McKay, Matthew, Ph.D., Martha Davis, Ph.D., and Patrick Fanning. *Messages: The Communication Book*. Oakland, CA: New Harbinger Publications, 1983. $9.95.

Workbook on communications. Many family and work issues are discussed.

Masters and Johnson. *Human Sexual Inadequacy*. Boston: Little, Brown, 1970.

The original researchers and their information about sexual dysfunctions.

Paulsen, K. and R. A. Kuhn, eds. *The Women's Almanac*. New York: Lipincott, 1976.

No-nonsense therapy for six sexual malfunctions.

CHAPTER SEVEN

Midlife Transitions & Stress

Introduction

SOMEWHERE BETWEEN young adulthood and old age, at the halfway point of the average human life span, the time called midlife occurs. Although this is a time when life continues to present many changes and challenges, it is also the time when most people begin to experience their limitations. "Midlife crisis" is the term used to describe the state of mind that results when certain particular stresses develop. These midlife stressors appear as people begin to understand that they have new limitations in their lives that they did not have when young. In order to not feel victimized by these frustrating limitations, it is important to understand our body's responses and to know what we can do to maximize our continued feelings of vigor and well-being.

Usually the first signs of midlife change are physical. The changes may be subtle, but they are definitely measurable. Bodily strength, stamina, energy, agility, flexibility, and adaptability diminish or are less available, even though there may be no outward sign of these changes. Youthful attractiveness wanes. Gradual increases in weight create a more solid appearance. People begin to lose height, hair, muscle tone, skin tone, and resiliency.

The body in midlife may become more brittle and subject to entirely new sets of aches and pains. If throwing a baseball, when young, resulted in a sore arm, the arm would usually heal in a day or two. The same injury might take one or two weeks to heal in midlife because healing takes more time the older we are. Clearly, midlife is a time of changing expectations and learning how to live within new limitations.

The emotional changes of midlife are frequently more intensely felt than the physical ones, especially those resulting from a changing self-image because of aging. Many people begin to think of time differently; they view their life span not in terms of how old they are or how many years they've lived, but in terms of how much time they have left. This changed attitude about time can affect every other aspect of life.

Attitudes about work, for example, can change radically. Most working people, especially men, are at their peak earning years during midlife, but often they find that making lots of money does not bring the happiness or satisfaction it did when they were younger. Midlife men often shift their self-definition away from simple job identification and want to expand their personalities. They may become more sensitive, nurturing, and dependent on social contacts. Some men take on leadership roles and find younger protégés with whom to share their business insights and experiences.

Women, on the other hand, at midlife often become more assertive, independent, and more willing to put their needs above the needs of others, particularly if their children are grown. Emotional insecurities may surface, however, due to declining physical abilities and sexual attractiveness. The expectations of youth must be reassessed and modified or discarded. This can be a very stressful experience for the woman who has defined herself by her youthful vigor and attractiveness.

For men and women, midlife requires a great deal of flexibility and the ability to change perspectives. Although the youthful expectation was that midlife would be more secure and easier than youth, many people find that life does not get easier. While certain stresses become less pronounced as career and family become more established, other stresses appear to take their place. In spite of the higher incomes enjoyed by midlifers, this is also a time of high expenses, and money may be a problem. Children in college, insurance rates, mortgages, retirement planning which can no longer be postponed, and rising health costs are all part of the midlife financial picture. And there may be less energy available to deal with these concerns.

Relationships are another area in which significant change can occur during midlife. As children grow up and leave home, the weaknesses of a marriage that were formerly tolerated may become very trying. Divorce rates soar in middle age partly because without the children's needs acting as a buffer, the imperfections of the marriage are felt more intensely. Both men and women, for many reasons, may feel stifled by a relationship which had previously provided security. With the realization that one's lifetime is finite, the desire for change and experimentation may now be felt more strongly than the need for stability and reliability. Then, too, as previously observed, this is a time for increased independence for women and increased interdependence for men, a fact that would naturally add stress to a marriage.

As relationships shift, often painfully, problems with alchohol or drug abuse may begin or become more acute. Often the patterns of alcohol or drug use have been in place for years without substantially interfering with one's life. But these patterns may become more pronounced and can become a serious problem if midlife is experienced as a time of disappointments and decreasing options.

Finally, the loss of family members, particularly parents and close friends, may begin in midlife. Mortality is a concept that all humans learn to live with from early childhood on, but midlife appears to be the time when aging and dying begin to be taken seriously. Naturally, these concerns are very stress-provoking.

Midlife is not only a story of diminishing energies and increased stress, however; distinct advantages will be felt, too. These middle years are often the most productive part of life because experience and maturity are the necessary conditions to work more efficiently and effectively. Confidence has grown and judgments are more reliable. Midlifers often feel a sense of control over their lives which is invigorating and can compensate for any decline in physical stamina.

Then, too, people often develop more well-rounded personalities at midlife. They may pay attention to parts of themselves they had neglected or overlooked in their youth. A midlife woman may return to school and give new priority to her intellectual and career development. A midlife man may read more or attend lectures on personal growth, activities which would have interested him less in earlier years. Letting go of old expectations or images of the self makes some people more open, tolerant, and accepting of others.

Midlife is also a time when many people begin or renew their religious/spiritual practices. This may result from the need for deeper social connections, or it may be due to the awareness that old age is approaching and the desire to accept aging with grace and serenity. Regardless of the motivation, a deepened religious/sprititual dimension to one's life can be immensely enriching.

Last but not least, the "crises" of midlife often provide the impetus one needs to make healthy lifestyle changes. This is a time when many people make a serious effort to change their diet, to exercise regularly, and to practice stress reduction techniques. The stresses that may be felt in midlife, if paid attention to, can encourage behavior changes that will make the second half of one's life a healthy, productive, and pleasurable time.

Stress Management Recommendations for Midlife

To survive the transitional stress of midlife crises as gracefully as possible, the following self-care strategies are recommended. The "big three"—relaxation, exercise, and a balanced diet—are the essential ingredients for a wellness program. Remember, you cannot control all of the stressors that come into your life, you cannot control the aging process, but you can control how you respond to stress.

Daily practice of stress management exercises can help to minimize the discomfort of the natural aging process, enabling you to feel better both physically and emotionally. The exercises presented in this chapter can help you control your heart rate, blood flow and blood pressure, muscle tension, and breathing. They can help lessen and even eliminate stress-related symptoms such as headaches, stomach problems, circulatory problems, anxiety, sleeplessness and pain.

Many people are skeptical of the value of stress reduction, or they claim they don't have enough time to do the exercises, or they simply give in to old behavior patterns and inertia. But making a commitment to regular practice of these stress reduction techniques is one of the simplest ways to improve your sense of well-being. Additionally, when practiced regularly, the relaxation techniques described in this chapter will cause an increase in self-acceptance and self-love. Self-acceptance is critical for the self-care that is needed to maintain health while aging. When you feel good about yourself, midlife stress can be tolerated, survived, and used as a pivot for future development and growth.

In addition to the stress reduction exercises presented in this chapter, regular physical exercise is also highly recommended to aid digestion, circulation, respiration, muscle tensions, and sleep problems. Jogging, swimming, bike riding, rope jumping, or rowing are excellent aerobic exercises if you can tolerate them. If you cannot, take regular walks or ride a stationary bike.

If you are unsure how much vigorous exercise is wise, or if you are not in excellent health, you should see a physician before beginning a strenuous exercise program. A complete physical examination, possibly including a treadmill "stress" test, will enable your doctor to recommend a program for you.

Some of the most common health concerns felt by both men and women during the midlife years are particularly responsive to regular physical exercise. For men, a regular exercise regimen can help counter the onset of heart disease or circulatory problems. For women, physical exercise, together with calcium supplements, can work to stop or slow the development of osteoporosis, a potentially crippling disease that afflicts 25% of postmenopausal women, as physical exercise stimulates the absorption and proper use of available calcium. Regular physical exercise during the midlife years and beyond can also lessen if not eliminate many of the uncomfortable symptoms of menopause. Osteoporosis needs to be prevented for there is no reliable cure. Even a condition such as diabetes, which sometimes flares up during midlife, may respond to a regular relaxation and physical exercise program, perhaps eliminating the need for insulin use.

Midlife is a good time to evaluate your diet. Often, dietary habits which have been formed in childhood or early adulthood, when you felt vigorous regardless of what you ate, need to be changed in these middle years. Now you feel more sluggish after a meal of pizza and beer, and you start to need several more cups of coffee to get you through the morning if you haven't eaten breakfast. You feel out of breath when climbing several flights of stairs, as your arteries may be increasingly clogged with fat deposits from too many fried foods. Even if you know that you should eat more fresh fruits, vegetables, and whole grains and fewer salty or fatty foods, it is not easy to change dietary habits, particularly when you are used to convenience foods to get you through your hectic day. And the body's cravings for sugar and salt are addictions which can seem as hard to break as an addiction to nicotine. But if you cut back gradually on the main culprits—foods high in sugar, salt, and fat—you will be amazed at how your cravings for these foods subside. The initial months are the hardest. After one year of substantially reducing your intake of foods with high sugar, salt, and fat contents, your body will cease to want these foods often, and you will be surprised how good fresh fruits and vegetables begin to taste! Several months of frustration are certainly worth a lifelong investment in better health.

Your use of caffeine, alcohol, and certain food additives should also be reevaluated in midlife. Long-term use of caffeine and alcohol can have a detrimental effect on liver, heart, and brain functions, and can lead to health problems such as hypertension, heart failure, kidney dysfunction, cirrhosis,

memory loss, and blackouts. Because food additives are in so many of the foods we eat and are so invisible, we often forget about them when we are thinking of the ways in which we can improve our diets. But it has been shown that common additives such as MSG, also known as meat tenderizer, can cause very severe stress reactions. It is best to avoid food additives and consume caffeine and alcohol, if at all, only in moderate quantities.

Many other drugs from diet pills to tranquilizers are frequently used when midlife crises are felt. These drugs can be dangerous, addictive, and are commonly abused. If they are prescribed, they should be used only as directed. If you find yourself thinking about that valium tablet in the medicine cabinet when you have a sleepless night because of difficulties in your marriage, think twice! Rather than depending on drugs, which only leads to a cycle of increased dependency and lowered self-esteem, learn to develop your own inner stength through stress reduction techniques and healthy activities.

Especially at midlife, it is important to realize that you need never stop growing. This is the time to get involved in activities that you have always meant to do "some day." Particularly if your children are grown, you can use your new freedom to develop a greater range of activities and social connections. Try to bridge the gap between generations. Socializing with people both older and younger than yourself will add color and depth to your life.

Teach a class or share information at work or at church. Becoming more deeply involved with an old hobby or special interest, or learning a new one, can be very rewarding at midlife. If possible, volunteer your services in community organizations where help is needed, such as schools, senior centers, or hospitals. The range of volunteer activities is enormous, from reading to the blind to coaching the junior-high school soccer team. Volunteering will increase your social contacts and make you feel good about yourself as well.

Above all else, keep active. The way to stay young and vigorous is to remain involved in all dimensions of life. New interests, hobbies, and activities will keep you growing, learning, and changing. Collecting, crafts, interest groups (from politics to computers), hiking, photography, camping, fishing, games (from chess to tennis), portrait painting, furniture restoration, nature study, auto repair, classes—the list could go on and on. New interests may even lead to financially lucrative adventures. But above all, pursuing any of these suggested activities can enrich your life and prevent you from feeling bored and listless. And all are pursuits that many people begin in midlife. You do not have to be a youngster to learn and grow.

Case Study #1

Bart and Jean were referred to me by a marriage counselor to learn stress management techniques and exercises. They had sought counseling because it had become clear to both of them that their marriage was in trouble. They are in their late forties and both are coping with midlife stress.

Although Bart had achieved recognition in his job at a large construction firm and was earning a great deal of money, he had lost his drive and his pleasure in his work. As a younger man, he always experienced a great deal of excitement and motivation with each new job. Now he felt lethargic and dissatisfied, even when new projects began. Concerned about his low energy level, he had sought medical advice, but his doctor reassured him that he was suffering only from midlife transitional stress.

Jean was also coping with her changing role in life. Both of her children were in their twenties, and the youngest was almost through with college. She found herself faced with the "empty nest" syndrome, as her children no longer relied on her skills as a homemaker. She had been trying to decide whether to return to school or to resume a career in real estate that she had left when she married.

Ever since their children had left home, Bart and Jean had had the most serious relationship problems in the entire course of their marriage. Bart had expressed a desire for greater closeness, but Jean wanted more independence. Financially, although they appeared well off, the combined payments on their house and insurance and retirement fund, and the cost of tuition for their youngest child left them with very little money.

After learning the background of their situation, I started Bart and Jean on a program of daily relaxation exercises. I began with the indirect relaxation, showing them how the exercise worked and then making a tape for them which they could take home and listen to once a day. They both felt comfortable with this exercise, and after four weeks I encouraged them to add a visualization exercise when they felt themselves to be completely relaxed. Jean, in particular, found the visualization to be extremely enjoyable and relaxing. She imagined herself on vacation on a beautiful beach in the warm sun, looking healthy, fit, strong, and energized. She saw herself feeling loved and desirable and being very active. Bart did not respond as well to the visualization, but he continued to enjoy the indirect relaxation. It took almost three months of practice, however, before he felt that he could control his relaxation response and use it as a tool whenever he needed. I assured him this was not unusual, as these techniques require consistent practice before their full results are felt.

I also encouraged Bart and Jean to get enough rest and to exercise regularly. They started taking long walks together each evening, an activity which also provided a good time for communication. We talked about their communication patterns, and I encouraged them to listen to each other's needs and thoughts and to look for cooperative ways to accommodate each other. For instance, instead of accusing the other person of spending too much, I suggested they work together to establish a budget and spending priorities, taking turns buying what each one wants if they disagree. I also encouraged Bart to be more open to communicating his feelings of tenderness for Jean instead of just taking care of business, as Jean seemed to need more support from Bart in this way. They began to plan romantic activities, and to make quality intimate time more of a priority.

We also talked about the importance of a healthy diet, and especially the importance of avoiding excessive use of alcohol and caffeine. And I encouraged both Bart and Jean to develop new interests and activities. Jean started classes at a local community college in computer studies and bookkeeping, and Bart began to play golf after not having played for ten years. In order to find an activity they would enjoy doing together, they began to talk about beginning a new garden. By supporting each other and working hard at their own health activities, they are surviving the physical and emotional changes and challenges of midlife.

Case Study #2

William runs his own business as an independent truck driver. Now in his late forties, he is feeling the typical physical changes of his age. He has put on some weight, lost some strength and agility, has less energy, and feels sore for long periods of time after engaging in his favorite sports. William has always been an avid athlete, playing tennis, golf, racquetball, and many other very active games. He has been upset to feel his body's changes, and rather than pacing himself and recognizing his body's natural limitations, William continues to expect to be able to live the way he did when he was in his twenties. As a result he has suffered some sports injuries which could have been avoided.

His worst problem is that he is developing a dependence on alcohol and drugs. In order to feel better, he has begun to drink too much and to use Valium and stimulants. His trucking business has suffered some setbacks in recent years, and his drug and alcohol use have increased as a result. His reliance on drugs has in turn lowered his ability to handle his business well. This vicious circle of self-defeat stirred up some long-standing emotional insecurities, and finally his family and friends encouraged him to seek counseling. At first, like many substance abusers, he denied having a problem. But as his business floundered and his relationships with family and friends became increasingly strained, he finally recognized that he did need help. He began seeing a counselor, and the counselor recommended relaxation training in addition to his counseling sessions.

I began William on a program of autogenic training, and when he felt comfortable with the exercise, we added visualizations in which he saw himself happy, healthy, physically fit, and not needing any alcohol or drugs to feel well. William often had time at work in which he was sitting in his truck, waiting for goods to be loaded or unloaded, so I suggested he get a portable tape player and use this time to do his relaxation exercises. He found this worked very well, and instead of feeling frustrated, impatient, or bored, he was able to use his idle time to relax.

In addition to the relaxation exercises, I encouraged William to reevaluate his priorities in life. I suggested he listen more carefully to what his body wanted and needed, such as more rest and exercise. In order to do this, it was very important that he not dull his body's messages with drugs or alcohol. He began to attend Narcotics Anonymous, and the organization soon became extremely important to him. The group not only provided him with much needed support, it enabled him to see the affects of substance abuse on other people, and made him very determined to not let the same things happen to him.

I also encouraged William to eat more fresh fruits and vegetables and fewer "fast foods," and to decrease his intake of coffee and sugar. The coffee, especially, I felt was contributing to William's mood swings and difficulty sleeping. As soon as he cut back, he did in fact find that he slept better and experienced a more consistent level of energy.

As he continued the relaxation exercises and visualizations, William gradually began to feel that he was getting back in control of his life. The visualizations, particularly, helped strengthen his self-esteem, and enabled him to feel that he could make needed changes. He began having fewer bouts of fatigue and depression than he had prior to beginning the relaxation program. His improved diet even caused his weight to slowly drop. His wife, doctor, and friends all praised him for his weight loss, and this was an unexpected boost to his morale. Most important, William gradually experienced a decrease in his desire for alcohol and drugs. As this dependency diminished, he felt an increasing sense of his ability to handle the changes of midlife in a positive, healthy way.

Relaxation Exercises for Midlife

MIDLIFE VISUALIZATION FOR SELF-ACCEPTANCE

The changes that come with midlife, particularly the waning of our physical stamina and attractiveness, often affect our self-image in a negative way. Negative feelings about ourself can be a drain on our energy and can inhibit our feelings of spontaneity, joy, and pleasure. On the other hand, learning to accept with grace our natural aging process and to appreciate the inner growth and maturity which comes with midlife will enable us to feel the continued and evolving richness of our lives. Learning to accept ourselves for who we are is an important part of the growth process called midlife. The following visualization is designed to increase feelings of self-love and acceptance. It includes an option for visualizing a change in a negative behavior pattern.

Visualization exercises can be used alone or they can be combined with one of the other deep relaxation techniques. You may want to use the visualization provided below at the end of a relaxation exercise, such as the indirect relaxation or autogenic training, before the wake-up suggestions. When the body is completely relaxed, the mind is particularly receptive to the images and positive suggestions the visualization offers.

Begin your visualization by becoming aware of your body. If you are using this visualization with a relaxation exercise, you should already be deeply relaxed. If you are starting with the visualization, settle into a chair or lie on a comfortable surface and let your body relax. Check the muscles of your face and head, letting go of any tension you may be holding. Make sure your neck and shoulders are relaxed. Let them sink back even further into whatever you are sitting or lying upon. Let the muscles in your arms and legs become loose and heavy.

When you are fully comfortable and relaxed, take a deep breath, inhaling fully and exhaling slowly and completely. Take another deep breath and slowly exhale. As you continue breathing slowly and deeply, try to clear your mind of the day's events. A good way to do this is to imagine that you are outdoors on a beautiful day gazing into the calm blue sky. As thoughts or mental distractions pass through your mind, imagine yourself letting them go as if they were colored helium-filled ballons. Let them drift up into the sky with every slow exhale of breath. Watch as they drift up and away, perhaps dancing in the warm breezes. As the balloons float higher and higher, watch them grow smaller. Eventually, you can watch as they blow over the horizon or become so small they simply drift from sight. Now the sky is calm and clear once again. Notice the soothing color of the blue sky as you continue to breathe slowly and naturally. You may even wish to imagine that you can breathe in the cool blue light of the sky as you continue to relax, just letting go.

Turn your attention, gently, to the warm rays of the sun and the gentle, warm breezes. Feel the warmth begin to relax you. Perhaps you can feel the warmth beginning to soak deep within you, allowing tension to melt away. Feel yourself sinking further into whatever you are sitting or lying upon. Imagine you are slowly breathing in the warmth and golden sunlight. As your body fills with this warming, healing light and energy, you can feel yourself recharging. Imagine every cell in your body is being bathed in oxygen and nutrients to help heal and recharge them. The cells soak up the perfect amount of nutrients, so they can grow healthy and strong, filling you with positive energy, health, and happiness. Even though you are filled with this positive energy, you remain relaxed and comfortable.

You can drift as long as you like in this state of relaxation, health, and happiness. Or you can imagine yourself doing something active in the sunshine, feeling healthy and strong. You are smiling and celebrating your positive energy and health. Remember that you can maintain this healing energy within you and use it anytime you wish. With practice you will find that this golden-white light and warm, healing energy can remain within your heart, as a reserve for whenever you need it. You will also find that within this positive energy dwells a special part of you. This part of you is the perfect being of love and light that people call the "soul." It can see and accept the many parts of you. It sees and accepts your strengths and weaknesses. Your strengths are the tools you have for growth and your weaknesses are the lessons you can also use for growth. As you remain relaxed and comfortable, bathed in love and light, see yourself accepting you strengths and your weaknesses, so that you can enjoy your life in a positive, healthy way. The ability to love and accept oneself comes slowly, but the end results can make a big difference in the quality of your life.

(If you want to change some negative behavior pattern, continue with the following visualization. Otherwise, proceed to the wake-up.) Now imag-

ine some negative behavior pattern that you want to change. Focus on that behavior. For instance, if you want to stop drinking, you may visualize yourself pouring a drink from your liquor cabinet. Now imagine yourself changing that behavior in the way you would like. Imagine yourself closing the door to the liquor cabinet and walking away, leaving the bottle unopened or the drink untouched. See yourself remaining relaxed and comfortable, as you move through this new, positive behavior. See yourself feeling strong and confident, fully comfortable with this new behavior. Feel a new self-love and respect developing in you as you continue to feel relaxed and comfortable.

Drift for a few more minutes in this pleasant state of relaxation and warmth, breathing slowly. When you wish to awaken, imagine that you can return to the room, letting the feelings of love and self-acceptance return with you. Let the feelings of relaxation and comfort remain with you throughout your day. When you wish to awaken completely, take a deep breath and stretch, letting the feelings of health, comfort, and joy return with you to a fully waking state. You may wish to take another deep breath and stretch, feeling wide awake, refreshed, and alert.

Continued practice with this technique makes it easier. The more difficult the negative behavior is to change, the more practice with this visualization you should allow. Do not expect instant results, but assure yourself that with continued practice you can positively affect the way you feel and act. With this exercise, you can learn to control and guide your behavior and feelings in a positive way.

BREATHING TECHNIQUES

These simple but powerful breathing techniques are designed for you to use throughout your day to prevent stress from accumulating in your body. By periodically releasing tension from your body, you avoid letting stress build to such a level that it contributes to physical problems such as backache or high blood pressure. You will also find that by practicing these exercises until they are second nature, under highly stressful situations you will automatically take a few deep breaths and begin to calm yourself. When you control your breath you also slow your heart rate, lower your blood pressure, relax your body's blood flow patterns, and help to control your mental activities. By focusing on your breathing, then, you can interrupt your body's stress response and induce the relaxation response instead.

#1. Try this. Lie down flat or stand up straight. Put one hand over your stomach and one hand over your chest, and see which way each hand moves

as you inhale. Now which way do your hands move as you exhale? Does your bottom hand move first and outward as you begin the inhale? Does the upper hand then move up and out? On the exhale, do you notice that both hands move in, perhaps forcing the last bit of air out? If so, then you are breathing very well and you can go on to the next breathing exercises. If not, you should practice a bit before you continue, as this breathing technique forms the basis of every stress management exercise.

#2. Now try breathing very slowly while you are in a comfortable position. As you inhale slowly but comfortably, count 1–4. Perhaps you can picture the numbers in you mind, or say them slowly to yourself. Now pause for a moment and count 1–4 again as you hold your breath (slowly, picturing the numbers in your mind if possible). And now as you exhale, slowly and comfortably count 1–8. Let your body relax more deeply as you exhale fully and completely, feeling the warm air as you exhale. You might want to repeat this for three breaths. Then check to see if you are feeling more relaxed. You may need to check the muscles of your shoulders, neck, and jaw. If you can let these muscle groups relax further, take another slow breath.

#3. Another breathing/counting exercise that works well is to take four slow breaths, counting to eight by counting one on the inhale, two on the exhale, three on the inhale, etc. Try to picture the numbers in your mind or say the numbers to yourself. After counting to eight, check your position, relax your jaw, forehead, neck, and shoulders and repeat the exercise one more time. Within about two minutes you can begin to feel more relaxed and open, releasing tension with each exhale. Remember, go slowly. Do not be in such a hurry to relax!

#4. Take three deep slow breaths. As you lie down or sit back comfortably, allow yourself to breathe slowly. Feel the cool air as you inhale, pause a moment, and then slowly exhale, feeling the warm breath carry away tensions or discomforts. You might try to feel the cool air at the tip of your nostrils. Exhale through your mouth, breathing away the warm air as if it will drift up into the sky like a helium-filled balloon. Let go slowly and easily, becoming more relaxed with every breath. Some people use this exercise not only to relax but to help them drift off to sleep.

These various breathing techniques work best when practiced on a regular basis. Find one or two that work well for you, and then use them consistently. This book is designed to increase your awareness of what you can do to take control of your body and your life, and to help you develop a practical relaxation program that will serve you as you go through the transitions of life.

INDIRECT RELAXATION FOR MIDLIFE

The following indirect relaxation exercise is a gentle approach to relaxation that should help you "let go" of the fears and anxieties of midlife crises. As you lower your anxiety level, you will find you have more energy for positive activities. When you practice this exercise on a regular basis, you will find that the sense of calmness and renewed energy will carry with you throughout your day. Don't expect results overnight, however. Four to six weeks of regular practice is usually needed before you begin to feel the benefits. Eight to twelve weeks of practice usually produces the maximum benefit. Remember as you drift off into the peaceful comfort of this relaxation that the rest of your day will be more enjoyable and rewarding because you have taken the time to care for yourself and to relax.

Read this exercise slowly (about half normal speaking speed). Pause at each (*). Do not be concerned by mispronunciations or verbal slips. Continue in a calm, even voice.

Find a quiet location where you will not be disturbed. Allow about twenty minutes for this exercise. Sit or lie back comfortably, allowing your arms and legs to remain uncrossed if possible. Let your head be supported and let your shoulders drop into a comfortable position. Check the muscles of your head and face. Let your forehead become calm and smooth. Allow the muscles around your eyes to loosen. Check the muscles of the mouth and jaw to make sure they are relaxed. Finally, allow your eyes to remain closed, remembering that you can open them whenever you need to use them.

Before we begin the relaxation, remember not to try to relax too quickly. In fact, do not try to relax at all. Without any effort you can allow yourself to relax by pleasantly letting go of tensions and discomforts, and then letting yourself drift deeper into a peaceful calmness. To begin the relaxation, take three deep breaths, pausing after you inhale, and then exhaling fully and completely. You might imagine that you release tensions and discomforts as you exhale by just breathing them away. * After you have finished these first three breaths, continue breathing slowly and naturally, relaxing more deeply with each slow exhale.

As you continue to breathe slowly and naturally, you may feel the relaxation beginning in your body. The most important thing to remember when dealing with midlife stress is that you can take control of your body through awareness and relaxation. So to begin this process, turn your awareness to the sensation of relaxation that is beginning in your arms and hands. You may feel that one arm is more relaxed than the other. * Perhaps one arm may feel a bit heavier than the other arm. The muscles may feel more loose or more flexible than in the other arm. * Or perhaps you feel that one arm is a bit warmer than the other arm. You may feel that the warmth of blood and energy may flow more easily down one arm, as if it were flowing through wide-open blood vessels, slowly but freely moving down into your hand and fingers. You may even feel it slowly pulsing down into your hand. * Or perhaps you find that both arms feel equally relaxed and this would be perfect as well. The only thing that matters is that you breathe slowly and gently as you let yourself drift deeper into that soothing dreamlike calmness. *

As you drift pleasantly, turn your awareness to the sensations of relaxation that may be beginning in your legs and feet. You might feel that one leg is slightly more relaxed than the other. Perhaps you notice that one leg feels a little heavier, as if the muscles of that leg were more loose or flexible than the other leg. * Or as you breathe slowly and gently, you may feel that one leg is slightly warmer, as if the blood and warmth could spread more easily down that leg, drifting down through wide-open blood vessels, * perhaps even pulsing slowly but freely down into your foot and toes. * Or perhaps your legs feel equally relaxed, and that would be perfect also. The only thing that really matters is that you continue to breathe slowly as you allow yourself to drift more deeply into that dreamlike calmness and comfort. *

You may even feel the gradual control of stress and tensions beginning as you sink back into whatever you are sitting or lying upon and the tension just melts away. *

You may even feel the muscles of your back beginning to loosen or soften, and as you breathe slowly, naturally, you might feel the relaxation spreading to the other muscles of your back. * Even your upper back and shoulders may begin to soften or loosen a bit further. Your shoulders may be able to drop into a more comfortable position. * You may feel the control growing stronger as your head sinks back into the pillow or chair, the muscles of your neck begin to let go, and you drift deeper into relaxation. *

As you pleasantly drift deeper into this comfort and calmness, you may be able to feel the muscles of your head and face beginning to relax even further. Continue to breathe slowly, allowing a soothing, healing wave of relaxation to gently spread down from the top of your head, soothing and cleansing every muscle and cell of your body. You can feel it slowly drifting down to relax the muscles of your forehead, * letting your forehead become calm and smooth. * Let this wave drift down to relax the muscles around your eyes, releasing the tension in these muscles. * The wave then drifts down helping to relax the muscles of your mouth, including your jaw. Let these muscles go loose and limp. * And as you breathe slowly, the wave slowly drifts down to relax the muscles of your neck. Even your shoulders can loosen a bit more. * The relaxation can begin to spread down your arms. * As the wave of relaxation gently drifts down your arms you may even be able to feel it pulsing into your hands. *

The wave of relaxation can drift down through your back and chest, spreading soothing comfort into your lower back. * Even your heartbeat feels more calm and regular as the relaxation gently spreads throughout your body. * The wave of relaxation can spread down through your pelvic area helping to loosen and relax the muscles of your legs even more. * The relaxation slowly drifts down through your legs. Perhaps you can feel it pulsing slowly into your feet, spreading the comfort down, washing the discomfort out of your body. *

As you allow yourself to drift more deeply in this calmness, the soothing relaxation can help you rest and recharge yourself. Perhaps you can imagine that you are outdoors in a perfect place, on a warm and beautiful day. Choose the most comfortable place to lie down. Feel the warmth from the sun. As you begin to soak up the warmth from the sun, feel your tensions and discomforts just melting away. * The warmth can fill you with healing energy and the golden-white light can help to recharge you fully and completely. Even though you remain at peace, you can feel the warmth of blood flowing more freely to every cell of your body, carrying oxygen and nutrients and healing energy to bathe every cell. Each cell, like a sponge, can soak up the perfect amount of nutrients and energy to help heal and recharge you. You may even begin to feel sensations of health, joy, and happiness burning more brightly within you, though you remain calm and comfortable. * Perhaps you can picture yourself filling with strength and energy as your body heals itself. * See yourself in a state of health and happiness, doing something active, perhaps smiling and celebrating in the sunshine. * As you practice this relaxation exercise you will become more comfortable with it, being able to relax more deeply and quickly. You will be more aware of tensions and begin to develop confidence that you can rid yourself of unnecessary anxieties whenever they may develop. The effects of the relaxation will begin to carry over throughout your day.

As you become comfortable with this relaxation, your awareness and control will continue with you throughout the day. You will feel more patient with any interactions that you experience. This patience will help to create a better environment at home. You will also experience more time and more

energy to do the things that you want to do. Remember that by taking this time for yourself, you will be able to feel greater acceptance of the changes of midlife. Your self-acceptance will enable you to make necessary adaptations and to continue to grow gracefully. Your awareness will also help you to identify your needs and find positive ways to have these needs met.

If you are using this exercise at bedtime you may wish to drift into a pleasant sleep, resting fully and awakening refreshed and alert. If you wish to drift off to sleep, continue breathing slowly and focus on the feelings of relaxation in your arms and legs. *

If you wish to awaken now, you can begin to do so. Let yourself gradually return to this room, feeling the bed or the chair beneath you. As you slowly awaken, you will bring the feelings of calmness, relaxation, health, and happiness back with you. Take a deep breath and stretch, letting the calmness return with you. Take another deep breath and stretch, allowing yourself to awaken feeling refreshed and alert, letting the relaxation and calmness continue with you.

AUTOGENIC TRAINING FOR MIDLIFE

If the changes of midlife feel beyond your control, these autogenic training phrases will help you feel you can regain control of your life. You may not be able to eliminate all sources of stress as you move through midlife transitions, but you will be able to affect the way your body responds to stress. The mental commands which you repeat in this exercise are in the first person, so they should help bolster the sense that you are in control. With practice, you will find yourself able to achieve a state of relaxation more quickly and easily. After six weeks of regular daily practice you will not only feel an increased calmness, but a sense of confidence that you don't have to be victimized by stress.

Read this exercise slowly (about half normal speaking speed). Pause at each (*). Do not be concerned by mispronunciations or verbal slips. Continue in a calm, even voice.

Find a quiet location where you will not be disturbed. Allow about twenty minutes for this exercise. Sit or lie back comfortably, allowing your arms and legs to remain uncrossed if possible. Let your head be supported and let your shoulders drop into a comfortable position. Check the muscles of your head and face. Let your forehead become calm and smooth. Allow the muscles around your eyes to loosen. Check the muscles of the mouth and jaw to make sure they are relaxed. Finally, allow your eyes to remain closed, remembering that you can open them whenever you need to use them.

Before we begin the relaxation, remember not to try to relax too quickly. In fact, do not try to relax at all. Without any effort you can allow yourself to relax by pleasantly letting go of tensions and discomforts, and then letting yourself drift deeper into a peaceful calmness. To begin the relaxation, take three deep breaths, pausing after you inhale, and then exhaling fully and completely. You might imagine that you release tensions and discomforts as you exhale by just breathing them away. * After you have finished these first three breaths, continue breathing slowly and naturally, relaxing more deeply with each slow exhale.

Repeat these phrases to yourself, exactly as they are written from this exercise, and try to feel your body responding to the commands. If you need to repeat the phrases more than three times to begin to feel results, then continue the repetitions a few additional times.

Repeat this mood phrase to yourself three times: "I am at peace with myself and fully relaxed." Continue breathing slowly and gently.

Begin to feel the muscles of your arms relax as you say, "My right arm is heavy * ... My right arm is heavy * ... My right arm is heavy * ..." Repeat this phrase slowly until you begin to feel the heaviness spreading through your arm. Now turn your awareness to your left arm as you breathe slowly and say to yourself, "My left arm is heavy * ... My left arm is heavy * ... My left arm is heavy * ..." Try to feel the heaviness starting in your arms or feel free to continue slowly repeating this phrase a few more times. Now proceed to your legs. Let them begin to relax as you breathe slowly. Feel the heaviness and relaxation starting in your legs as you slowly repeat, "My right leg is heavy * ... My right leg is heavy * ... My right leg is heavy * ..." You can repeat this several more times if you need to, until you begin to feel the relaxation and the heaviness. Now focus on the left leg and feel it beginning to relax as you say, "My left leg is heavy * ... My left leg is heavy * ... My left leg is heavy * ..." Repeat if needed. With practice you will feel the heaviness more quickly and easily. Now turn your attention to your neck and shoulders. Let them sink into a more comfortable position and let the muscles relax as you breathe gently and say, "My neck and shoulders are heavy * ... My neck and shoulders are heavy * ... My neck and shoulders are heavy * ..." Repeat if needed. Take a deep slow breath and feel the heaviness and relaxation as you begin to sink back into whatever you are sitting or lying upon.

Perhaps you can feel the blood beginning to flow more easily down into your hands or your feet as the blood vessels begin to dilate, as the smooth muscles in the walls of the arteries begin to relax. Focus on the feelings of warmth, or a pulse, or perhaps a tingling feeling in your right hand as you say, "My right arm is warm * . . . My right arm is warm * . . . My right arm is warm * . . ." Repeat this slowly several more times until you begin to feel the warmth or pulse. Heaviness is generally easier for most people to feel than warmth, but with continued practice you can begin to control the blood flow. Now turn your attention to your left arm and say to yourself, "My left arm is warm * . . . My left arm is warm * . . . My left arm is warm * . . ." Repeat if needed. Perhaps you can start to feel the warmth in your arms, and you may feel the blood flowing freely through your entire body. As you breathe slowly and gently, turn your awareness to your legs and say to yourself, "My right leg is warm * . . . My right leg is warm * . . . My right leg is warm * . . ." Repeat several more times to help develop this skill. Move your attention to your left leg and say, "My left leg is warm * . . . My left leg is warm * . . . My left leg is warm * . . ." Repeat if needed. Feel the heaviness and warmth in your arms and your legs as you breathe slowly and gently. Now turn your awareness to your neck and shoulders, and say, "My neck and shoulders are warm * . . . My neck and shoulders are warm * . . . My neck and shoulders are warm * . . ." Repeat if needed. Breathe slowly as you drift for a few moments, feeling the heaviness and warmth spreading pleasantly about your body.

Slow and calm your heart by slowly repeating to yourself, "My heartbeat is calm and regular * . . . My heartbeat is calm and regular * . . . My heartbeat is calm and regular * . . ." Repeat if needed. If you experience any discomfort with this phrase then change to the phrase "I feel calm * . . . I feel calm * . . . I feel calm * . . ." As you breathe slowly, begin to feel the peace and relaxation spreading to every part of your body.

To slow your breathing say to yourself as you breathe into your diaphragm, "My breathing is calm and regular * . . . . . . My breathing is calm and regular * . . . My breathing is calm and regular * . . ." Repeat if needed.

Become aware of the relaxation starting in your stomach region. As you breathe slowly say, "My abdomen is warm and calm * . . . My abdomen is warm and calm * . . . My abdomen is warm and calm * . . ." Repeat if needed. If you have any serious abdominal problems or diabetes, change this phrase to "I am calm and relaxed * . . . I am calm and relaxed * . . . I am calm and relaxed * . . ." Feel the sensations of warmth and relaxation beginning to spread through your abdomen.

Move on to your forehead and let the muscles of your head and face relax as you say, "My forehead is cool and calm * . . . My forehead is cool and calm * . . . My forehead is cool and calm * . . ." As you breathe slowly, feel the muscles around your eyes, mouth, and jaw loosen and then relax.

Let yourself drift pleasantly in this calmness. As you breathe gently, perhaps you can feel the heaviness in your arms and legs as the muscles relax. * Perhaps you can begin to feel the warmth or pulse of blood flowing more easily down into your hands and perhaps even your feet, like sunshine or a bath gently warming you. Some people feel the warming as if it were a tingling sensation spreading blood more easily into the extremities. * As you enjoy the relaxation you can feel that your heartbeat is calm and regular. *

With practice, you can feel the relaxation more easily and quickly. The warmth of blood flowing into your hands and feet gradually grows easier to control, until you will be able to consistently warm your hands to 93 degrees and your feet to 90 degrees. The relaxation will then carry over with you throughout your day.

Though you are experiencing the changes of midlife, you can control your response to these changes. By letting go of stress you can feel healthy and energized. Your skill at relaxation can also lead to greater self-awareness and self-acceptance. You can appreciate both your strengths and your weaknesses, and gradually change negative behaviors. You can become more accepting of all the parts of yourself as your sense of calmness and relaxation grows.

At the end of this relaxation exercise, awaken yourself slowly. Feel the bed or chair beneath you and say, "I am refreshed and completely alert * . . . I am refreshed and completely alert * . . . I am refreshed and completely alert * . . ." Then take a deep breath and stretch, allowing yourself to wake fully, and let the relaxation carry over with you into a fully waking state. You may wish to take another deep breath and stretch, letting the relaxation return with you.

BIBLIOGRAPHY

Green, Sadja, M.D. *Menopause Naturally: Preparing for the Second Half of Life*. San Francisco: Volcano Press, 1984. $10.00.

Very complete book about the physical changes of menopause for women in this stage of midlife adjustment. Many helpful suggestions.

Levinson, Daniel J., with Charlotte Darrow, Edward Klein, Maria Levinson, and Braxton McKee. *The Seasons of a Man's Life*. New York: Ballantine Books, 1978. $9.95.

Midlife crisis and aging issues for men are examined very well. Worth checking into if you need information and support.

Nichols, Michael P., Ph.D. *Turning 40 in the '80's: Personal Crisis, Time for Change.* New York: Fireside, 1986. $8.95.

A psychologist's view of midlife adjustment for men and women. With awareness of midlife issues, the transition can be more graceful.

Pesmen, Curtis, *How a Man Ages: Growing Older: What to Expect and What You Can Do About It.* New York: Ballantine Books/Esquire Magazine, 1984. $7.95.

Information and suggestions for dealing with midlife crisis and the aging process.

AUDIOCASSETTE TAPES

Mason, L. John, Ph.D. *High Blood Pressure Relaxation, Relaxation for Pain*, and *Relaxation for Sleep.* 1988. All are $11.95 and can be ordered from the author.

Specially formulated relaxation exercises designed to help reduce if not eliminate the specific concerns. These guided techniques are most beneficial when practiced regularly.

CHAPTER EIGHT

Aging & Stress

Introduction

UNTIL RECENTLY, old people were respected and highly valued members of society. The knowledge and wisdom they had acquired during their lives were considered valuable resources. They were consulted for their opinions and their guidance was frequently followed. Today, in our fast-paced world, old people are not valued. On the contrary, their life experiences are thought to be irrelevant to today's complex problems and their wisdom is denied by our youth-worshipping culture.

This shift in attitude is the result of changes in many areas of our society. Some of these changes are easily apparent, such as the media's intense glorification of youthful exuberance and sexuality or the rapid changes in technology, which can cause one's expertise in a particular field to become outmoded overnight. But other changes are more subtle, though nonetheless significant.

For example, after World War II ended, housing styles changed. Large houses with live-in attics and spare rooms went out of style. The new ranch houses of suburbia and the two-bedroom apartments of the cities were designed to accommodate small families. Couples with children no longer had the room to house aging parents or other elderly relatives. So, beginning in the sixties, retirement villages and senior citizen's complexes sprang up to meet the housing needs of retirees who could not live with their families.

Because older people no longer lived with their extended families, when women began entering the work force in large numbers, they sent their children to daycare centers instead of relying on grandparents to care for them. In the sixties also, many large companies began mandating compulsory retirement at age sixty-five, so the contact between young and old people in the work force diminished, too. Gradually, without anyone planning it, the elderly were unofficially separated from the rest of the population. When we do not share our lives closely with someone, it becomes harder to know them well and to value their special resources and attributes.

While all these social changes were taking place, another enormous medical/biological change was occurring: because of improvements in our diets and living standards, people started living longer. Today, the average life span in the United States has increased so much that gerontologists must distinguish between the "young old," those in their late sixties and seventies, and the "old old," those in their eighties and nineties. Some statistical predictions hold that by the year 2035, every fourth American will be "elderly"—if sixty-five and older continues to be the definition of that term. And, by the middle of the twenty-first century, there will be some sixteen million people over the age of eighty-five! (*Our Aging Society: Paradox and Promise,* A. Pifer and L. Bronte, eds., New York: W. W. Norton & Co., 1986, p. 4).

Clearly, our aging society will need the contributions its older citizens can make. With long lives stretching far ahead for most of us, we have an urgent need to stay healthy and productive as long as we can. Let's take a closer look at just what is involved in the aging process.

Physically, human beings age at different rates. Some people seem aged and infirm by their late fifties. Others, who, judging by their birth certificates, are way past retirement age, remain spry and energetic and show few signs of even slowing down. These differences are mostly due to genetic inheritances, but lifestyle, nutrition, exercise, and stress levels certainly contribute to the rate at which individuals age.

Aging is the continuation of the process that actually started with physical maturation: energy decline, diminishing physical abilities, and the slowing down of repair mechanisms. In the typical aging body, the cardiovascular system exhibits lower heart output and slower, possibly blocked, circulation. Changes in the endocrine system affect kidney functioning and cause a decrease in hormone production. An aging nervous system causes a reduction in sensory functioning, so that the five senses become duller and lose some degree of sensitivity. Sexual activity usually decreases. Muscles show reduced levels of strength and flexibility. The skeleton becomes brittle and bone breaks heal more slowly. The respiratory system slows down and functions much less efficiently. Metabolism slows, and weight loss is common. Digestive patterns change and function erratically.

These inevitable changes continue as the body ages until one or more of the body's major life systems—circulatory, repiratory, digestive, etc.—wears out completely and death occurs. In people living past the age of sixty-four, heart disease is the most common cause of death, followed by cancer, respiratory diseases, and accidents. All of these are related to the aging body's reduced capacities. But we also know that the breakdown of the body's major life systems is influenced by lifestyle behaviors, such as smoking, drinking, drug abuse, poor diet, lack of exercise, and emotional stress. By improving these lifestyle behaviors, then, we can have an impact on the rate at which our body ages and the degree of health we experience in our older years.

The physical aspects of aging are documented and well understood. But the mental and emotional aspects, which greatly affect the physical changes, are equally important. By understanding the typical emotional patterns of aging, we can more readily deal with them. The pleasures and enjoyments of life do not have to disappear because of age.

One of the major emotional changes of old age is the change in self-image. Too often, the older person's self-image shifts from a positive to a negative view because of the physical changes described above. Resentment is a fairly natural reaction to the slowing down of old age. But resenting sloweddown systems won't speed them up, and the stress of resentment can contribute to illness.

Society's negative attitudes about old age also add to an older person's negative self-image. We all need to shift our images of the elderly, but elderly people who project positive self-images can help these attitudes to change. A positive self-image is a prerequisite for enjoying life. One of the best ways to maintain a positive self-image is to make a self-care program a high priority.

Careful monitoring of one's diet and exercise program, and staying as active as possible, will contribute to high self-esteem. But even if strength and health diminish because of aging, keeping up appearances is still a worthwhile activity. Rightly or wrongly, we are judged by how we look; this doesn't change no matter how old we become. If we wear inappropriate clothing, or are careless and slovenly, other people will not treat us respectfully. Flattering outfits are available for all ages. By caring about the impres-

sion we make on others, we continue to care for ourselves, and we keep ourselves in better shape. We can't help but feel good about ourselves when other people respond positively to us.

Financial concerns are another common emotional stress for older people. In spite of senior citizens' broad work experiences and skills, in spite of their honesty and availability, it is very hard for them to find work after retirement. And, many retirees are finding that after adjusting for inflation and the rising cost of living, their retirement benefits do not meet their needs adequately. The recent rash of stories about the Social Security Administration's financial difficulties have added to the financial stress of many older people.

Nevertheless, some very determined senior citizens have found employment for themselves after retirement. Some work at night, some part-time. Some are sharing jobs. They are supplementing their incomes by working at daycare centers or as teachers' aides; they housesit for pets, plants, and houses; they provide live-in care for the "old old" or for invalids or children; they do carpentry, plumbing, or bookkeeping. The list could go on and on. The law says that it is illegal to deny employment to someone because of age, and the courts have been upholding the older person's right to work.

The fact that the aging population is also a large part of the voting population suggests that as the ranks of the aging swell, we may see federal aid or subsidies for the elderly. Groups like the Gray Panthers have been politically active for some time and these groups appear to be growing stronger as the population of the old increases. In some communities, the Gray Panthers have organized programs that connect older people with working mothers to provide grandparentlike services—an arrangement that satisfies needs of both young and old.

Almost all communities have an area agency on aging that will provide outreach advocacy programs to assist the elderly—especially the low-income elderly. They provide health services, homemaker/chore services, home-delivered meals, housing/home repair services, and transportation. Also, most churches and synagogues run assistance programs for their elderly members. Organizations like the Lions, the Odd Fellows Lodge, the Masons, and many veterans organizations offer a wide variety of support services for the older people of their communities. Most large cities support a Meals-On-Wheels program for independent older people who cannot cook nutritious meals for themselves.

These services and others are not just for the poor, and there should be no stigma attached to making use of them. All public and private social agencies are staffed with social workers whose job it is to inform senior citizens about the services available to them. Entitlement may depend upon income, assets, and need, but a wide range of support programs for the elderly is available in every city.

Another aspect of aging that is very stressful to older people is their vulnerability to crime. Senior citizens, especially in the larger cities, have been victimized in horrifying numbers because of their fragility. Most police and sheriff's departments have officers who will inspect a home and give advice about making it safe from intruders. Some older people, in addition to following commonsense precautions such as locking windows as well as doors, and never leaving a key under a doormat, start or join telephone networks.

A telephone network is a group that provides a phone call every day at a specific time to check on the member's well-being. Failure to answer brings another phone call within a few minutes. Failure to answer the second call will result in a call to a neighbor or friend who is available to go directly to the member's house to check on him or her. This system has had great results in both large cities and small towns.

Perhaps the most depressing problem people experience as they age is loneliness. As spouses, relatives, and friends grow old and die, the impact on the survivors can be devastating. The loss of a lifetime companion can have a physical as well as emotional impact. Statistics on cancer patients show a very high incidence of tumor development six to eighteen months after the death of a loved one. Some people seem to lose their will to live after such a death. And, recent research points to a decrease in the immune system's natural defense mechanisms after the loss of a loved one.

Grief is a terrible experience, and no one should be pressured to pass through a mourning period faster than his or her own needs will dictate. But after the necessary time has passed, most people realize that expressions of grief and sorrow do not celebrate a loved person's memory as well as picking up the pieces and continuing to live as well as one can. Of course, it is extremely difficult to resist giving in to self-pity, and it is even harder to be sensible and direct one's attention to other people and events. But, after a time, that is exactly what needs to be done.

Preparing for just such an eventuality as the loss of one's friends or family is another reason that retired people should strive to fill their lives with interesting activities and enjoyable pursuits. Most recreational activities usually include companionship with people who have similar interests. It is important for older folks' physical and emotional health to get out of the house for a change of scene and a variety of activities.

There are many kinds of participatory activities as well as spectator entertainments at which the elderly can meet new friends or join old ones. Community organizations can often help inform people of these activities. Senior drop-in centers, often run by local organizations such as the Council on Aging, are safe, comfortable places for seniors to gather for companionship. Those who do not wish to participate in any activities can read or watch TV in companionable company. Loneliness is not the inevitable accompaniment to old age.

Stress Management Recommendations for Aging

A self-care wellness program to cope with aging should include several different strategies. The first and most important should be to nurture your own will to live. Finding a purpose in life and positive reasons for living are essential coping mechanisms.

Consider sharing your time, energy, and wisdom with other people. Remember that younger generations *need* to hear the wisdom of experience even if they do not fully understand or appreciate it. Sharing your perspective on things may offer younger people an entirely new way of looking at troubling events. Fresh perspectives are always valuable, and even though you may not have solutions to offer, your time and concern may help in and of themselves. Although younger people may appear to be disrespectful, they need your viewpoint. Individuals and society need to experience continuity; without continuity, life loses a lot of its meaning.

Volunteering your time and service can provide you with a much needed purpose in life at the same time that it provides a valuable resource to your community. Service can take many forms. If you drive, you can offer to drive someone who doesn't to the supermarket or to church. If your energy level is high and you like working with young children, perhaps volunteering to be a "foster grandparent" would suit you. Maybe working with your local conservation organization, or the political party of your choice would interest you. Whatever you select, finding some outer-directed activity that benefits others is often the way to achieve a stronger desire to live.

Developing new skills, hobbies, and interests also helps to develop positive attitudes. New experiences challenge your resources and keep you functioning optimally. We are never too old to learn, or to enjoy discovering new things about the world. One of the best strategies for developing a positive attitude is to set goals for yourself. If the goals are within reason, they can provide a sense of purpose and an extra incentive to live. Such a goal might be to visit your family or friends, or it might be to plan a trip to exotic places. You might even want to study another language. Setting goals and meeting them is the best way to live in the present and to look forward to the future.

Once the will to live is firmly established, learning to control your stress response will minimize the impact of the physical and emotional changes that accompany aging. The relaxation exercises listed in this chapter, when practiced on a regular basis, help to reconnect mind and body and to improve self-acceptance and self-esteem. Review them carefully, find the ones that work best for you, and integrate them into your life. You will be amazed at what a difference in well-being you can experience from regular practice of these exercises. They can even help eliminate or decrease the need for certain medications. Also listed are specific relaxation exercises that are useful for dealing with chronic pain, high blood pressure, and sleeping problems.

Keeping as physically fit as possible is essential to feeling good in old age. The healthiest old people I know are always active. As you age, your need for physical exercise does not change, although your expectations and practices will need to be adapted to your changing body. Regular exercise helps to combat degenerative diseases like diabetes, high blood pressure, heart disease, osteoporosis, and certain mental/emotional conditions.

Walking and dancing are fine physical activities for older people. Many local organizations hold dances for seniors during the daytime. Daytime outings to museums, plays, historical sites, and amusement parks are sponsored by many local groups and afford plenty of physical exercise as well as entertainment. Swimming is good exercise for seniors, especially if a warm pool is available. Bike riding outdoors, or indoors on a stationary bike, is also excellent. If your doctor okays it, jogging, rowing, skating, and jumping rope are fine in moderation. If you and your doctor agree on the value of competitive sports for you, like tennis, lawn bowling, or golf—fine. But take care not to allow the competitiveness to vex you emotionally. You will lose the sport's therapeutic value if you blow your stack!

Three times a week is the minimum amount of regular exercise prescribed for a wellness program. Daily exercise, if you can tolerate it, is even better. Remember to stay within reasonable limits. Overdoing it adds unnecessary stress to your life. Exercise properly done, whether it is walking, bike riding, folk dancing, t'ai chi, or calisthenics can also take on a meditative quality that will energize you spiritually as well as physically. Exercise is the closest we have come to an antiaging, antidisease pill.

Good nutrition is another essential aspect of a self-care wellness program. Every *body* regardless of its age requires a well-balanced diet. Older people, especially those living alone, often forget to eat properly, or refuse to take the time and effort to prepare well-balanced meals for themselves. This is a great mistake. The evidence is overwhelming that proper diet can minimize and, in some cases, even eliminate many digestive disorders. Conditions such as bowel cancer, hypertension, ulcers, constipation, and diarrhea are all linked to improper diet.

In a proper diet, fresh fruits and vegetables are as important as protein and carbohydrates. The vitamins, minerals, fiber, and iron they provide are essential. Foods high in calcium, such as milk and cheese, are also important to the older person's diet. If you can't tolerate dairy products, calcium supplements can be used instead. Caffeine, sugar, alcohol, salt, fats, and certain food additives like MSG should be used sparingly, if at all.

Red meat, wine, wheat, dairy products, and chocolate have been known to cause allergic reactions in some people. Observe how your body reacts to these foods and delete them from your diet if necessary. The aging body is increasingly sensitive to and less tolerant of poor food habits.

The fact that basal metabolism declines with age also means that an older body needs less food to sustain it than a younger one does. The old folk saying "The wider the waistline, the shorter the lifeline" is true! Moderation in food and drink are even more essential in old age than earlier, as the extra weight you carry further burdens your body's systems. If you have to lose weight, restrict your calories by combining nutritional needs with the foods you crave. Most weight problems have to do with the *amount* you eat, not what you eat. But remember that food is frequently one of life's greatest pleasures, and don't deny this pleasure too severely. A deprivational diet ignores emotional needs of the dieter and is bound to fail. One of the most successful ways to lose weight is to liberate yourself from guilt and give yourself permission to enjoy occasional food cravings. Just remember that moderation is absolutely essential. If you want assistance in constructing and maintaining a diet, I recommend consulting your local Weight Watchers. Their program recognizes the need for flexibility and allows for a wide variety of menus. The group support they offer can also be very valuable to dieters.

Older people need to remember, too, that commonly prescribed drugs, from diet pills to tranquilizers, are dangerous, addictive, and frequently abused. Even if your doctor prescribes them, you should try to find more

healthful substitutes. For example, some people have found lecithin and spirulina to be effective in curbing appetite. And meditation and relaxation exercises are a healthful substitute for tranquilizers if you are nervous and tense.

Finally, remember that if you are embarked on a wellness program to care for yourself physically, emotionally, mentally, and socially, you must not neglect the care of your spirit. Mind, body, emotions, and spirit all interact to create health or disease. Your spiritual pursuits may involve a church or they may not. There is a spirit energy in everyone, and we call it by various names—God, The Light, the life-force—and invoke it in different ways, according to our religious practices. It heals and protects us if we cherish and acknowledge it. As we practice self-acceptance, our spirit teaches us to accept others. As we accept ourselves and others, self-conflict and conflict with others is reduced and harmony increases.

The peace of mind that we can achieve through awakening our spirituality offers great hope in even the most difficult of times. Spiritual development will not solve all problems, nor will it answer all questions. But it does lead us toward a more centered consciousness, which will help us deal with life's transitions in more loving and conscious ways.

Case Study #1

Henry and Betty were moving into that uneasy transition from middle age to retirement when they contacted me. They had made a commitment to each other to change their lifestyle, and they wanted my help. They were both justifiably concerned about their health problems, which although not severe, could easily have become so. Betty was suffering from a mild sleep disorder. She had trouble falling asleep and would frequently wake during the night worrying about her family. Henry had high blood pressure, and his doctor was watching him closely for signs of diabetes. In recent years, he had put on quite a bit of weight.

Henry and Betty had been married for more than thirty years, and their three children were grown and had left home. Henry planned to retire the following year from his lifelong job as a warehouseman. Betty had already retired from her job with an insurance company, but had gone back to work part-time to boost her future Social Security benefits. Although they had looked forward to retirement and had made plans to travel around the country in a trailer, they were becoming increasingly worried about finances and about how retirement would affect them emotionally.

Their children, two of whom had just started their own families, were in no position to help them out. In fact their middle child, whom they felt lacked direction in life, was still a worry to them. Henry and Betty were also concerned that they did not have enough time or energy to devote to their grandchildren, and this added to their general worries.

After discussing their concerns, we talked about the components of a wellness program—exercise, improved diet, and relaxation techniques. They both knew they needed to exercise more, and I encouraged them to take walks each day and find some other outdoor activity they enjoyed as well. Henry had been an avid golfer at one time, and he expressed interest in getting back out on the golf course. Betty enjoyed gardening and began making plans for some new garden projects.

Improving their diet was not an easy undertaking, as they were used to eating foods high in fat, such as red meat and butter, and high in salt and sugar, such as sodas and chips. We made a list of the foods they wanted to omit from their diet, starting with the ones which contributed most to high blood pressure, those highest in cholesterol. Then we made a list of foods high in fiber which they wanted to add to their diet, such as whole grains and fresh fruits and vegetables. Each week they were to eliminate one item from the first list and substitute one from the second. In this way they wouldn't feel too deprived of their favorite foods, and could adjust to the changes gradually.

I also introduced Henry and Betty to indirect relaxation and encouraged them to practice the technique for twenty minutes a day. When they had become comfortable with the exercise, after about six weeks of practice, I added a visualization for each of them. I encouraged Henry to visualize his blood flowing freely through wide open blood vessels. Betty focused on a visualization of herself in a beautiful setting, feeling healthy, energetic, and vibrant. Both Henry and Betty enjoyed the relaxation and visualizations and made them a permanent part of their daily routine.

As they learned to "let go" of physical tension, they experienced an emotional letting go as well, a letting go of anxiety. After two months, Henry began to see a slight decline in his blood pressure, probably due mostly to the relaxation exercises. He was having difficulty changing his diet as much as he knew he should, and was still eating more meat and butter than was advisable. Betty was sleeping more soundly and feeling less anxious about her family concerns. Although she and Henry had come in to see me in order to deal with stress, it was becoming clear to all of us that underlying the stress symptoms, Betty had been depressed. Her spirits had been much improved just knowing that she and Henry had started to take better care of themselves. She felt they would provide a good example to their children and grandchildren as well.

Case Study #2

Frances was eighty-five when her doctor sent her to see me because of her high blood pressure, which he was concerned might lead to a stroke. Frances showed rather severe symptoms of artereosclerosis, or hardening of the arteries, caused by both hereditary factors and a lifelong diet high in cholesterol. Though her doctor knew these organic causes of hypertension could not be reversed by relaxation techniques, he felt some of her blood pressure elevation might be linked to stress, and he thought relaxation exercises might help.

When I first met with Frances we talked briefly about the sources of stress in her life. She had lost her husband seven years earlier, and had been living alone since then. However, over the last several years she had experienced some short-term memory loss as well as increased clumsiness and had had several minor accidents at home as a result. Her daughter had been urging her to move into a mother-in-law apartment which adjoined the daughter's house so Frances would be closer to her family. At the time I began to work with Frances she had just decided to move in with her daughter, but she expressed a great deal of anxiety about the move. This was clearly a major transition for her, and not an easy one.

Frances was worried that giving up her own home would mean losing her independence. She was also fearful that she might become a burden to her daughter. She had always been a very active woman and the loss of memory and agility that she was experiencing made her very fearful of losing her physical abilities. Her hearing and eyesight were not as sharp as they had been, and this increased her fears and also made her feel somewhat isolated as she sometimes could not participate in group conversations or activities.

I began by introducing Frances to temperature biofeedback combined with autogenic phrases to increase the blood flow to the hands and feet. When blood flow to the extremities is increased, this indicates a relaxing of the blood vessels and should result in lower blood pressure. First I taped a fish tank thermometer to the outside of her index finger to measure the temperature of her hands. Then I taught her to use the autogenic relaxation exercise, emphasizing phrases which encouraged the blood vessels to relax and the blood to flow freely into the extremities. After she completed the exercise, we again measured the temperature in her hands to see if it had increased as a result of the relaxation and increased circulation.

Frances practiced the autogenic relaxation at home for twenty minutes a day, and I saw her each week for the next month, each time measuring the temperature of her hand, leading her through the autogenic exercise, and then measuring her hand temperature again. Even after a month of practice, she seemed unable to significantly increase the temperature in her extremities as a result of the relaxation.

I had also asked Frances's daughter to take her mother's blood pressure each day at home to see how it fluctuated and to possibly correlate the fluctuations with certain events in her life. I wanted to see, for instance, if her blood pressure was higher on days when she was around the frenetic energy of her grandchildren a great deal, or on days when she felt particularly anxious about her health. We were unable to detect any such correlation.

I began to suspect that hardening of the arteries, not stress, was responsible for Frances's high blood pressure. In younger adults, approximately 70% of hypertension cases are linked to stress and anxiety in their lives. These people can do a great deal to lower their blood pressure by changing lifestyle behaviors and using relaxation techniques. When organic problems such as artereosclerosis are causing the blood pressure elevation, however, stress reduction techniques have minimal impact.

Though we were unable to significantly lower Frances's blood pressure, the regular use of autogenic relaxation definitely had a positive effect on her well-being. She began to feel less anxious about the transition she was going through and more self-accepting. She overcame her fears of being dependent on her family and began to feel good about being closer with them. She realized that even though she couldn't care for her grandchildren, by talking with them and spending time with them she was making a contribution to their lives. Our society does not encourage or emphasize this kind of contribution, so it is easily overlooked.

Frances began to sleep more soundly and to have more energy during the day. She was able to reduce the level of the medications she had been taking to help her relax, and she felt more clearheaded as a result, as grogginess was a side effect of these medications. In general, her level of fear and anxiety was lowered and she felt an increased peace of mind as she moved through the transition of old age.

Relaxation Exercises for Aging

PROGRESSIVE RELAXATION WITH SELF-ACCEPTANCE VISUALIZATION

This relaxation exercise can be used to gain control over the stresses associated with the aging process. You cannot stop your body from aging, but you can control your response to your body's changes. Progressive relaxation helps you to achieve a deep state of comfort and serenity. Once you are fully relaxed, the visualization will help you develop the peace of mind and self-acceptance that will enable you to move through the aging process with grace and equanimity. The visualization presents positive images of health and happiness that will help heal and recharge you. When your body and mind feel relaxed, you will find you have more energy and can handle life's challenges with a positive attitude.

Daily practice for eight to twelve weeks will bring the maximum benefits. If you continue using the exercise on a regular basis beyond this time, you may help prevent future health problems.

Read this exercise slowly (about half normal speaking speed). Pause at each (*). Do not be concerned by mispronunciations or verbal slips. Continue in a calm, even voice.

Find a quiet location where you will not be disturbed. Allow about twenty minutes for this exercise. Sit or lie back comfortably, allowing your arms and legs to remain uncrossed if possible. Let your head be supported and let your shoulders drop into a comfortable position. Check the muscles of your head and face. Let your forehead become calm and smooth. Allow the muscles around your eyes to loosen. Check the muscles of the mouth and jaw to make sure they are relaxed. Finally, allow your eyes to remain closed, remembering that you can open them whenever you need to use them.

Before we begin the relaxation, remember not to try to relax too quickly. In fact, do not try to relax at all. Without any effort you can allow yourself to relax by pleasantly letting go of tensions and discomforts, and then letting yourself drift deeper into a peaceful calmness. To begin the relaxation, take three deep breaths, pausing after you inhale, and then exhaling fully and completely. You might imagine that you release tensions and discomforts as you exhale by just breathing them away. * After you have finished these first three breaths, continue breathing slowly and naturally, relaxing more deeply with each slow exhale.

As you continue to breathe slowly and gently, begin to focus your atten-

tion on the muscles in your feet. You may want to move your toes briefly to see how these muscles feel. Let them rest in the most comfortable position and then use your imagination to see or feel these muscles relaxing even further. Slowly exhale, breathing away energy or tension in your toes. As you breathe slowly, imagine these muscles becoming more soft and flexible. *
Turn your awareness to the muscles of the arch of your foot. The muscles from the ball of your foot below the big toe down to the heel can relax even further. Take a slow breath and then imagine that as you exhale you release the tensions from these muscles. * Now feel the sides and the top of your foot. Can you feel your shoes or socks touching your foot? As you breathe slowly and naturally, you can let the muscles of your foot relax more. You might even be able to feel a pulse or tingling sensation gradually spreading warmth and relaxation to every muscle of your foot. *

Turn your awareness to your lower leg. Can you feel your ankles, * your calves, * your shin bones? * Feel the muscles of your lower legs, and notice that you can relax these muscles even further. Breathe slowly as you feel the muscles softening. You may even feel the knee starting to relax into a more comfortable position. As your awareness increases, your skill at relaxing will also. You will feel your control increasing as you practice letting these muscle groups relax even more. * Now become aware of your upper legs. Feel the large muscles of the sides and top of your legs relax slowly as you exhale the unwanted energies and tensions. * You can now relax the big muscles of the back of your upper legs. As these muscles relax, you might even feel the relaxation spreading up through your pelvic area into the lower back. The big muscles of the leg may loosen so that you can feel the sensation of heaviness down the length of your leg. * Breathe slowly and gently. You might even feel the pulse of blood flowing more freely and easily down your leg into your foot and toes. *

The relaxation can now begin to spread up into your lower back. As the muscles of your back begin to soften, you might feel the relaxation spreading to the other muscles of the back. Feel the muscles of your upper back, including your shoulders, let go even further. Your shoulders may be able to drop down into a more comfortable position. * Feel your head sinking back into the chair or pillow, totally supported, as the muscles of your neck let go even more. * Continue breathing slowly and gently as you feel the relaxation spreading down through your arms. * The muscles of your upper arms may feel loose and comfortable. * Your lower arms, even your wrists, can relax further. As you breathe slowly, feel the sensation of heaviness as your arms sink back into the bed or chair. * The relaxation can slowly drift down into your hands and fingers. * You may feel a pulse of blood flowing

freely and easily down into your hands. Feel your hands warm comfortably, letting you drift deeper into comfort and relaxation. *

The muscles of your head and face may be able to relax even more. Your forehead may feel more calm and smooth. * The muscles around the eyes can let go. * Even the muscles of the mouth and the jaw might be able to relax even further. * Slowly breathing away stress, you can control these tensions through relaxation. * The sensations of peace and harmony grow stronger as you allow yourself to drift deeper in this peaceful calmness. *

The relaxation can drift down into your chest. As you breathe slowly, you might feel the relaxation gently spreading into the other muscles of the torso. You can feel your heartbeat, calm and regular. * The relaxation spreads down into your stomach region. * You may be able to feel the sensation of warmth glowing gently in the stomach region. * Continue breathing slowly and gently as you drift peacefully.

VISUALIZATION FOR SELF-ACCEPTANCE

As you continue breathing slowly and deeply, try to clear your mind of the day's events. A good way to do this is to imagine that you are outdoors on a beautiful day gazing into the calm blue sky. As thoughts or mental distractions pass through your mind, imagine yourself letting go as if they were colored helium-filled ballons. Let them drift up into the sky with every slow exhale of breath. Watch as they drift up and away, perhaps dancing in the warm breezes. As the balloons float higher and higher, watch them grow smaller. Eventually, you can watch as they blow over the horizon or become so small they simply drift from sight. Now the sky is calm and clear once again. Notice the soothing color of the blue sky as you continue to breathe slowly and naturally. You may even wish to imagine that you can breathe in the cool blue light of the sky as you continue to relax, just letting go.

Turn your attention, gently, to the warm rays of the sun and the gentle, warm breezes. Feel the warmth begin to relax you. Perhaps you can feel the warmth beginning to soak deep within you, allowing tension to melt away. Feel yourself sinking further into whatever you are sitting or lying upon. Imagine you are slowly breathing in the warmth and golden sunlight. As your body fills with this warming, healing light and energy, you can feel yourself recharging. Imagine every cell in your body is being bathed in oxygen and nutrients to help heal and recharge them. The cells soak up the perfect amount of nutrients, so they can grow healthy and strong, filling you with positive energy, health, and happiness. Even though you are filled with this positive energy, you remain relaxed and comfortable.

You can drift as long as you like in this state of relaxation, health, and happiness. Or you can imagine yourself doing something active in the sunshine, feeling healthy and strong. You are smiling and celebrating your positive energy and health. Remember that you can maintain this healing energy within you and use it anytime you wish. With practice you will find that this golden-white light and warm, healing energy can remain within your heart, as a reserve for whenever you need it. You will also find that within this positive energy dwells a special part of you. This part of you is the perfect being of love and light that people call the "soul." It can see and accept the many parts of you. It sees and accepts your strengths and weaknesses. Your strengths are the tools you have for change and your weaknesses are the lessons from which you learn and grow. As you remain relaxed and comfortable, bathed in love and light, see yourself accepting your strengths and your weaknesses, so that you can enjoy your life in a positive, healthy way.

As you drift in this peaceful state of calmness, acceptance, and health, remember that the pains and fears of life can be lessened by your new awareness and control. These difficulties may not leave completely, but you will be able to let them pass from your mind rather than letting them be a weight within you which drains your energies. You can replace these worries and fears with love, energy, and the positive new plans and goals you are making for yourself. You remain young and alive as you explore these new activities and celebrate each day anew. Light and energy grow bright within you as you feel new energy and peace.

Drift for a few more minutes in this pleasant state of relaxation and warmth, breathing slowly. When you wish to awaken, imagine that you can return to the room, letting the feelings of love and self-acceptance return with you. Let the feelings of relaxation and comfort remain with you throughout your day. When you wish to awaken completely, take a deep breath and stretch, letting the feelings of health, comfort, and joy return with you to a fully waking state. You may wish to take another deep breath and stretch, feeling wide awake, refreshed, and alert.

Continued practice with this technique makes it easier. Do not expect instant results, but assure yourself that with continued practice you can positively affect the way you feel and act. With this exercise, you can learn to control and guide your behavior and feelings in a positive way.

AUTOGENICS FOR CONTROL OF HIGH BLOOD PRESSURE

This exercise is formulated to help you control your high blood pressure through relaxation and visualization. You should use the exercise in conjunction with your doctor's treatment program. If you are currently taking medication to control your blood pressure, continue taking the medication, but inform your doctor that you are practicing relaxation exercises. Together you can monitor your progress to see whether your need for medication decreases. Hopefully, if you practice the exercise consistently, you can eliminate your need for medication. But do not make a decision to decrease or eliminate medication without your doctor's knowledge and authorization.

Eight to twelve weeks of daily practice is usually needed before you will see significant results from this exercise. As you do the exercise, concentrate particularly on increasing the blood flow and warmth to your hands and feet. Most people find it easier to increase the warmth in their hands; however, the best results occur when your're able to consistently feel increased warmth in your feet.

Read this exercise slowly (about half normal speaking speed). Pause at each (*). Do not be concerned by mispronunciations or verbal slips. Continue in a calm, even voice.

Find a quiet location where you will not be disturbed. Allow about twenty minutes for this exercise. Sit or lie back comfortably, allowing your arms and legs to remain uncrossed if possible. Let your head be supported and let your shoulders drop into a comfortable position. Check the muscles of your head and face. Let your forehead become calm and smooth. Allow the muscles around your eyes to loosen. Check the muscles of the mouth and jaw to make sure they are relaxed. Finally, allow your eyes to remain closed, remembering that you can open them whenever you need to use them.

Before we begin the relaxation, remember not to try to relax too quickly. In fact, do not try to relax at all. Without any effort you can allow yourself to relax by pleasantly letting go of tensions and discomforts, and then letting yourself drift deeper into a peaceful calmness. To begin the relaxation, take three deep breaths, pausing after you inhale, and then exhaling fully and completely. You might imagine that you release tensions and discomforts as you exhale by just breathing them away. * After you have finished these first three breaths, continue breathing slowly and naturally, relaxing more deeply with each slow exhale.

Repeat these phrases to yourself, exactly as they are written from this exercise, and try to feel your body responding to the commands. If you need to repeat the phrases more than three times to begin to feel results, then continue the repetitions a few additional times.

Repeat this mood phrase to yourself three times: "I am at peace with myself and fully relaxed." Continue breathing slowly and gently.

Begin to feel the muscles of your arms relax as you say, "My right arm is heavy * . . . My right arm is heavy * . . . My right arm is heavy * . . ." Repeat this phrase slowly until you begin to feel the heaviness spreading through your arm. Now turn your awareness to your left arm as you breathe slowly and say to yourself, "My left arm is heavy * . . . My left arm is heavy * . . . My left arm is heavy * . . ." Try to feel the heaviness starting in your arms or feel free to continue slowly repeating this phrase a few more times. Now proceed to your legs. Let them begin to relax as you breathe slowly. Feel the heaviness and relaxation starting in your legs as you slowly repeat, "My right leg is heavy * . . . My right leg is heavy * . . . My right leg is heavy * . . ." You can repeat this several more times if you need to, until you begin to feel the relaxation and the heaviness. Now focus on the left leg and feel it beginning to relax as you say, "My left leg is heavy * . . . My left leg is heavy * . . . My left leg is heavy * . . ." Repeat if needed. With practice you will feel the heaviness more quickly and easily. Now turn your attention to your neck and shoulders. Let them sink into a more comfortable position and let the muscles relax as you breathe gently and say, "My neck and shoulders are heavy * . . . My neck and shoulders are heavy * . . . My neck and shoulders are heavy * . . ." Repeat if needed. Take a deep slow breath and feel the heaviness and relaxation as you begin to sink back into whatever you are sitting or lying upon.

Perhaps you can feel the blood beginning to flow more easily down into your hands or your feet as the blood vessels begin to dilate, as the smooth muscles in the walls of the arteries begin to relax. Focus on the feelings of warmth, or a pulse, or perhaps a tingling feeling in your right hand as you say, "My right arm is warm * . . . My right arm is warm * . . . My right arm is warm * . . ." Repeat this slowly several more times until you begin to feel the warmth or pulse. Heaviness is generally easier for most people to feel than warmth, but with continued practice you can begin to control the blood flow. Now turn your attention to your left arm and say to yourself, "My left arm is warm * . . . My left arm is warm * . . . My left arm is warm * . . ." Repeat if needed. Perhaps you can start to feel the warmth in your arms, and you may feel the blood flowing freely through your entire body. As you breathe slowly and gently, turn your awareness to your legs and say to yourself, "My right leg is warm * . . . My right leg is warm * . . . My right leg is warm * . . ." Repeat several more times to help develop this skill. Move your attention to your left leg and say, "My left leg is warm * . . . My left leg is warm * . . . My left leg is warm * . . ." Repeat if needed. Feel the heaviness and warmth in your arms and your legs as you breathe slowly and gently. Now turn your awareness to your neck and shoulders, and say, "My neck and shoulders are warm * . . . My neck and shoulders are warm *

... My neck and shoulders are warm * ..." Repeat if needed. Breathe slowly as you drift for a few moments, feeling the heaviness and warmth spreading pleasantly about your body.

Slow and calm your heart by slowly repeating to yourself, "My heartbeat is calm and regular * ... My heartbeat is calm and regular * ... My heartbeat is calm and regular * ..." Repeat if needed. If you experience any discomfort with this phrase then change to the phrase "I feel calm * ... I feel calm * ... I feel calm * ..." As you breathe slowly, begin to feel the peace and relaxation spreading to every part of your body.

To slow your breathing say to yourself as you breathe into your diaphragm, "My breathing is calm and regular * ... My breathing is calm and regular * ... My breathing is calm and regular * ..." Repeat if needed.

Become aware of the relaxation starting in your stomach region. As you breathe slowly say, "My abdomen is warm and calm * ... My abdomen is warm and calm * ... My abdomen is warm and calm * ..." Repeat if needed. If you have any serious abdominal problems or diabetes, change this phrase to "I am calm and relaxed * ... I am calm and relaxed * ... I am calm and relaxed * ..."

Move on to your forehead and let the muscles of your head and face relax as you say, "My forehead is cool and calm * ... My forehead is cool and calm * ... My forehead is cool and calm * ..." As you breathe slowly, feel the the muscles around your eyes, mouth, and jaw loosen and then relax.

Let yourself drift pleasantly in this calmness. As you breathe gently, perhaps you can feel the heaviness in your arms and legs as the muscles relax. * Perhaps you can begin to feel the warmth or pulse of blood flowing more easily down into your hands and perhaps even your feet, like sunshine or a bath gently warming you. Some people feel the warming as if it were a tingling sensation spreading blood more easily into the extremities. * As you enjoy the relaxation you can feel that your heartbeat is calm and regular. *

With practice, you can feel the relaxation more easily and quickly. The warmth of blood flowing into your hands and feet gradually grows easier to control, until you will be able to consistently warm your hands to 93 degrees and your feet to 90 degrees. The relaxation will then carry over with you throughout your day. You will even be able to remain more comfortable when your blood pressure is taken in your doctor's office. You will be able to breathe slowly in stressful situations, to help release any tensions, just letting go of the stress.

At the end of this relaxation exercise, awaken yourself slowly. Feel the bed or chair beneath you and say, "I am refreshed and completely alert *

. . . I am refreshed and completely alert * . . . I am refreshed and completely alert . . ." Then take a deep breath and stretch, allowing yourself to wake fully, and let the relaxation carry over with you into a fully waking state. You may wish to take another deep breath and stretch, letting the relaxation return with you.

RELAXATION FOR IMPROVED SLEEP

Sleeping difficulties are often linked to the many stresses in our lives. If our minds are swimming with worries and concerns, it is hard to achieve the relaxed state in which we can easily fall asleep. Though people of any age can experience difficulty falling asleep or staying asleep, as we age poor sleep patterns often become more acute. And the older person is often less able to tolerate loss of sleep.

This relaxation, practiced before bedtime, should aid you in getting to sleep, staying asleep, and waking feeling refreshed. I suggest you have a tape of this exercise by your bed so that you can listen to it whenever it may be needed. If possible, use a tape recorder which shuts off automatically at the end so you do not have to wake up to turn it off. With practice, you will learn the technique so well that you will be able to go through the relaxation without using the tape.

Read this exercise slowly (about half normal speaking speed). Pause at each (*). Do not be concerned by mispronunciations or verbal slips. Continue in a calm, even voice.

Find a quiet location where you will not be disturbed. Lie back comfortably, allowing your arms and your legs to remain uncrossed. (You may require a different position for comfort, so please feel free to adjust your position for the comfort needed to sleep.) Let your head be supported and let your shoulders drop into a comfortable position. Check the muscles of your head and face. Let your forehead become calm and smooth. Allow the muscles around your eyes to loosen. Check the muscles of the mouth and jaw to make sure they are relaxed. Finally, allow your eyes to remain closed, remembering that you can open them whenever you need to use them.

Before we begin the relaxation, remember not to try to relax too quickly. In fact, do not try to relax at all. Without any effort you can allow yourself to relax by pleasantly letting go of tensions and discomforts, and then letting yourself drift deeper into a peaceful calmness. To begin the relaxation, take three deep breaths, pausing after you inhale, and then exhaling fully and completely. You might imagine that you release tensions and discomforts as you exhale by just breathing them away. * After you have finished these first three breaths, continue breathing slowly and naturally, pleasantly relaxing more deeply with each slow exhale.

As you continue to breathe slowly and naturally, you may feel the relaxation beginning in your body. The most important thing to remember when dealing with stress is that you can take control of your body through awareness and relaxation. So to begin this process, turn your awareness to the sensation of relaxation that is beginning in your arms and hands. You may feel that one arm is more relaxed than the other. * Perhaps one arm may feel a bit heavier than the other arm. The muscles may feel more loose or more flexible than in the other arm. * Or perhaps you feel that one arm is a bit warmer than the other arm. You may feel that the warmth of blood and energy may flow more easily down one arm, as if it were flowing through wide-open blood vessels, slowly but freely moving into your hand and fingers. You may even feel it slowly pulsing down into your hand. * Or perhaps you find that both arms feel equally relaxed and this would be perfect as well. The only thing that matters is that you breathe slowly and gently as you let yourself drift deeper into that soothing dreamlike calmness. *

As you drift pleasantly, turn your awareness to the sensations of relaxation that may be beginning in your legs and feet. You might feel that one leg is slightly more relaxed than the other. Perhaps you notice that one leg feels a little heavier, as if the muscles of that leg were more loose or flexible than the other leg. * Or as you breathe slowly and gently, you may feel that one leg is slightly warmer, as if the blood and warmth could spread more easily down that leg, drifting down through wide-open blood vessels, * perhaps even pulsing slowly but freely down into your foot and toes. * Or perhaps your legs feel equally relaxed, and that would be perfect also. The only thing that really matters is that you continue to breathe slowly as you allow yourself to drift more deeply into that dreamlike calmness and comfort. *

You may even feel the gradual control of stress and tensions beginning as you sink back into whatever you are lying upon and the tension just melts away. *

You may even feel the muscles of your back beginning to loosen or soften, and as you breathe slowly, naturally, you might feel the relaxation spreading to the other muscles of your back. * Even your upper back and shoulders may begin to soften or loosen a bit further. Your shoulders may be able to drop into a more comfortable position. * You may feel the control growing stronger as your head sinks back into the pillow, the muscles of your neck begin to let go, and you drift deeper into relaxation. *

As you pleasantly drift deeper into this comfort and calmness, you may be able to feel the muscles of your head and face beginning to relax even further. * Continue to breathe slowly, allowing a soothing healing wave of relaxation to gently spread down from the top of your head, soothing and cleansing every muscle and cell of your body. You can feel it slowly drifting down to relax the muscles of your forehead, * letting your forehead become calm and smooth. * Let this wave drift down to relax the muscles around your eyes, releasing the tension in these muscles. * The wave then drifts down helping to relax the muscles of your mouth, including your jaw. Let these muscles go loose and limp. * And as you breathe slowly, the wave slowly drifts down to relax the muscles of your neck. Even your shoulders can loosen a bit more. * The relaxation can begin to spread down your arms. * As the wave of relaxation gently drifts down your arms you may even be able to feel it pulsing into your hands. *

The wave of relaxation can drift down through your back and chest, spreading soothing comfort into your lower back. * Even your heartbeat feels more calm and regular as the relaxation gently spreads throughout your body. * The wave of relaxation can spread down through your pelvic area, helping to loosen and relax the muscles of your legs even more. * The relaxation slowly drifts down through your legs. Perhaps you can feel it pulsing slowly down into your feet, spreading the comfort down, washing the discomfort out of your body. *

As you allow yourself to drift more deeply in this calmness, the soothing relaxation can begin to rest and recharge you. Perhaps you can imagine that you are outdoors in a perfect place, on a warm and beautiful day. Choose the most comfortable place to lie down. Feel the warmth from the sun. As you begin to soak up the warmth you can feel your tensions and discomforts just melting away. * The warmth can fill you with comforting energy and the golden-white light can help to recharge you fully and completely. Even though you remain at peace, you can feel the warmth of blood flowing more freely to every cell of your body, carrying oxygen and nutrients and energy to bathe every cell. Each cell, like a sponge, can soak up the perfect amount of nutrients and energy. You may even begin to feel sensations of comfort, acceptance, and happiness burning more brightly within you, though you remain calm and comfortable. * Perhaps you can picture yourself filling with the joy and peace that relaxation can bring to you. * See yourself in a state of harmony and happiness, doing something active, perhaps smiling and celebrating in the sunshine. * As you practice this relaxation exercise you will be able to relax more deeply and more quickly. You will be more aware of tensions and begin to develop confidence that you can rid yourself of unnecessary anxieties whenever they may develop. The effects of the relaxation will begin to carry over throughout your day.

As you become more comfortable with this relaxation, things that used to bother you will be more tolerable. As you take care of yourself in this special way you will gradually learn to see and to accept the many parts of yourself, your strengths and your weaknesses. As you feel acceptance, you will free yourself to grow in a spiritual way. Letting go of fears and pains will become easier, and you will feel more peaceful. You can move through difficult transitions with grace and dignity.

You can feel yourself drifting into a pleasant sleep, knowing you will rest fully and awaken refreshed and alert. Continue breathing slowly and focus on the feelings of relaxation in your arms and legs. * Continue to breathe slowly and gently as you feel the heaviness of your arms and legs. Let yourself drift in this dreamlike state as you sleep deeply and peacefully, resting well so you can awaken refreshed in the morning.

INDIRECT RELAXATION TO CONTROL PAIN

This relaxation/visualization is included to assist people who may be suffering from aches and pains that are made worse by stress. The exercise can be highly effective in helping to eliminate certain types of stress-related pain. But even if it does not completely eliminate the pain, it will help to lessen the anxieties that make pain more intense. With practice, this relaxation will even help reduce the severity of chronic pain. The main purpose of the exercise is to help you gain control over your body and your life, as this control may have been lessened by the fight with pain.

Read this exercise slowly (about half normal speaking speed). Pause at each (*). Do not be concerned by mispronunciations or verbal slips. Continue in a calm, even voice.

Find a quiet location where you will not be disturbed. Allow about twenty minutes for this exercise. Sit or lie back comfortably, allowing your arms and legs to remain uncrossed if possible. Let your head be supported and let your shoulders drop into a more comfortable position. Check the muscles of your head and face. Let your forehead become calm and smooth. Allow the muscles around your eyes to loosen. Check the muscles of the mouth and jaw to make sure they are relaxed. Finally, allow your eyes to remain closed, remembering that you can open them whenever you need to use them.

Before we begin the relaxation, remember not to try to relax too quickly. In fact, do not try to relax at all. Without any effort you can allow yourself to relax by pleasantly letting go of tensions and discomforts, and then letting yourself drift deeper into a peaceful calmness. To begin the relaxation, take three deep breaths, pausing after you inhale, and then exhaling fully and completely. You might imagine that you release tensions and discomforts as you exhale by just breathing them away. * After you have finished these first three breaths, continue breathing slowly and naturally, relaxing more deeply with each slow exhale.

As you continue to breathe slowly and naturally, you may feel the relaxation beginning in your body. The first step to controlling pain and discomfort is to be able to release tensions that may be intensifying the pain or symptom. Control starts with awareness, followed by the ability to let go of stress, knowing that you can lessen if not eliminate the discomfort. So to begin this process, turn your awareness to the sensation of relaxation that is beginning in your arms and hands. You may feel that one arm is slightly more relaxed than the other. * Perhaps one arm may feel a bit heavier than the other arm. The muscles may feel more loose or more flexible than in the other arm. * Or perhaps you feel that one arm is a bit warmer than the other arm. You may feel that the warmth of blood and energy may flow more easily down one arm, as if it were flowing through wide-open blood vessels, slowly but freely moving down into your hand and fingers. You may even feel it slowly pulsing down into your hand. * Or perhaps you find that both arms feel equally relaxed and this would be perfect as well. The only thing that matters is that you breathe deeper into that soothing dreamlike calmness. * As you drift pleasantly, turn your awareness to the sensations of relaxation that may be beginning in your legs and feet. You might feel that one leg is slightly more relaxed than the other. Perhaps you notice that one leg feels a little heavier, as if the muscles of that leg were more loose or flexible than the other leg. * Or as you breathe slowly and gently, you may feel that one leg is slightly warmer, as if the blood and warmth could spread more easily down that leg, drifting down through wide-open blood vessels, * perhaps even pulsing slowly but freely down into your foot and toes. * Or perhaps your legs feel equally relaxed, and that would be perfect also. The only thing that really matters is that you continue to breathe slowly as you allow yourself to drift more deeply into that dreamlike calmness and comfort. *

You may even feel the gradual control of pain and discomfort beginning as you sink back into whatever you are sitting or lying upon and the tension just melts away. *

You may even feel the muscles of your back beginning to loosen or soften, and as you breathe slowly, naturally, you might feel the relaxation spreading to the other muscles of your back. * Even your upper back and shoulders may begin to soften or loosen a bit further. Your shoulders may be able to drop into a more comfortable position. * You may feel the control growing stronger as your head just sinks back into the pillow or chair, the muscles of your neck begin to let go, and you drift deeper into relaxation. *

As you pleasantly drift deeper into this comfort and calmness, you may be able to feel the muscles of your head and face beginning to relax even further. * Continue to breathe slowly, allowing a soothing, healing wave of relaxation to gently spread down from the top of your head, soothing and cleansing every muscle and cell of your body. You can feel it slowly drifting down to relax the muscles of your forehead, * letting your forehead become calm and smooth. * Let this wave drift down to relax the muscles around your eyes, releasing the tension in these muscles. * The wave then drifts down helping to relax the muscles of your mouth, including your jaw. Let these muscles go loose and limp. * And as you breathe slowly, the wave slowly drifts down to relax the muscles of your neck. Even your shoulders can loosen a bit more. * The relaxation can begin to spread down your arms. * As the wave of relaxation gently drifts down your arms you may even be able to feel it pulsing down into your hands. *

The wave of relaxation can drift down through your back and chest, spreading soothing comfort into your lower back. * Even your heartbeat feels more calm and regular as the relaxation gently spreads throughout your body. * The wave of relaxation can spread down through your pelvic area, helping to loosen and relax the muscles of your legs even more. * The relaxation slowly drifts down through your legs. Perhaps you can feel it pulsing slowly down into your feet, spreading the comfort down, washing the discomfort out of your body. *

As you allow yourself to drift more deeply in this calmness, the soothing relaxation can help you rest and recharge yourself. Perhaps you can imagine that you are outdoors in a perfect place, on a warm and beautiful day. Choose the most comfortable place to lie down. Feel the warmth from the sun. As you begin to soak up the warmth, you can feel your tensions and discomforts just melting away. * The warmth can fill you with healing energy and the golden-white light can help to recharge you fully and completely. Even though you remain at peace, you can feel the warmth of blood flowing more freely to every cell of your body, carrying oxygen and nutrients and healing energy to bathe every cell. Each cell, like a sponge, can soak up the perfect amount of nutrients and energy to help heal and recharge you. You may even begin to feel sensations of health, joy, and happiness burning more brightly within you, though you remain calm and comfortable. * Perhaps you can picture yourself filling with strength and energy as your body heals itself. * See yourself in a state of health and happiness, doing something active, perhaps smiling and celebrating in the sunshine. * As you practice this relaxation exercise you will be able to relax more deeply and quickly. You will be more aware of tensions and you will develop confidence that you can rid yourself of unnecessary pains and discomforts. The effects of the relaxation will begin to carry over throughout your day.

If you are using this exercise at bedtime you may wish to drift off into a pleasant sleep, resting fully and awakening refreshed and alert. If you wish to drift off to sleep, continue breathing slowly and focus on the feelings of relaxation in your arms and legs. *

If you wish to awaken now, you can begin to do so. Let yourself gradually return to this room, feeling the bed or the chair beneath you. As you slowly awaken, bring the feelings of calmness, relaxation, health, and happiness back with you into a more fully waking state. Take a deep breath and stretch, letting the calmness return with you. Take another deep breath and stretch, allowing yourself to awaken feeling refreshed and alert, letting the relaxation and calmness continue with you.

BIBLIOGRAPHY

Averyt, Anne C., with Edith Furst and Donna Dalton Hummel. *Successful Aging: A Sourcebook for Older People and Their Families*. New York: Ballantine Books, 1987. $9.95.

A resource book with useful information about services and activities for aging people.

Clark, Etta. *Growing Old Is Not for Sissies: Portraits of Senior Athletes*. Corte Madera, CA: Pomegranate Calendars and Books, 1986. $16.95.

This inspirational book challenges standard ideas about the limitations imposed by aging!

Leshan, Eda. *Oh, to Be 50 Again!: On Being Too Old for a Mid-Life Crisis*. New York: Times Books / Random House, 1986. $16.95 (hardback).

Gentle awareness of the issues, concerns, and adjustments of aging. Many practical suggestions.

Painter, Charlotte (text) and Pamela Valois (photos). *Gifts of Age: Portraits and Essays of 32 Remarkable Women*. San Francisco: Chronicle Books, 1985. $14.95.

Beautiful book about strong able women. Inspirational!

AUDIOCASSETTE TAPES

Mason, L. John, Ph.D. 1) *High Blood Pressure Relaxation*, 2) *Relaxation for Pain*, and 3) *Relaxation for Sleep*. 1988. Each is $11.95 and can be ordered from the author.

Specially formulated relaxation exercises designed to help reduce if not eliminate the specific concerns. These guided techniques are most beneficial when practiced regularly.

CHAPTER NINE

Death & Dying

Introduction

THIS IS THE most difficult chapter of this book for me to write, not for lack of information, but because the emotions evoked by death and loss are painful to confront. Yet, at some time in our lives, we will all most likely have to face the death of a loved one. And certainly we will all eventually confront our own mortality. The purpose of this chapter is to share information which may help reduce the anxiety of the death experience. It is written both for the person making this ultimate life transition, and the person who is suffering the loss of a friend or family member. Stress management can assist the person entering the transition of death by helping to reduce anxiety and pain and to increase feelings of acceptance. When death can be seen as a life completing experience, it offers the opportunity for spiritual growth and expanded awareness. Stress management can help the person going through the grieving process to feel a sense of control over her responses at a time when she may feel so little control over other areas of her life. It also helps her to continue living with a renewed sense of purpose and meaning and to deal with the alterations in her life in a positive way.

Our society spends a great deal of energy denying the existence of death. Our youth-oriented culture does not like to acknowledge or discuss this ultimate transition. Strong taboos exist against talking about the feelings evoked by death and against allowing the death experience to be an integral part of our lives. Whereas Grandpa used to be cared for at home during his last illness and death, with his grandchildren, children, neighbors, and friends walking in and out of his home daily, he is now shuttled off to an old folk's home or to a sterile hospital when his health deteriorates. His natural transition into death is viewed as unseemly or as something his family cannot cope with, and only those closest to him witness this final stage of life. Even those who go through the experience with him talk of it only in hushed whispers, and usually only to clergy or close family members.

When death is not an integral, accepted part of our lives, we do not learn how to respond to it appropriately, and this adds to the confusion and anxiety for everyone involved. Fortunately, in the last ten years, our society has begun to recognize the importance of the death experience and to urge that many of the taboos cloaking this experience be lifted. Increasingly, people speak of "death with dignity," and new emphasis has been placed on the importance of allowing the dying person to remain at home, in a familiar and comfortable environment, surrounded by friends and family.

One outgrowth of this new emphasis on dying as a natural part of life has been the development of hospice organizations. The word "hospice" orginally referred to a shelter or lodging for travelers. Hospice organizations attempt to serve the dying person's needs, just as the original hospice shelters, usually run by monks, served the needs of the traveler. The term "hospice" also suggests a positive view of the dying person as a traveler through life's ultimate journey.

In cities across the country, trained hospice staff—nurses, social workers, home-help aides, chaplains, volunteers—provide practical, emotional, and medical assistance to the dying person and his family so that the terminally ill person can remain at home and in comfort as long as possible. Nurses may administer medication or monitor the person's illness, staying in close communication with the doctors at the hospital. Social workers provide counseling or information about available resources, such as Medicare or other programs, and how to use them. Home-help aides may assist the terminally ill person with personal grooming or eating. Volunteers may provide relief to caregivers, so they can leave the home for a few hours or run other errands. Nondenominational chaplains may encourage families to talk more freely about the emotions which accompany death and loss. All of these services allow people to feel they are not alone with their pain and grief, but are part of a supportive community and a larger, meaningful life experience.

Elisabeth Kübler-Ross, a psychiatrist and authority on death who has worked with many dying patients, has done a great deal to bring the awareness of death as a growth experience to the broader public. Her book, *On Death and Dying*, is used as a guide for trained staff and laypersons alike. In it she identifies four common stages of grief which both the terminally ill person and his family and friends experience. Initially, many people tend to deny the fact of impending death. Next, as reality sinks in, the person may feel anger and frustration. "Why me?" is a common utterance, as the terminally ill person and his loved ones feel resentful and victimized. Ultimately, the dying person and those around him move through a stage of grief and then acceptance, in which they are able to transcend their initial feelings and find peace. I highly recommend that anyone coping with death and dying read Kübler-Ross's book.

Kübler-Ross and other experts on death and dying emphasis the importance of finding value in the death experience. This will mean different things to different people, but often finding value and meaning in death is related to spiritual growth and development. One's spiritual growth may be shaped by the beliefs of organized religion, or it may be a personal process which lies outside of a specific religious practice. We all have within us a "soul" or "spirit" which connects us to all other living things and which, when nurtured, can become a powerful ally in dealing with the anxieties surrounding death. This special part of our consciousness radiates the acceptance and pure energy of love. It enables us to see our strengths and our weaknesses and to accept them. When we open ourselves to this inner light, we can find meaning in suffering and richness of experience in life's final stage.

Sometimes those approaching death will fight the inevitable. Particularly when people have a powerful reason to live, this challenge to mortality can be positive, helping to prolong life. We've all heard stories, for instance, of the dying person who holds onto life until his family is able to gather around his bedside, or the person filled with courageous desire to live who defies and outlives her prognosis.

But sometimes the inability to accept impending death may be spurred by feelings of anger, resentment, or fear. These negative feelings can interfere with the ability to move more peacefully through this transition, and can prolong an uncomfortable situation for the dying person and his whole family. Learning to acknowledge and then express the feelings which are causing someone to hold on to life in a painful way can be liberating for everyone involved. Moving toward an acceptance of death does not imply resignation, but trust of the process through which one is moving.

Learning to view death as freeing and uplifting rather than morbid or fearful can also help the dying person feel open to and accepting of the final stage of life. Indeed, recent study of the death experience has revealed some astounding visions of the transition from life to death, visions which counter many of our society's prevailing images of death as painful or frightening. Researchers have studied the experiences of people who were resuscitated after a near-death experience (NDE). Some of these people had actually been legally dead, showing no life functions, before they regained their vital signs. The stories which these people relate upon returning from "death" seem to defy our morbid conceptions of death. The general consensus is that death is not frightening, but warm and inviting. Many who returned to life expressed regret about having to leave the feeling of complete freedom, love, and acceptance as they were "yanked back" by their medical saviors. Many told of a warm, bright light that invited them forward through a dark tunnel. They often felt they were assisted or guided in their journey by friends or family who had died in the past. These "survivors" also reported a feeling of being connected with all other living or conscious beings in a "oneness" unknown in life. Almost without exception, the "survivors" reported changed attitudes upon returning to life. They expressed a new lack of fear or anxiety about living because they knew the ultimate outcome, death, would be peaceful. They felt greater harmony and acceptance in their daily lives than they had ever known before.

If you want to know more about these near death experiences and what they can teach us about life and death, read the books listed in this chapter's bibliography, particularly Ken Moody's *Life after Life*, and Ken Ring's *Life at Death* and *Heading Toward Omega*. These books are fascinating and powerful. The picture which they provide of death as comforting and freeing rather than morbid and painful can not only help us confront our own death or the death of others, it can free us to live with a greater acceptance and appreciation of life.

Finally, I would like to make special mention of the feelings surrounding the death of a child or an unexpected, sudden death of a younger family member. Unplanned for, sudden loss of a loved one often leaves deep scars for those left behind. Anger, frustration, anxiety, and depression are common emotions of people whose lives have been suddenly, inexplicably bereaved. Often these people have difficulty searching for the "meaning" of a death which seems so particularly unfair. Margaret Miles and Eva Crandall have worked with bereaved parents and described their coping processes. Miles and Crandall found that those who could not find meaning in their loss felt a subsequent lack of purpose in their own lives, lacked trust, and often felt sui-

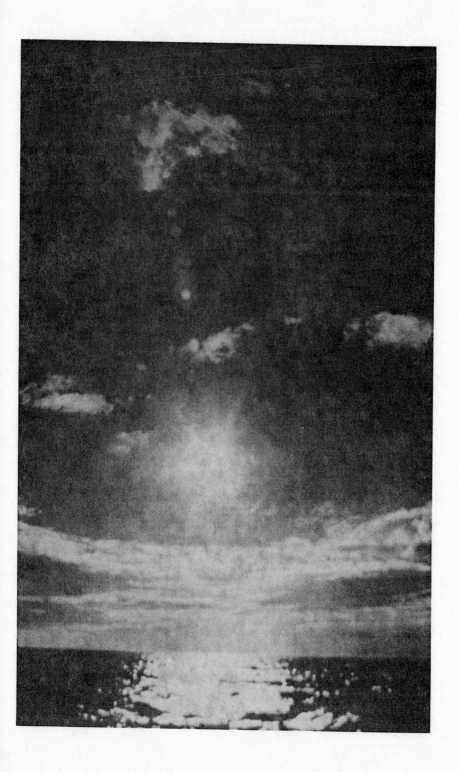

cidal. Those bereaved parents who were able to find meaning in their loss learned to live each day to the fullest, to be more understanding of others who had experienced loss, to feel more loving toward others, to have a stronger faith, and to experience life as precious. These findings certainly underscore the need for support during the grieving process, whether it be from a church or synagogue, individual or group therapy, from other health professionals, or from family and friends. The self-care suggestions outlined in this chapter are also critical tools for coping with grief and eventually transforming negative feelings into feelings of hope, faith, and affirmation.

Stress Management Recommendations for Dying and Grieving

The recommendations offered here for coping with the stresses of death and dying apply both to the dying person and to people who are experiencing the loss of a loved one. Because the process of death and dying is one that usually feels truly beyond control, it is vital that you feel able to take control of your responses to the situation in which you find yourself. The experience of death is perhaps one of the most trying experiences you will ever go through. The fears, anxieties, pain, and suffering which can accompany death can elicit severe stress responses. These responses are normal and indicate that you are moving through a vital life transition. They also signal an opportunity for personal growth. By learning to control your stress response through relaxation exercises, you can move through this often difficult journey with greater balance.

For both the dying person and her friends and family, controlling the stress response means reducing pain and anxiety. By controlling pain and anxiety you also lessen fear, and this in turn enables you to be more open to finding meaning in this difficult time. You may feel freer to experience the spiritual growth and insights which accompany death. As you learn to relax, you will also find your communication with those you love can improve, and greater closeness can result. Controlling your stress response may reduce your need for medication, enabling you to be more clearheaded. It can also help you to sleep better and to have more energy to deal with difficult situations.

These exercises may not solve all your problems, but they can help you to cope with these problems more effectively, and can offer a respite from the emotional turmoil produced by death and loss. I encourage you to find the exercise that works best for you and practice it daily. Finding the motivation to begin the exercise and to stick with it may be difficult when your energies are absorbed in a trying and painful situation, but taking the time to relax and care for yourself will improve both your physical and emotional well-being.

In addition to daily practice of relaxation exercises, I recommend that you reach out to support networks that are available to you. Your family and friends are a natural support system. Even if your relations with them are sometimes strained, this may be a time to repair relationships and establish a closeness that will not only help you deal with loss but will continue to enrich your life. Church groups are another source of support for many people. Local hospice organizations may be a valuable resource for the entire family. Check with your hospital to find out about the hospice center in your area. Many communities, either through hospitals, hospices, or private therapy organizations, offer special support groups for terminally ill people, and for people coping with the loss of a loved one. The opportunity to talk with other people who are going through similar experiences can help combat feelings of isolation and loneliness. Often, trained counselors may be able to assist the entire family with the dynamics of bereavement, explaining what feelings are common and helping family members to communicate openly.

Open communication is perhaps one of the most important ways to release the accumulated stresses caused by loss and pain. Often such strong emotions of guilt, anxiety, anger, or fear are aroused by terminal illness and death that these feelings are difficult to even acknowledge let alone articulate. But it is important to begin talking about these feelings as soon as they arise. Often, too, we simply don't know what to say when confronted with a situation that we can do nothing to change. We may feel helpless and inadequate in the face of death, and words may seem empty or fruitless. Yet great comfort can result from frank and loving communication, and sometimes this may be the greatest gift that one can offer. The guidance of a chaplain, counselor, or hospice staff member can be of great help in promoting meaningful communication. Also, I encourage you to read as much as possible about the experience of death and grieving. The more you know about what to expect and what other people have experienced, the easier it is to feel comfortable with your own experience and to be able to talk about it. The books listed at the end of this chapter are all valuable resources as well as being very moving.

Elisabeth Kübler-Ross has found, in her work with dying patients, that the desire for honest communication from one's doctor, family, and friends is a recurrent theme. Patients want kindness, but they also want to know what is happening to them and what they can expect in the future. There is power in knowledge, and because the dying person may feel a loss of personal power, access to information may become a critical expression of one's continuing integrity.

Another frequently expressed concern of dying patients is the fear of being a burden to other people. Dependency is a very real outcome of severe illness, and the feelings that dependency raise, for both the person who is ill and the person caring for him, are often among the most difficult to deal with. Again, frank communication is perhaps the best way to cope with this issue. Children often feel guilt rather than fear of dependency. The dying child may sense his parents' extreme distress and know that she is the cause of this unhappiness. If the parents can reassure the child, through open communication, that they will be all right, the child may more easily be able to let go and find peace.

Positive action is another way for those struggling with loss to transform feelings of depression and anger into an opportunity for growth. When Candy Lightner's daughter was killed by a drunk driver in 1980, Candy was overcome with grief and rage. Yet rather than sink into lethargy or succomb to feelings of life's meaninglessness, she decided to put her emotions into productive use. She founded Mothers Against Drunk Drivers (MADD), an organization which is now nationwide and has done a great deal to lobby for tougher laws pertaining to driving and drinking and stronger enforcement of these laws. Though she lost her daughter, she has worked to see that other parents would not suffer the same loss, and in this way she can feel that her bereavement was not in vain and can find new meaning and purpose in her own life.

You may not respond to your loss by founding a national organization, but perhaps you will want to do volunteer work for your church to help others in need, or become involved in an organization whose cause you believe in. Or perhaps you will feel more sensitive to other people's grief and pain, and will be able to offer your faith and strength to them. When you turn your loss into positive action, you feel a greater appreciation of life and are able to accept life's difficult lessons, find meaning in them, and continue living with renewed affirmation.

It is important to remember, too, that your body's need for proper diet and exercise does not diminish in a time of grief. Even if you are keeping a bedside vigil, don't neglect your need for fresh air and a change of scenery. If you have been exercising regularly, try to keep up your exercise schedule. If not, at least get out for a fifteen or twenty minute walk once a day. And

though the last thing you may be thinking about is food preparation, try not to skip meals or eat fast foods that are high in sugar and fat. Now more than ever, your body needs good, high-energy nourishment. Studies have shown that emotional stress actually uses up body protein, so you may want to increase your protein intake. Eating protein, fresh fruits and vegetables, and whole grains and avoiding sugar, fat, caffeine, and alcohol will help you feel stronger during this intense, emotional time.

Finally, learning how to "let go" is a vital skill for both the dying person and the grieving person. "Letting go" means releasing thoughts, tensions, memories, and emotions which can make one hold onto life in a negative way, and allowing the life-completing process to follow its course. When the dying person can truly let go, he can drift into deep and peaceful eternal rest. Leaving the body behind, he can find real freedom. When the grieving person is able to let go, he is less likely to be overcome by anger, bitterness, or debilitating remorse and more able to continue life in a positive way.

Case Study #1

I received a call one afternoon from a woman named Mary whom I had worked with several years earlier for job-related stress. She sounded extremely distraught, and immediately told me that her twenty-year-old nephew, John, had been seriously injured in an auto accident and she was very concerned about the effect this was having on the family, particularly her sister, Martha, the boy's mother. John was in the hospital in a coma with serious head injuries and was not expected to recover. Mary asked me if I would come to the hospital to talk with the family and see if I could help them deal with their pain.

When I walked into the hospital room, you could cut the air with a knife, so thick was the emotion. John's aunt, mother, father, nineteen-year-old sister, and several friends were sitting around the bed where John lay unconscious, on a respirator. They were clearly in shock, grief-stricken. Yet it was also clear that all of the anguish they were feeling was bottled up inside. I introduced myself and spoke with them quietly for about half an hour. They seemed glad I had come, but were unable to express the powerful emotions that were churning inside. They had been sitting and watching John for a week, and I sensed their enormous feeling of helplessness. Nothing they could do would change things or make John better.

I talked with them, gently, about the things they could do for themselves to handle their grief more positively. I encouraged them to get out for fresh air, to take walks, and take a break from the hospital environment. Martha, particularly, looked haggard, and she said she had not slept much in the last week. I gave her a tape of a progressive relaxation exercise which I explained would help her fall asleep more easily. The progressive relaxation exercise is very simple and straightforward, and I felt it would be the easiest, least demanding exercise for her to use. I told the family I would check back with them in a couple of days.

I continued to visit John's family several times a week over the next couple of months. John's condition was unchanged, and the continued vigil and grief were taking a toll on the whole family. On several occasions I took a walk with Martha and had a chance to talk with her a little more about her feelings. John had been very well liked and had a lot of friends in the community who were extremely upset by the accident. Martha felt that she had to be a source of comfort and support for this extended community of mourners, as well as for her own family. It was clear that her own needs were being buried under the responsibility she felt for others. I continued to stress to her the importance of taking care of herself, of eating well, exercising, and using the relaxation exercise at least once daily. She did feel that the relaxation was helping her to fall asleep more easily. I encouraged her to see a professional counselor, too, and she decided to contact the pastor of her church.

As Martha and I got to know each other a little better, she began to express to me feelings of fear that John might stay in a coma for a long time, neither recovering nor dying. She knew this state of limbo was tearing her family apart, but felt guilty expressing the sentiment that it might be better if John died. She also sensed that John was unprepared for and fearful of death, and that perhaps he was hanging onto life because of his fears and his concern about the well-being of his family and friends. We talked about the need for expressing these feelings among the family members and to John, but Martha was reluctant to do this. Finally I suggested that I could speak to John for the family if she wanted me to. She welcomed this idea.

Back in the hospital room, I sat beside John and stroked his hand. I told him that his family did not want him to be frightened of death, and that if he needed to leave that would be okay. His family loved him and his death would be difficult for them, but he didn't need to hang on to take care of them. I assured him that it was okay to let go. I did not know if he really heard me or if he could respond to my words, but somehow I felt a slight change from him, almost a sigh of relief.

A short time later John died of pneumonia. His death was peaceful, a beautiful release. His family was sad yet relieved. I spoke with Martha periodically over the next six months, and was pleased to find her moving on with her life and finding positive meaning in her loss. She and her husband and daughter had joined a group for bereaved families offered through their church, and felt that they had learned to open up to each other in a way they never had before. The family's communication was more honest and complete, and they knew they would never again leave anything unsaid to the people they loved. The whole family had become closer, had learned not to blame each other for what happened, and had learned not to fear death, but to see it as a lesson in appreciating life.

Case Study #2

When I met first met with Tom, he was in his late fifties. He had had a successful business career, and had built his small manufacturing company into a lucrative endeavor. Yet his face reflected much strain and suffering. By Tom's accounts, life had not treated him fairly.

He had married his college sweetheart in his midtwenties, after graduating with a masters in business from a highly respected college. For several years Tom worked for other people, learning valuable business skills. Then he branched out on his own, starting a manufacturing company. His wife gave birth to two sons, and with his family and new business thriving, Tom's future looked bright.

Then, when his older boy was six years old, the younger boy, aged two, developed leukemia. The boy battled the disease for two years and then died. The entire family suffered from this devastating experience, but Tom felt especially angered and embittered. Unable to find any positive meaning in his son's death, he expressed his anger and frustration by immersing himself in his work. Though he loved his wife and remaining son, he began to spend much less time with them, and their relationships suffered. The boy, particularly, was hurt by his father's neglect, and he began to have emotional problems. Yet Tom continued to ignore his family's needs, finding his only satisfaction in his work.

When she was in her early fifties, Tom's wife developed severe health problems. Tom again felt life was dealing him an unfair blow. He loved his wife very much, yet he seemed unable to show her this love. She died after a two-year illness, in which she showed little will to live.

Tom took the death of his wife very hard. He began to open his eyes to what he had been missing in life. Tom realized that he had let the irreplaceable love of his family slip from his heart. His older son was the only remaining family member to whom he could reach out, and he tried to reconnect with him. The son, however, blamed Tom for his mother's death, and would not accept his father's overtures. Now Tom felt even more grief and loss.

A little more than one year after Tom's wife died, he was diagnosed as having cancer. His doctor gave him only several months to live, as he had a rapidly growing liver tumor, and recommended that Tom contact the hospital's hospice organization. The phone call Tom made to the hospice organization was probably one of the most important calls he had ever made.

Tom was very moved by the support which was offered to him by the hospice workers as he fought his illness. They helped him turn a situation which could have been the ultimate, devastating blow, into a time of renewed growth. With their encouragement, he developed a very positive, fighting spirit, and his cancer temporarily went into remission. One of the hospice nurses recommended that Tom try relaxation exercises to find greater peace of mind and to help control pain, and it was at this point that Tom came to see me.

I made an indirect relaxation tape for Tom and added a visualization for self-acceptance and to control pain. When I know I don't have much time to work with someone, I use the indirect exercise because the relaxation suggestions, being "indirect," do not produce much internal resistance, and most people find it easy to be comfortable with this exercise. The indirect exercise also seems to get people into their bodies very quickly. Tom did respond well to the tape and practiced the exercise on a daily basis. He felt that it helped him to open up emotionally as well as to control pain.

Although Tom rallied through several brief remissions, his tumor did continue to grow, causing him to become increasingly weak. It became clear that he had only weeks to live. In these last few weeks I continued to meet with Tom, helping him with the exercises as well as talking with him about the spiritual side of life. He became much more open spiritually than he'd ever been, and was able to let go of some emotional blocks and not feel angry or embittered by what he was going through. He began to come to terms with his son's and wife's deaths, and finally with his own situation, too. In the last weeks of his life he reached out to his remaining son in a most beautiful and loving way, and the son finally was able to accept his father's caring. They spent these last days together, sharing in ways they never had before. Toward the very end Tom seemed to hallucinate, as if he were already halfway into another world. He told his son he saw a warm, white light, and that his wife was waiting for him. Tom died peacefully. Although his son grieved the loss of a newly rediscovered relationship, we had all learned much about love and life from sharing Tom's death.

Relaxation Exercises for Dying and Grieving

Special relaxations for improving sleep and pain control can be found in Chapter Eight.

PROGRESSIVE RELAXATION WITH ACCEPTANCE VISUALIZATION

This special relaxation is designed to help you control the stresses and anxieties that may accompany the process of dying. It is written both for the patient and for those who are losing a loved one. The relaxation is initiated by a simple progressive relaxation. If you desire, you can substitute the indirect suggestion relaxation for the progressive relaxation. The visual images which follow the relaxation will help you let go of negative thoughts and fears so you can feel recharged with a powerful sense of love and warmth. This positive energy will enable you to feel greater acceptance of the dying process, and to move through this time gracefully. While fighting and struggle are important to some stages of life, acceptance and letting go are vital to the last stage of life. Parts of us die every day and are reborn again and again. This is how we grow, mature, and change. Death is simply one more stage in this growth process.

Read this exercise slowly (about half normal speaking speed). Pause at each (*). Do not be concerned by mispronunciations or verbal slips. Continue in a calm, even voice.

Find a quiet location where you will not be disturbed. Allow about twenty minutes for this exercise. Sit or lie back comfortably, allowing your arms and your legs to remain uncrossed if possible. Let your head be supported and let your shoulders drop into a comfortable position. Check the muscles of your head and face. Let your forehead become calm and smooth. Allow the muscles around your eyes to loosen. Check the muscles of the mouth and jaw to make sure they are relaxed. Finally, allow your eyes to remain closed, remembering that you can open them whenever you need to use them.

Though you may find yourself going through the most difficult period of your life, please be good to yourself. With proper self-care, you can find the inner peace and the strength to make this experience valuable and as graceful as you possibly can.

Before we begin the relaxation, remember not to try to relax too quickly. In fact, do not try to relax at all. Without any effort you can allow yourself to relax by pleasantly letting go of tensions and discomforts, and then letting yourself drift deeper into a peaceful calmness. To begin the relaxation, take three deep breaths, pausing after you inhale, and then exhaling fully and completely. You might imagine that you release tensions and discomforts as you exhale by just breathing them away. * After you have finished these first three breaths, continue breathing slowly and naturally, pleasantly relaxing more deeply with each slow exhale.

As you continue to breathe slowly and gently, begin to focus your attention on the muscles in your feet. You may want to move your toes briefly to see how these muscles feel. Let them rest in the most comfortable position and then use your imagination to see or feel these muscles relaxing even further. Slowly exhale, breathing away any energy or tension in your toes. As you breathe slowly, imagine these muscles becoming more soft and flexible. * Turn your awareness to the muscles of the arch of your foot. The muscles from the ball of your foot below the big toe down to the heel can relax even further. Take a slow breath and then imagine that as you exhale you release the tensions from these muscles. * Now feel the sides and the top of your foot. Can you feel your shoes or socks touching your foot? As you breathe slowly and naturally, you can let the muscles of your foot relax more. You might even be able to feel a pulse or tingling sensation gradually spreading warmth and relaxation to every muscle of your foot. *

Turn your awareness to your lower leg. Can you feel your ankles, your calves, * your shin bones? * Feel the muscles of your lower legs, and notice that you can relax these muscles even further. Breathe slowly as you feel the muscles softening. You may even feel the knee starting to relax into a more comfortable position. As your awareness increases, your skill at relaxing will also. You will feel your control increasing as you practice letting these muscle groups relax even more. * Now become aware of your upper legs. Feel the large muscles of the sides and top of your legs relax slowly as you exhale the unwanted energies and tensions. * You can now relax the big muscles of the back of your upper legs. As these muscles relax, you might even feel the relaxation spreading up through your pelvic area into the lower back. The big muscles of the leg may loosen so that you can feel the sensation of heaviness down the length of your leg. * Breathe slowly and gently. You might even feel the pulse of blood flowing more freely and easily down your leg into your foot and toes. *

The relaxation can now begin to spread up into your lower back. As the muscles of your back begin to soften, you might feel the relaxation spreading to the other muscles of the back. Feel the muscles of your upper back, including your shoulders, let go even further. Your shoulders may be able to drop down into a more comfortable position. * Feel your head sinking back into the chair or pillow, totally supported, as the muscles of your neck let go even more. * Continue breathing slowly and gently as you feel the relaxation spreading down through your arms. * The muscles of your upper arms may feel loose and comfortable. * Your lower arms, even your wrists, can relax further. As you breathe slowly, feel the sensation of heaviness as your arms sink back into the bed or chair. * The relaxation can slowly drift down into your hands and fingers. * You may feel a pulse of blood flowing freely and easily down into your hands. Feel your hands warm comfortably, letting you drift deeper into comfort and relaxation. *

The muscles of your head and face may be able to relax even more. Your forehead may feel more calm and smooth. * The muscles around the eyes can let go. * Even the muscles of the mouth and the jaw might be able to relax even further. * Slowly breathing away stress, you can control these tensions through relaxation. * The sensations of peace and harmony grow stronger as you allow yourself to drift deeper in this peaceful calmness. *

The relaxation can drift down into your chest. As you breathe slowly, you might feel the relaxation gently spreading to the other muscles of the torso. You can feel your heartbeat, calm and regular. * The relaxation spreads down into your stomach region. * You may even be able to feel the sensation of warmth glowing gently in the stomach region. * Continue breathing slowly and gently as you drift peacefully.

VISUALIZATION FOR ACCEPTANCE

As you continue breathing slowly and deeply, try to clear your mind of all stressful thoughts. A good way to do this is to imagine that you are outdoors on a beautiful day gazing into the calm blue sky. As thoughts or mental distractions pass through your mind, imagine yourself letting them go as if they were colored helium-filled ballons. Let them drift up into the sky with every slow exhale of breath. Watch as they drift up and away, perhaps dancing in the warm breezes. As the balloons float higher and higher, watch them grow smaller. Eventually, you can watch as they blow over the horizon or become so small they simply drift from sight. Now the sky is calm and clear once again. Notice the soothing color of the blue sky as you continue to breathe slowly and naturally. You may even wish to imagine that you can breathe in the cool blue light of the sky as you continue to relax, just letting go.

Turn your attention, gently, to the warm rays of the sun and the gentle, warm breezes. Feel the warmth begin to relax you. Perhaps you can feel the warmth beginning to soak deep within you, allowing tension to melt away. Feel yourself sinking further into whatever you are sitting or lying upon. Imagine you are slowly breathing in the warmth and golden sunlight. As your body fills with this warming, healing light and energy, you feel flooded with love and acceptance.

You can drift as long as you like in this state of relaxation and comfort. Or you can imagine yourself smiling and celebrating the love which surrounds you. Remember that you can maintain this healing energy within you and use it anytime you wish. With practice you will find that this golden-white light and warm, healing energy can remain within your heart, as a reserve for whenever you need it. You will also find that within this positive energy dwells a special part of you. This part of you is the perfect being of love and light that people call the "soul." It can see and accept the final transition of life. As you remain relaxed and comfortable, bathed in love and light, see yourself accepting this life-completing experience, knowing that you are surrounded by love.

As you drift in this peaceful state of calmness and acceptance, remember that the pains and fears of this final transition can be lessened by your new awareness and control. You can replace these worries and fears with love and acceptance. You will be able to maintain this balance and calmness as you pass through the transition of death. When the experience presents itself, you will be able to let go even more, moving into a state of complete calmness, peace, harmony, and acceptance. As you let go, you will see the light of unconditional love, peace, and acceptance burning brightly. You will allow yourself to move to the light and become one with it. Within the light you will find peace, freedom, and loving acceptance.

Drift for a few more minutes in this pleasant state of relaxation and warmth, breathing slowly. When you wish to awaken, imagine that you can return to the room, letting the feelings of love and self-acceptance return with you. Let the feelings of relaxation and comfort remain with you. When you wish to awaken completely, take a deep breath and stretch, letting the feelings of peace and acceptance return with you to a fully waking state. You may wish to take another deep breath and stretch, feeling peaceful and full of love.

INDIRECT RELAXATION

This exercise can help you feel more in control of your body's responses to stress at a time when so many things may feel beyond your control. It will help you reduce the fears and anxieties that accompany death and grieving, and can be useful for either the dying person or the person who is losing a loved one. If you like, this indirect relaxation can be used instead of the progressive relaxation to precede the acceptance visualization.

Read this exercise slowly (about half normal speaking speed). Pause at each (*). Do not be concerned by mispronunciations or verbal slips. Continue in a calm, even voice.

Find a quiet location where you will not be disturbed. Allow about twenty minutes for this exercise. Sit or lie back comfortably, allowing your arms and legs to remain uncrossed if possible. Let your head be supported and let your shoulders drop into a comfortable position. Check the muscles of your head and face. Let your forehead become calm and smooth. Allow the muscles around your eyes to loosen. Check the muscles of the mouth and jaw to make sure they are relaxed. Finally, allow your eyes to remain closed, remembering that you can open them whenever you need to use them.

Before we begin the relaxation, remember not to try to relax too quickly. In fact, do not try to relax at all. Without any effort you can allow yourself to relax by pleasantly letting go of tensions and discomforts, and then letting yourself drift deeper into a peaceful calmness. To begin the relaxation, take three deep breaths, pausing after you inhale, and then exhaling fully and completely. You might imagine that you release tensions and discomforts as you exhale by just breathing them away. * After you have finished these first three breaths, continue breathing slowly and naturally, relaxing more deeply with each slow exhale.

As you continue to breathe slowly and naturally, you may feel the relaxation beginning in your body. The most important thing to remember when dealing with stress is that you can take control of your body through awareness and relaxation. So to begin this process, turn your awareness to the sensation of relaxation that is beginning in your arms and hands. You may feel that one arm is more relaxed than the other. * Perhaps one arm may feel a bit heavier than the other arm. The muscles may feel more loose or more flexible than in the other arm. * Or perhaps you feel that one arm is a bit warmer than the other arm. You may feel that the warmth of blood and energy may flow more easily down one arm, as if it were flowing through wide-open blood vessels, slowly but freely moving down into your hand and fingers. You may even feel it slowly pulsing down into your hand. * Or perhaps you find that both arms feel equally relaxed and this would be perfect as well. The only thing that matters is that you breathe slowly and gently as you let yourself drift deeper into that soothing dreamlike calmness. *

As you drift pleasantly, turn your awareness to the sensations of relaxation that may be beginning in your legs and feet. You may feel that one leg is slightly more relaxed than the other. Perhaps you notice that one leg feels a little heavier, as if the muscles of that leg were more loose or flexible than the other leg. * Or as you breathe slowly and gently, you may feel that one leg is slightly warmer, as if the blood and warmth could spread more easily down that leg, drifting down through wide-open blood vessels, * perhaps even pulsing slowly but freely down into your foot and toes. * Or perhaps your legs feel equally relaxed, and that would be perfect also. The only thing that really matters is that you continue to breathe slowly as you allow yourself to drift more deeply into that dreamlike calmness and comfort. *

You may even feel the gradual control of stress and tensions beginning as you sink back into whatever you are sitting or lying upon and the tension just melts away. *

You may even feel the muscles of your back beginning to loosen or soften, and as you breathe slowly, naturally, you might feel the relaxation spreading to the other muscles of your back. * Even your upper back and shoulders may begin to soften or loosen a bit further. Your shoulders may be able to drop into a more comfortable position. * You may feel the control growing stronger as your head sinks back into the pillow or chair, the muscles of your neck begin to let go, and you drift deeper into relaxation. *

As you pleasantly drift deeper into this comfort and calmness, you may be able to feel the muscles of your head and face beginning to relax even further. * Continue to breathe slowly, allowing a soothing, healing wave of relaxation to gently spread down from the top of your head, soothing and cleansing every muscle and cell of your body. You can feel it slowly drifting down to relax the muscles of your forehead, * letting your forehead become calm and smooth. * Let this wave drift down to relax the muscles around your eyes, releasing the tension in these muscles. * The wave then drifts down helping to relax the muscles of your mouth, including your jaw. Let these muscles go loose and limp. * And as you breathe slowly, the wave slowly drifts down to relax the muscles of your neck. Even your shoulders can loosen a bit more. * The relaxation can begin to spread down your arms. * As the wave of relaxation gently drifts down your arms you may even be able to feel it pulsing into your hands. *

The wave of relaxation can drift down through your back and chest, spreading soothing comfort into your lower back. * Even your heartbeat

feels more calm and regular as the relaxation gently spreads throughout your body. * The wave of relaxation can spread down through your pelvic area helping to loosen and relax the muscles of your legs even more. * The relaxation slowly drifts down through your legs. Perhaps you can feel it pulsing slowly into your feet, spreading the comfort down, washing the discomfort out of your body. *

As you allow yourself to drift more deeply in this calmness, the soothing relaxation can help you rest and recharge yourself. Perhaps you can imagine that you are outdoors in a perfect place, on a warm and beautiful day. Choose the most comfortable place to lie down. Feel the warmth from the sun. You are well protected and safe from any harm or distractions. As you begin to soak up the warmth from the sun, feel your tensions and discomforts just melting away. * Allow yourself to let go even further, letting yourself drift into a perfect place of comfort and loving warmth. The warmth can fill you with comforting energy and the golden-white light, helping to recharge you fully and completely. Even though you remain at peace, you can feel the warmth of blood flowing more freely to every cell of your body carrying oxygen and nutrients and energy to bathe every cell. Each cell, like a sponge, can soak up the perfect amount of nutrients and energy. You may even begin to feel sensations of comfort, acceptance, and happiness burning more brightly within you, though you remain calm and comfortable. * Perhaps you can picture yourself filling with the joy and peace that relaxation can bring to you. * See yourself in a state of harmony and happiness, perhaps smiling and celebrating in the sunshine. *

As you practice this relaxation exercise you will become more comfortable with it, being able to relax more deeply and quickly. You will be more aware of tensions and begin to develop confidence that you can rid yourself of unnecessary anxieties whenever they may develop. The effects of the relaxation and the comfort will begin to carry over throughout your day.

As you become comfortable with this relaxation, your awareness and control will continue with you throughout the day. You will feel more balence and patience through any interactions that you experience. Things that used to bother you will be more tolerable. As you take care of yourself in this special way, you will gradually learn to see and to accept the many parts of yourself, your strengths and your weaknesses. You will find acceptance and so free yourself to grow in a spiritual way. Letting go of fears and pains grows easier, so you are more peaceful. You can move through this time with grace and dignity.

If you are using this exercise at bedtime you may wish to drift into a pleasant sleep, resting fully and awakening refreshed and alert. If you wish to drift off to sleep, continue breathing slowly and focus on the feelings of relaxation in your arms and legs. *

If you wish to awaken now, you can begin to do so. Let yourself gradually return to this room, feeling the bed or the chair beneath you. As you slowly awaken, you will bring the feelings of calmness, relaxation, love, and acceptance back with you. Take a deep breath and stretch, letting the calmness return with you into a fully waking state. Take another deep breath and stretch, allowing yourself to awaken feeling calm and refreshed, letting the relaxation and calmness continue with you.

BIBLIOGRAPHY

Kübler-Ross, Elisabeth. *Death: The Final Stage of Growth*. New York: Simon & Schuster, 1975. $6.95.

A philosophical, positive view of death. Inspiring case histories.

Kübler-Ross, Elisabeth. *On Death and Dying*. New York: Macmillan, 1969. $4.95.

First of Kübler-Ross's major works on death and dying. Describes the typical stages of the dying process and gives the background of Kübler-Ross's work.

Kübler-Ross, Elisabeth. *Working It Through: An Elisabeth Kübler-Ross Workshop On Life, Death and Transition*. New York: Collier Books, 1982. $5.95.

Illustrates the transformative process of Kübler-Ross's workshops. Shows how people share and overcome their fears. With photographs by Mal Warshaw.

Ring, Kenneth. *Heading Toward Omega: In Search of the Meaning of the Near-Death Experience*. New York: Quill, 1984. $6.95.

An amazing and powerful spiritual statement based on hundreds of interviews with near-death survivors.

Ring, Kenneth. *Life at Death: A Scientific Investigation of the Near-Death Experience*. New York: Quill, 1980. $7.50.

Profound series of interviews exploring the experiences of near-death survivors. Helps to paint a different picture of what death and dying is actually about.

AUDIOCASSETTE TAPES

Mason, L. John, Ph.D. 1) *High Blood Pressure Relaxation*, 2) *Relaxation for Pain*, and 3) *Relaxation for Sleep*. 1988. Each is $11.95 and can be ordered from the author.

Specially formulated relaxation exercises designed to help reduce if not eliminate the specific concerns. These guided techniques are most beneficial when practiced regularly.

GUIDED RELAXATION TAPES
FOR STRESS MANAGEMENT

Learn to handle stress and tension. The tapes guide you into peaceful states by identifying tension and giving instruction on releasing suppressed energy. Feel how good it is to relax completely.

#101: *Basic Progressive Relaxation (Passive).* Day and night versions. Sit back and peacefully relax.

#102: *Basic Autogenic Training Phrases.* Side 2: *Autogenics and Deepening Techniques.* Gain control of your body's "relaxation center." Learn to relax at will.

#103: *Ten to One (10-1) Count Down (Progressive Relaxation).* Day and night versions. Listen inwardly in deepening relaxed awareness.

#104: *Visualization for Deep Relaxation.* Day and night versions. Mental images of peaceful scenes to induce calmness.

YOU MAY ORDER THESE TAPES DIRECTLY FROM THE AUTHOR FOR **$9.95 EACH** OR GET A SET OF ALL **4 FOR $36.00**

– NEWLY RELEASED –

Health Series:

Specially formulated relaxations for stress management useful for these specific conditions. Side 1 is accompanied by relaxation music. Side 2 uses ocean sounds as a background.

#201: *Prenatal Stress Management* (11.95)
#202: *Stress Management for Chronic Pain* (11.95)
#203: *Stress Management for High Blood Pressure* (11.95)
#204: *Stress Management for Sleep* (11.95)

Business Series:

#301: *Ten Minute Stress Management for Work* (11.95) Side 1 contains stress management information. Side 2 is an exercise to fit into a busy work schedule.

#302: *Commuter Stress Management* (11.95) This tape is designed to help commuters relax; appropriate for drivers as well as riders.

YOU MAY ORDER THE NEWLY RELEASED TAPES DIRECTLY FROM THE AUTHOR FOR **$11.95 EACH** OR ANY **2 TAPES FOR $22.00** (SAVE $2.00) OR ANY **4 TAPES FOR $40.00** (SAVE $8.00)

California residents add 6% sales tax. Include $1.00 per tape for shipping and handling. You may pay by check, payable to L. John Mason, Ph.D. or by credit card (VISA or MasterCard). If paying by credit card, please send your account number, expiration date, and your signature.

MAIL ORDERS TO:

L. John Mason, Ph.D.
author of *Guide to Stress Reduction* & *Stress Passages*
Biofeedback • Stress Reduction Consulting
315 East Cotati Avenue, Suite F, Cotati, CA 94928
(707) 795-2228

L. John Mason, Ph.D., has been in practice as a stress management consultant and biofeedback therapist since 1977. He founded the Stress Education Center in 1978 where he has his private practice and is the director of *Transitional Counseling Training*. John is also a consultant for the Redwood Center for Pain Management in Santa Rosa, California, where he heads the psychophysiology department. His first book, *A Guide to Stress Reduction*, Celestial Arts, and his stress management audio cassettes have assisted thousands of people. John also enjoys invitations to continue his work in lecturing and stress management consulting.